HED

HOW STUDENT DEBT HAS IMPAIRED A GENERATION AND WHAT TO DO ABOUT IT

David E. Linton

FOREWORD BY JOHN KATZMAN

J.ROSS
PUBLISHING

Copyright © 2023 by David E. Linton

ISBN-13: 978-1-60427-189-8

Printed and bound in the U.S.A. Printed on acid-free paper.

10 9 8 7 6 5 4 3 2 1

Library of Congress Cataloging-in-Publication Data

Names: Linton, David E., 1982– author.
Title: Crushed : how student debt has impaired a generation and what to do about it / David E. Linton.
Description: Plantation, FL : J. Ross Publishing, Inc., [2023] | Includes bibliographical references and index. | Summary: "Crushed is a timely and insightful work that sheds light on the state of American universities and their graduates. It takes readers on a fascinating and reflective journey into the current student debt crisis and how it has become a major burden to American society. Beyond just describing how we got into this huge mess, Crushed also offers actionable public-policy steps to help fix this ever-growing problem"— Provided by publisher.
Identifiers: LCCN 2022050905 (print) | LCCN 2022050906 (ebook) | ISBN 9781604271898 (paperback : acid-free paper) | ISBN 9781604278415 (epub)
Subjects: LCSH: Student loans—United States. | College costs—United States. | College graduates—United States. | BISAC: EDUCATION / Educational Policy & Reform / General | STUDY AIDS / Financial Aid
Classification: LCC LB2340.2 .L56 2023   (print) | LCC LB2340.2   (ebook) | DDC 378.3/62—dc23/eng/20230221
LC record available at https://lccn.loc.gov/2022050905
LC ebook record available at https://lccn.loc.gov/2022050906

Direct all inquiries to J. Ross Publishing, Inc., 151 N. Nob Hill Rd., Suite 476, Plantation, FL 33324.

Phone: (954) 727-9333
Fax: (561) 892-0700
Web: www.jrosspub.com

Dedication

First, to my parents—without whom I would not have learned the value of an education—I am immensely grateful for your guidance and support. I am exceedingly fortunate that, unlike most in my generation, I completed my postsecondary education without student debt. Thank you!

Second, to my children, Matthew, Joshua, and Leah—without whom I would not be so concerned about the cost of college—I wish you to be good, brave, and happy. Watching you grow has brought me immense joy, and I hope one day you might dust off this book, browse through it, and ask me why it does not have more pictures.

Finally, to my readers—without whom this book would have no utility—I appreciate you have decided to spend your personal time reading this work and I hope you gain insight that may improve your (or your children's) educational outcome.

Contents

Part I. How Did We Get Here?   1

Foreword

I have been involved in higher education for decades. As the founder and CEO of The Princeton Review, 2U, and now Noodle, I've gotten to know hundreds of administrators and professors. With few exceptions, they are smart, honest, hard-working, and committed to the public good. They compete hard with one another, if in an appropriately collegial way. This competition has led to significant advances in the "student experience," including an expansion of course offerings and an explosion in peripheral services offered by colleges and universities, but few administrators or their respective boards have focused on efficiency or cost rationalization. As a result, tuition has risen at a rate commensurate with the breadth of services offered by universities, but not necessarily at a rate commensurate with the value of the education.

I met David Linton a couple of years ago and I was skeptical that another set of eyes on college finance would help solve the problem. I warmed to *Crushed* as it clearly described the scope and impact of the student debt problem and its burden to both students and society. David discusses in clear terms how we got into this mess, and he explains what parents and students should know before enrolling in college. As a businessman who works with colleges, what gets me excited about *Crushed* is the analysis of various policy proposals. David provides creative ways to mitigate and eventually eliminate runaway tuition inflation and the overwhelming stock of student debt. As a parent, I appreciate how David answers head-on all the questions I (and others) have about college:

- Is it worth it?
- Who should go to college, and when?
- What are the common pitfalls parents and students make, and how can you avoid those mistakes?
- How can you (or your child) get the most out of college?

It's reasonable to question if college is worth it. After all, it is one of the most expensive things you'll ever purchase. David addresses this question in a more nuanced way, but the simple answer is yes. As he notes, it's still a compelling return on students' time and (usually) money by measures as diverse as economics, health, and happiness—especially if a student picks a good school that aligns their interest and opportunity. But as David notes, this is true *on average*, and generally only if a student completes their degree without assuming a crushing debt load in the process.

Whether you're a parent facing the cost of educating your family, a higher education administrator, or a policymaker wrestling with the public good, the question is where to go from here. Most important, how do we make a great college experience less expensive, and who and how do we best pay for it? David comes at these issues as a gifted economist. *Crushed* is politically neutral, unbiased, calm, and balanced; he has no ax to grind. Armed with a truckful of data, he's keen to offer insight that will improve student outcomes and will answer a lot of questions you probably have.

Unsustainable things always seem to stick around much longer than we think they will. As we approach $2 trillion in student debt, it's clear that we need to do something different for both students and society. *Crushed* offers solutions, all of which are thoughtful and reasonable, and some of which might work.

—John Katzman, founder of The Princeton Review

Introduction

IT'S PERSONAL

Juli immigrated to the United States as a child. Interested in interior design, as a high school senior Juli and her parents toured the New England Institute of Art (NEIA), a for-profit institution in Brookline, Massachusetts, a suburb of Boston. While there, Juli and her family were led to believe that the NEIA would be instrumental in allowing Juli to secure an internship and full-time employment at graduation; thus, she could go on to achieve the American dream of home ownership and financial security. Juli was a good candidate for admission to the NEIA, but not for the reasons that she assumed at the time. Because Juli's parents were of modest means and because her family had little knowledge of the American postsecondary education system, Juli's family would likely receive Pell Grants and could be convinced to assume federal student debt. Consequently, that's what happened; in what Juli describes as a high-pressure situation, Juli asked her father—who didn't speak English—to cosign student loan documents. Juli graduated on time with a degree in interior design in 2012, but she was unable to find work in her chosen field. The NEIA meanwhile stopped enrolling students in 2015 and closed in 2017. Now, after 10 years, Juli is still struggling to repay student loans and has been unable to work as an interior designer, in part because her diploma is of dubious value now that the NEIA is no longer an accredited college.

James' parents didn't go to college, but the idea that a college degree was the path to financial success was taught to him from an early age. In high school, James wasn't a great student but he scored well on standardized tests. He was initially hesitant to go to college—what would he study, and how would he afford it? After learning about the GI Bill, James joined the Air Force in 1997, and after serving four years was honorably discharged. James then chose to attend a small college in South Carolina. Each semester's tuition at the time was only $2,200, which was fully covered by the GI Bill. However, by the time he graduated, the tuition has risen more than 100 percent to $4,500 per semester, which wasn't fully covered by his government allowance. So, James borrowed $15,000 and graduated in 2007 with a BS in Management. James got a job but was laid off in 2008 during the Great Recession. He found employment again, but was laid off a second time shortly thereafter. During these periods, he got behind on his payments and began incurring penalties and significant interest charges. He later defaulted on his debt, which after 10 years grew to over $60,000. James reports that his credit is ruined, he's regularly hassled by collections agencies, and that he doesn't believe he can achieve any of his personal goals including financial security. This has all taken a major toll on his mental health leading to thoughts of suicide.

After graduating from college, Haylee took a job with a local government. Haylee assumed significant student debt to pay for college, and her plan to repay her debt was to enroll in an income-driven repayment plan in order to maintain eligibility in the Public Service Loan Forgiveness (PSLF) program. This government program would allow her to jettison her remaining student debt after ten years of (or 120) consecutive on-time student loan payments. After graduating Haylee contacted her servicer, FedLoan, and confirmed that her loans qualified for the PSLF program and that she was on her way to full loan forgiveness. However, after three years of payments, Haylee received a note from FedLoan indicating that her loans may be eligible for PSLF, something she thought (correctly) she already knew. Confused, she contacted her servicer and was (mis)informed that to be eligible for forgiveness, she would have to consolidate her loans. However, by doing this, she also consolidated loans that already had 32 qualifying payments, meaning her payment history would *restart*. She wasn't informed of this at the time. Now, despite having been misinformed regarding her loan forgiveness eligibility, and despite adhering to all criteria as disclosed to her, she finds she's starting over with respect to her student debt payments. With $85,000 in debt, she fears she won't be able to buy a home, get married, have kids, or live on her own.*

IT'S MASSIVE

Juli, James, and Haylee's stories are not unique. In fact, they are in the majority. The College Board estimates that 55 to 57 percent of bachelor's degree recipients have student debt at graduation (depending on the type of school). The average balance of student debt at graduation is $26,700 if the student attended a public four-year school, and $33,600 if the student attended a private four-year school.[i] That's pretty high, but it may be worse; the Institute of

---

* These student debt stories, and many others, can be found at www.studentdebtcrisis.org/stories/.

College Access and Success estimated that in 2016, the share of people who have student debt at graduation is closer to 66 and 68 percent for public and non-profit schools, respectively. For-profit schools have even worse statistics with an estimated 83 percent of students graduating with student debt, and the average student balance at graduation was $39,900.[ii] And those are the lucky students! Why? The College Board figures hide a dirty secret: they are estimating the amount of debt *at graduation*. However, these figures don't include the students that fail to earn a degree but assume debt along the way. That's a nontrivial population; nearly one in three students entering a public four-year program, and nearly three in four students entering a for-profit program, will fail to earn a degree![iii] Most of those students took on debt as well, and now they have little to show for it.

This issue is massive. There are roughly 43 million people with student debt in the United States.[iv] Just to wrap our heads around that number, there are more student debtors than residents of Florida (21.8 million), Texas (29.5 million), or California (39.2 million).[v] There are more student debtors than registered Independents (34.7 million) or Republicans (35.7 million), and almost as many student debtors as registered Democrats (48.0 million).[vi] There are more student debtors than Americans who live in the largest 25 American cities *combined* (38.6 million).[vii] And how much debt do they have? Around $1.8 trillion. Just to wrap our heads around *that* number, $1.8 trillion is roughly the entire annual economic output of Texas ($1.8 trillion), New York ($1.8 trillion), and greater than all of the New England states combined ($1.1 trillion).[viii] There is more student debt than credit card debt ($890 billion) or auto loans ($1.5 trillion).[ix]

And this problem is impairing a generation of young adults. The studies that have connected student debt to impaired student outcomes can fill a small library. Student debt has been linked to delayed household formation, delayed home purchases, delayed marriages, delayed family formation, fertility issues, lower entrepreneurship and economic dynamism, greater economic inequality, impaired career choices, lower job satisfaction, and damaged physical and mental health. I summarize many of these findings later in this book.

IT'S PREDICTABLE

Berkshire Hathaway Vice Chairman Charlie Munger is credited with saying, "Show me the incentive and I'll show you the outcome." To this, he added in a 2020 interview, "If you have a dumb incentive system, you get dumb outcomes."[x] To anybody who is adversely impacted by student debt, it is self-evident that the current postsecondary education system, with its associated on-demand student debt system, is dumb. Really dumb.

At the beginning of the process of writing this book, a colleague asked me why I thought I was qualified to write it. To be fair, my stint as an adjunct professor at a large university was relatively brief, and I am an investment manager by education and trade. To my colleague, I responded: I'm not an academic, reporter, or tragic victim of this system (as most contributors to this topic are)—I'm an economist. So, why does being an economist make me qualified to write on this topic? Because, if we're going to figure out how we got into this mess and what we need to do about it, we need calm, rational, thoughtful analysis paired with actionable solutions. And how do we get this kind of analysis and potential solutions? We, my dear reader, have to employ a process that I call the *economic method*, which is the economic cousin of the scientific method.

When fully analyzing a system and employing the economic method, any economist who is worth his or her salt begins by measuring outcomes. Then, we ask, "Is this outcome *optimal*?" We generally define optimal as leading to the highest amount of *utility* or happiness among people. So, if we measure an outcome that's not optimal, our focus turns to identifying how we arrived at an outcome. A foundational assumption in the economic method is that all outcomes are driven by incentive structures. So, to address a poor outcome, we must identify every stakeholder and identify each stakeholder's incentive structure. If we want to get a different outcome, we simply need to thoughtfully change the incentives in a targeted manner.

For this book, I analyzed the incentives and motivations of students, parents, guidance counselors, endowments, university faculty, university boards, banks, and politicians. I then asked (as Charlie Munger described), "Are these good or *dumb* incentives?" Unfortunately for America's youth, there is a whole host of misaligned (i.e., dumb) incentives. Of all the aforementioned stakeholders, few if any are incentivized to ensure that students graduate on time, with little or no debt, and with degrees that elevate their economic opportunities. On the contrary—student outcomes of secondary or tertiary consideration and incentives are aligned to maximize the quantity of students graduating with student debt. Don't believe me? Then ask yourself, "Why are there 44 million indebted Americans with $1.8 trillion in student debt?"

IT'S CORRECTABLE

Altering outcomes by influencing economic incentives has a proven track record of success. How does this look in practice? There are two approaches—tax (disincentivize) what leads to bad outcomes and subsidize (incentivize) what leads to good outcomes. Consider the following two examples. California considers smoking to be a public health nuisance, yet, while smokers primarily impact their own health, they also consume a disproportionate amount of healthcare services, which creates a financial burden on nonsmokers. So, in 1998, California voters passed a $0.25 tax on each pack of cigarettes, with the objective of reducing smoking. The following year, cigarette sales fell by 9.4 percent and continued to decline in subsequent years.[xi] The tax functioned as a disincentive to engaging in a behavior that caused public harm, and it worked. Conversely, financial incentives can lead to a dramatic increase in activity. In 2005, in an attempt to increase all forms of domestic energy consumption (as reliance on foreign oil was a geopolitical concern), Congress passed the Energy Policy Act. This act included a provision that created a 30 percent tax credit on residential and commercial solar systems. In other words, for every $100 spent on installing solar panels, a person or business could deduct $30 from their year-end tax bill. Following the creation of this subsidy (positive incentive), the solar panel industry experienced a major surge in growth. Solar installations increased at an average rate of 77 percent *per year* from 2006 to 2012, and the total workforce in the United States who were employed in the solar industry jumped from under 20,000 to nearly 120,00 over the same period.[xii]

That's interesting, but what does this have to do with the student debt crisis? The answer is that legislative solutions have the ability to dramatically eliminate the use of student debt for future generations if the legislation effectively realigns stakeholders' incentives. Policy reform must ensure that the government, banks, students, and universities are all incentivized to create a well-educated, debt-free, highly productive, equitable society. In order to do this, each and every stakeholder in the postsecondary system must gain when this objective is achieved and share in the pain when this objective is not achieved. The thoughtful and appropriate policy solutions proposed in this book will take years (or even decades) to manifest in the form of superior outcomes, but these policy solutions have the potential to ensure that student debt becomes a relic of a bygone era.

What if you're picking up this book because you want to gain a better understanding of the American postsecondary education system? Or, if you want to know what you should and should not do when it comes to applying to college? Then you're in luck. As a father of three (likely) college-bound kids, I wrote the final chapter explaining what I learned while researching this topic, and how I will guide my kids when we decide on their postsecondary path.

Thank you for your time. We can achieve great things when we work together, and by picking up this book, you're contributing to an effort to end our *crushing* student debt crisis.

About the Author

David E. Linton is an author and economist. Mr. Linton is a Faculty Lecturer
at the University of Texas McCombs
School of Business, where he teaches
Investment Management, and he is a
former professor at the University of
Southern California's Marshall School
of Business. His first book, *Foundations
of Investment Management*, has become
a mainstay among aspiring professionals who want to bridge the gap between an academic understanding and
the practical application of investment
management strategies.

Mr. Linton is currently a senior portfolio manager at a multinational financial technology firm where he shares responsibility for the management
of both corporate and customer cash assets. Previously, he was the direc-
tor of Portfolio Construction and Manager Research at Pacific Life Fund
Advisors LLC. Prior to this, Mr. Linton was a vice president and portfolio
manager at PIMCO.

Mr. Linton is a CFA® charterholder with a BS in Business Administration from the University of Southern California and an MBA from the University of Chicago Booth School of Business.

At J. Ross Publishing we are committed to providing today's professional with practical, hands-on tools that enhance the learning experience and give readers an opportunity to apply what they have learned. That is why we offer free ancillary materials available for download on this book and all participating Web Added Value™ publications. These online resources may include interactive versions of material that appears in the book or supplemental templates, worksheets, models, plans, case studies, proposals, spreadsheets and assessment tools, among other things. Whenever you see the WAV™ symbol in any of our publications, it means bonus materials accompany the book and are available from the Web Added Value Download Resource Center at www.jrosspub.com.

Downloads for *Crushed* include the figures and tables from the book, including supporting data.

Part I

How Did We Get Here?

1

A Brief History of the Growth of the American University System

WHY REVIEW HISTORY?

The crisis of insolvency, stunted career trajectories, delayed household formation, and mental health issues directly attributable to student debt is unique to this generation. There are no empirical data we can examine to calculate the long-term adverse effects of this phenomena because never before has so much debt been assumed by so many young adults. With respect to the university system, both the breadth of course offerings at universities, as well as the percentage of the population that has obtained or attempted to obtain an advanced degree, is greater than at any time in history. So, what is the point of reviewing the history of the American university system? We will find no robust discussions of student debt in the dusty archives of university libraries, nor will we find policy solutions in the Library of Congress.

The answer to this question is: A review of the history of the American university provides both context and the intuition regarding the trajectory of the American university system, its costs, and the debt assumed by its students. In addition, to determine the magnitude of the student debt problem, diagnose its cause, and offer solutions, we must first closely examine postsecondary education in the United States. More specifically, what is the cost of a university degree? Is this excessive? Is it sensible to ask students to assume debt to achieve this degree? How have both the cost of a postsecondary degree and the value it confers to its recipient changed over time? Where are we headed? And, if you're a parent or a policy maker, what should you know or do?

However, if we hope to fully answer these questions, we should consider digging even deeper—we must begin with a discussion of the university itself. Specifically, what purpose do junior colleges, colleges, and universities serve? Do these institutions serve their students or their societies, and are students expected to utilize the knowledge they gain to advance themselves, serve society, both, or neither? And most important, are institutions of higher learning upholding their tacit societal contract, and if not, why? While we can answer these questions without a review of history (I answer these questions at the end of the chapter), a review of history adds helpful context and color to later discussions.

While readers who are most interested in policy solutions to the student debt crisis and parents who are looking to advise their children are welcome to skip over this chapter, those who follow me from the beginning will emerge with a far greater understanding as to how we got here and what we can and should do about it.

COLONIAL PERIOD THROUGH THE CIVIL WAR

Higher education in America began in 1636 with the establishment of Harvard College in Cambridge, Massachusetts. Within years of having settled in Massachusetts Bay, the English Puritans turned their attention to the establishment of a university. According to American historian Samuel Morison, "Enthusiasm for education was one aspect of that desire to know and do the will of God that bound the puritans together . . . their Congregational churches must have a learned clergy, cost what it might." In addition to Theology, early disciplines at Harvard included Rhetoric and Logic, Ethics and Politics, Arithmetic and Geometry, as well as the study of Latin, Greek, and Hebrew.[i] In fact, while the emphasis on the training of a learned ministry continued to be viewed as *essential* in the early days of Harvard College, by the 1660s the expectation was that the university would address a broad range of the needs of the colony.[ii]

The second institution of higher education that was founded in the American colonies was the college of William and Mary, chartered in 1693. Named in honor of the reigning monarchs King William III and Queen Mary II, this institution is located in Williamsburg, Virginia. Alumni of William and Mary include sixteen members of the Continental Congress (including George Washington and Thomas Jefferson), and four signers of the Declaration of Independence, earning it the nickname: *the Alma Mater of the Nation*.[iii] On the eve of the Revolutionary War, the number of institutions of higher learning in the Thirteen Colonies had grown to nine while its population was estimated at 2.5 million people.[1,iv] There were also around 3,000 living college graduates, meaning about 11 in every 10,000 people had college degrees.[v] Figures 1.1 and 1.2 chart the growth of degree-granting postsecondary institutions as well as the number of living baccalaureate graduates as a percentage of the population.

The Revolutionary War years were a challenge for U.S. colleges; Nassau Hall at Princeton was occupied by both the British forces and the continentals, the President at King's College (later Columbia University) was run out of the city by an angry mob, and William and Mary College was closed during the siege of Yorktown with one of its buildings set on fire by French forces. However, once the war ended, interest in higher education returned and from 1782 to 1802, nineteen colleges that are still in existence today were chartered.[vi] The success of the American Revolution, acceptance of European Enlightenment ideas centering on the sovereignty of reason and the de-emphasis of the divine, and a general decline in the religious orthodoxy among the newly established United States of America all contributed to a rethinking of the purpose of American colleges.

According to American Historian Frederick Rudolph, "colleges were now serving a new responsibility to a new nation: the preparation of young men for responsible citizenship in a republic that must prove itself, the preparation for lives of usefulness of young men who also intended to prove themselves."[vii] The first institution among the colonial colleges to revise its curriculum to reflect this shifting viewpoint was the college of William and Mary. Four years *prior* to the war's conclusion, then Virginia Governor Thomas Jefferson put forward a series of proposals for the college including the establishment of a professorship of law and policy (public administration), anatomy, medicine, and chemistry. By reshaping its faculty and curriculum, Jefferson hoped visitors would be free from "the royal prerogative, or the laws of the kingdom of England; of the canons or the constitution of the English church."[viii] Many colleges adopted similar changes to their curriculums in the years following the American Revolution. Yet, while educational focus of the American college would move away from educating graduates to serve congregants, this does not mean that colleges would educate young men to serve only themselves. On the contrary, at the birth of the nation, a higher calling remained embedded within the fabric of the colleges throughout the country,

---

[1] The U.S. Census Bureau estimates that there were 2.2 million people in 1760 and 2.8 million people in 1770. However, the first census was conducted in 1790. The statistic of 2.5 million people appears on the U.S. Census Bureau website.

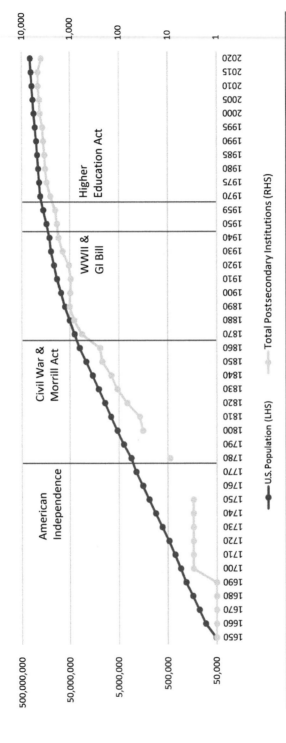

Figure 1.1   U.S. Population and Total Postsecondary Institutions.

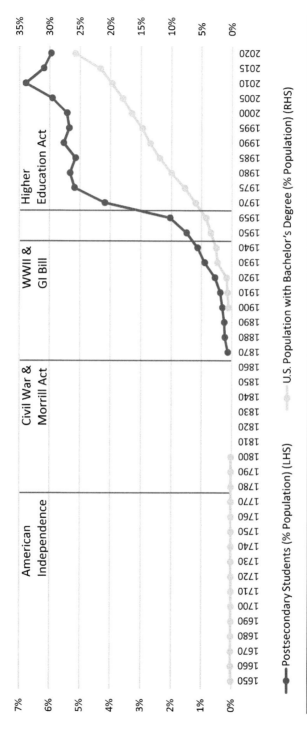

Figure 1.2   Postsecondary Students and Holders of Bachelor's Degrees (% of U.S. Population).

with universities expecting their graduates to still serve society (although not necessarily from an altar).[ix]

The charting of new colleges in the early 1800s continued with zeal as the U.S. population rapidly grew; across the country, America opened the doors of higher education in the same spirit as canal-building, farming, gold-mining, and other activities that echoed the belief in endless progress. Frequently, as towns grew on the western frontier, colleges were chartered not by local necessity, but with the hope of either spreading Western theology or recreating New England-type towns.[x]

THE CIVIL WAR THROUGH WWII

By 1860, the number of operating colleges in the United States had grown to around 250.[xi] With 31.4 million[xii] people in the United States, this equates to approximately one institution of higher learning for every 125,000 people—up from one institution for every 277,000 people at the beginning of the Revolutionary War. A college degree was still largely unobtainable for anyone but the children of the wealthiest, those fortunate to find a benefactor, or those entering the clergy. In fact, the requirement of proficiency in Latin and Greek as a prerequisite for admission generally functioned as an insurmountable barrier for most Americans. However, if knowledge of dead languages functioned as a barrier to entry, the cost of the education generally did not. In 1851, the first president of the University of Michigan, Henry Tappan, observed, "We have cheapened education—we have reduced it to cost—we have put it below cost—we have even given it away. The public has given money so liberally, and made education so nearly gratuitous, that, taking Harvard College as an illustration, every graduate costs the public nearly one thousand dollars."[xiii] Similar to conditions during the Revolutionary War, the Civil War adversely impacted institutions of higher learning. Washington and Lee College (then Washington College) located in Lexington, Virginia, was damaged by Union forces who destroyed books and laboratory equipment, defaced buildings, and stole property.[xiv] Meanwhile, Emory University in Atlanta, Georgia, was closed in 1861; its campus was later used as a Confederate hospital and then occupied by Union forces near the war's conclusion.[xv]

In the years following the Civil War, colleges again began to rethink their purpose and utility in the country. While the Protestant Second Great Awakening (early 1800s) had been the impetus for opening new colleges and infusing religion into their curriculum, the pendulum reversed direction following the Civil War as the nation rebuilt. At the time, many leaders of new and existing institutions believed that the current curriculum was "too narrow, elementary, or superficial." There was a general desire to move away from the sectarian and toward the democratic. In addition, insufficient attention was given to research and topics that were both technical and practical. Only in the South were colleges simply content to maintain operations after having lost students, faculty, and financial support.[xvi]

The desire to increase both the availability of and the usefulness of the college education was codified in the Morrill Act of 1862—named after Representative Justin Smith Morrill of Vermont. This act was instrumental in shaping the trajectory of college education in America in the post-Civil War era with the United States becoming a global leader in technical education within 50 years of the bill's passage.[xvii] At the time of the bill's passage, the federal government was cash-poor but land-rich; so, the solution to enable the federal government to support institutions of higher learning was the distribution of federal land to be used for the establishment of colleges. Under the act, each eligible state received 30,000 acres of federal land for each member of congress the state had as of the census of 1860. Ninety percent of the capital raised by the sale of the land would seed each college's endowment, which was mandated by law to fund the college in perpetuity at a rate of five percent.[xviii] A further condition of this grant was that the college curriculum must reflect the occupational needs of the growing country—farming and engineering.[xix]

Between 1862 and 1879, 26 land-grant institutions were established,[xx] and the number of students graduating with engineering degrees began expanding dramatically; by 1910, Americans who earned an engineering degree had grown from 87 to around 2,100 per year. By comparison, in 1911 the 11 technical schools in Germany graduated approximately 1,800 engineers per year.[xxi] While the study of engineering flourished during that time, many remained skeptical of the usefulness of attending college to study agriculture.[xxii] While new colleges rapidly opened their doors in the post-Civil War years, existing institutions of higher learning continued to evolve. The most material development was the pivot away from a predefined (generally classical) curriculum to which students must strictly adhere and toward a more flexible elective curriculum. The most vocal (and successful) proponent of this evolution was Charles Eliot, president of Harvard University from 1869 to 1909. The rationale for the elective system was a combination of necessity, principle, and preference.[xxiii] Across the nation, other institutions reconsidered their own course requirements and began adopting elective systems.[xxiv]

In total, 432 colleges and universities were established from 1860 to 1899—186 of those institutions (151 private) opened from 1860 to 1879, and 246 of them (197 private) opened from 1880 to 1899.[xxv] By 1900, the number of colleges in the United States expanded to 977.[xxvi] Meanwhile, the number of living baccalaureate graduates had grown to over 400,000, which equated to roughly 53.5 graduates per 10,000 people.[xxvii] While the percentage of Americans with college degrees was still limited (0.5% of the population), the college system had evolved dramatically by 1900. No longer designed to educate future clergy and/or the wealthiest Americans in the classics, colleges dramatically expanded their curriculums to ensure both greater societal relevance and utility. Yet, for all the benefits this evolution would confer to its students and the society, this transformation came with a loss of both purpose and identity among colleges themselves.[xxviii]

Enrollment in colleges and universities continued at a remarkable trajectory, growing five-fold from 1890 to 1940. Class sizes grew rapidly to accommodate the increase in enrollment, with the average number of students at public universities growing from 415 to 2,810 between 1897 and 1934 while the average number of students at private universities grew from 256 to 858 during the same period. Public institutions experienced a disproportionate share of the growth in enrollment, owing in part to state support and lower tuition expenses.[xxix] Female enrollment also expanded during this period with women comprising 40 percent of the 1939 fall enrolled class.[xxx] As enrollment and course offerings expanded rapidly, the American institute of higher education continued to evolve and become distinctly *American*. Universities in Europe generally took three forms: the classical studies of British universities, the scientific training of French grand ecoles, and the graduate and research institutes of Germany. By contrast, the American university combined each of these components and served a multitude of simultaneous functions. Furthermore, during that period, independent schools of theology and denominational institutions continued to decline in popularity while a majority of the professional schools (those educating primarily lawyers, dentists, pharmacists, and doctors) closed and were replaced by departments that were serving the same function at larger universities.[xxxi] While completion of secondary education and entrance exams remained the primary barriers of entrance to a university, the explicit cost of higher education was not prohibitively high. In-state tuition plus fees for undergraduates in 1933 was $61 at public sector institutions and $265 at private institutions.[xxxii] By comparison, a contemporary estimate of household income in 1930 in the United States was $2,438.[xxxiii] Meanwhile, from 1902 to 1940, total state and local government expenditures supporting higher-education institutions increased from 1.3 percent to 3.1 percent of total government expenditures.[xxxiv]

Johns Hopkins University, established in 1876, is considered the first research university in the United States. When the university first opened its doors, nearly its entire faculty had studied in Germany.[xxxv] Despite the growing success and prestige of research produced by Johns Hopkins prior to WWII, university reforms centered on broadening curriculum and not on enhancing research efforts. As such, only four of the 92 Nobel Prizes awarded between 1901 and 1931 were won by Americans.[xxxvi] However, this began to change in the 1930s. The ascendence of Nazi Germany generated an exodus of well-educated Jewish faculty from some of the world's most prestigious institutions, including the University of Berlin and University of Göttingen. Most of these faculty came to America and propelled forward American higher education standards.[xxxvii] So, while the American university was not widely respected internationally among scholars and researchers, the foundation had been established that would turn select American universities into the world's leading research institutions following WWII.

Another concurrent development that would shape the American university was the Great Depression. Beginning in 1929 and lasting approximately a decade, the Great Depression was a global phenomenon among developed countries that was characterized by a dramatic decline in income, tax revenue, prices, international trade, and an increase in unemployment. Meanwhile, many universities cut expenses; in 1933, Marietta professors proposed and received a salary cut of 50 percent. In response, the student newspaper wrote that the faculty had "come a lot nearer to a common feeling with the students. Now everyone on campus can admit quite freely that he is broke."[xxxviii] Meanwhile, social criticism became increasingly popular among students who were disillusioned with the state of the global economy. Students joined picket lines, organized labor unions, pledged not to go to war, criticized their schools' endowments for holding investments in companies considered predatory, and engaged in a variety of other extracurricular activities and demonstrations.[xxxix]

Despite the economic hardships created by the Great Depression, and despite the disillusionment that students felt toward their country and established institutions, enrollment did not decline during the Great Depression, nor did a great number of universities close. While some students postponed or ceased their university studies, others remained in college longer or earned master's degrees. In fact, the number of institutions of higher education grew by 299 to 1,708 between 1930 and 1940 while the total enrollment of students grew by roughly 400,000 to 1.5 million during the same period.[xl] By 1940, over 3.4 million Americans had college degrees, which was 258 graduates per 10,000 residents, up from 71 per 10,000 in 1910.[xli]

POST-WWII THROUGH THE 1970s

On December 8, 1941, Harvard University President James B. Conant spoke before a large audience in Sanders Theatre. He proclaimed, "The United States is now at war . . . We are here tonight to testify that each one of us stands ready to do his part in insuring that a speedy and complete victory is ours. To this end I pledge all the resources of Harvard University."[xlii] The motivations for such a proclamation were likely two-fold: (1) a patriotic desire to demonstrate loyalty to the American war effort and (2) a realization that Harvard would need to quickly adapt to the changing needs of the country or else it would face financial ruin. Harvard was not unique in this assessment, as WWII would reduce civilian enrollment by over 60 percent, rob schools of faculty, and generate other financial strains. However, despite the existential threat the war posed, a vast majority of colleges were able to adapt and survive. Hundreds of colleges that participated in training programs conducted by the Army, Navy, and Army Air forces, continued to operate (albeit with some financial strain). Meanwhile, over two-thirds of the few colleges that did not participate in government programs also survived; institutions that were forced to close were mostly small liberal arts colleges.

During this time, curriculums changed to better suit the needs of the military. For example, in addition to offering German, colleges added courses in Chinese, Russian, and Japanese. Liberal arts studies declined in favor of applied studies or the application of disciplines. Summer vacations were eliminated by many colleges by transitioning to a trimester system; students not enrolling in the third trimester had extra time to work (i.e., support the war effort) during the summer. Universities also became highly active in research. Prior to WWII, most university research was privately funded and was medical in application. However, during WWII (and beyond) university research departments received significant federal support in order to address material wartime needs. During this time, American universities developed synthetic rubber, advanced dehydration processes to store and transport food, developed new technologies to mass produce penicillin, developed pesticides to eliminate mosquitoes and combat malaria and other diseases, just to name a few.[xliii]

One full year prior to V-J Day, marking the conclusion of the war, President Roosevelt signed into law the Serviceman's Readjustment Act of 1944, colloquially known as the *GI Bill*. Proposals for what became the GI Bill were put forward by both a committee of college presidents as well as the American Legion, the non-profit organization formed in 1919 that advocates for veterans. Motivations for passing the GI Bill were many and included both a desire to reward servicemen for their sacrifice, dramatically increase the educational attainment of the population, increase the long-term productivity of the country, and avoid a dramatic surge in unemployed veterans following the war's conclusion. With respect to this final objective, the GI Bill would be a mechanism for keeping veterans out of the labor market until the economy could fully absorb them.

Benefits offered by the GI Bill to all servicemen who had served at least 90 days included subsidized low-interest mortgages, subsidized low-interest loans to start a business, and most famously, monthly payments to subsidize the cost of attending high school, college, or vocational school. An annual living stipend was increased in 1945 to $780 ($65 per month) for single veterans and $1,080 ($90 per month) for married veterans. In addition to this, veterans received $500 per year toward tuition and other educational expenses.[xliv] These figures may seem modest today; however, at the time, these figures far exceeded the cost to attend most universities. For example, in 1944 quarterly tuition, room, and board fees were as follows: University of Kansas ($225), University of California ($238), Northwestern University ($461), and Stanford University ($353). A few opponents of the GI Bill noted that many colleges responded to the increased willingness and ability to afford higher tuition by raising their tuition to the maximum allowable under the GI Bill (this is a recurring theme that we'll examine in the next chapter). Others at the time noted that veterans generally attended the most expensive college to which they had gained admission, while some veterans purchased unnecessary supplies if their $500 education stipend hadn't been exhausted. Regardless of any inefficiencies caused by this program, it was highly effective in increasing college enrollment. In the autumn of 1946, over one million veterans enrolled in college while over 2.2 million veterans (about one in eight) attended college by 1956 when support from the GI Bill concluded.[xlv]

Between 1940 and 1950, the number of Americans with a bachelor's degree increased by 1.9 million to 5.3 million, and the number of living graduates per 10,000 increased from 258 to 351.[xlvi] A majority of the post-WWII increase in enrollment were men, and by 1950 approximately 70 percent of students were male (up from 60%) in 1940, thereby temporarily reversing a trend toward parity between the genders.[2,xlvii] While the magnitude of the impact that the GI Bill had in college enrollment can be debated, what cannot be debated is how the dramatic increase in college enrollment and the coincident evolution in the political and societal view of college forever altered the trajectory of postsecondary education in the United States. In July of 1946, President Truman appointed a commission to "reexamine our system of higher education in terms of the objectives methods, and facilities; and in the light of the social role it has to play."[xlviii] Just over one year later, the first of the commission's

---

[2] By 1980, women had achieved parity in college enrollment.

six-volume report was returned to the president. Titled *Higher Education for American Democracy*, its recommendations included:

> . . . the abandonment of European concepts of education and the development of a curriculum attuned to the needs of a democracy; the doubling of college attendance by 1960; the integration of vocational and liberal education; the extension of free public education through the first 2 years of college for all youth who can profit from such education; the elimination of racial and religious discrimination; revision of the goals of graduate and professional school education to make them effective in training well-rounded persons as well as research specialists and technicians; and the expansion of Federal support for higher education through scholarships, fellowships, and general aid.[xlix]

In response to both the surge in post-WWII enrollment as well as the recommendations found in the *Higher Education for American Democracy* report, many states passed bills expanding existing institutions, built branch (satellite) campuses for existing universities, increased funding for research at universities, and many created statewide coordinating governing boards for universities and colleges.[l] Between 1940 and 1960, the number of institutions grew by 296 to 2004 (+17%), while fall enrollment grew by 2.1 million to 3.6 million (+144%).[li]

In 1958, the National Defense Education Act (NDEA) was signed into law; this act was passed in response to the successful launch of Sputnik by the Soviet Union as well as a countrywide shortage of mathematicians and engineers. This act provided funding to colleges to expand science, mathematics, and foreign language instruction; it also provided loans to students as well as national defense fellowships.[lii] The program was highly successful at increasing the educational attainment of students in the field of language and moderately successful at increasing the number of mathematicians. In 1960, universities conferred 5,405 (1.4% of total) foreign languages bachelor's degrees nationwide, while in 1970, universities conferred 20,895 (2.6% of total) degrees. By contrast, in 1960, universities conferred 11,399 (2.9% of total) mathematics bachelor's degrees nationwide, while in 1970, universities conferred 27,442 (3.5% of total) degrees.[liii]

Six years later, with support in both houses of Congress, President Lyndon B. Johnson began passing a series of major spending programs addressing medical care, urban development, rural poverty, transportation, and education. Known as the *Great Society* agenda, this domestic agenda aimed to improve and advance all areas of American life; policy initiatives included a "war on poverty," the creation of Medicare and Medicaid, further expanding welfare benefits, and increased spending on elementary through postsecondary education (to name a few).[liv] As part of the Great Society agenda, the Higher Education Act (HEA) of 1965 was drafted "to strengthen the educational resources of our colleges and universities and to provide financial assistance for students in postsecondary and higher education."[lv] In practice, this bill provided significant taxpayer support to implement many of the policy recommendations found in the *Higher Education for American Democracy* report from twenty years prior. Following its adoption, the HEA became the main legislative tool through which Congress now directly impacts higher education because every institution that receives federal funds must adhere to all its terms and conditions. The Act has been reauthorized roughly every five years since 1968, with the exception of 2014 through today.[lvi]

In the first of its eight titles (sections), the 1965 HEA appropriated a modest $25 million its first year and $50 million thereafter for grants used by states to "strengthen community service programs of colleges and universities." Other appropriations included grants to improve college libraries (Title II), support smaller colleges that are struggling financially (Title III), support the training of teachers who work in low-income areas (Title V), and make improvements to college campuses through building remodels, acquisition of equipment (Title VI), and expansion enrollment capacity (Title VII).[lvii] During the HEA's second reauthorization in 1972, Title IX was added; this addition corrected an oversight from the Civil Rights Act of 1964 whereby discrimination based on sex was prohibited in employment and public accommodations; however, this prohibition did not extend to education institutions. In 1964, women were underrepresented among university professional staff, comprising only 22% of its workforce.[lviii] The text from the Educational Amendments of 1972 reads: "No person in the United States shall, based on sex, be excluded from participation in, be denied the benefits of, or be subjected to discrimination under any education program or activity receiving Federal financial assistance."[lix] Title IX did not reference college athletics (for which it is well known today).[3]

Perhaps the most impactful component of the 1965 HEA that directly contributed to today's student loan crisis (which we will explore more fully in Chapters 2 and 5) was Title IV. This title provided $70 million in grants to be offered to high school students who were qualified to enter college but lacked the financial means to pay for it. The Title further charged states with administering one or more programs to ensure students had access to student loans that carried a federal guarantee. The loan sizes (offered on an annual basis) were $1,500 for graduate students and $1,000 for all other students,

---

[3] May 20, 1974, Senator Tower (R-Texas) introduced an amendment to exempt revenue-producing sports from being included in the determination of Title IX compliance. The amendment was rejected.

with a maximum balance of $7,500 and $5,000, respectively; the interest rate on loans was capped at either six or seven percent. Since these loans were federally guaranteed, the federal government offered to repay the lender in full should a borrower default, become permanently disabled, or die.[lx] Certainly, the framers of this act were well-intentioned and believed (rightly so) that the extension of federal guarantees to student loan administrators would expand the availability of loans to students. The framers also correctly ascertained that this extension of credit would enable students who might otherwise not attend college to earn an advanced degree; as shown in Figure 1.2, enrollment in higher education more than doubled between 1960 to 1970![lxi] However, as we will explore later, this Act has had several unintended consequences which have enabled the rapid growth in both college tuition expenses as well as the stock of debt utilized to pay college-related expenses.

THE 1970s THROUGH THE 2020s: GROWTH OF COMMUNITY, PUBLIC, AND PRIVATE COLLEGES

Growth of Community Colleges

While not a focus of this chapter, community colleges (also called junior colleges) currently occupy a highly relevant place in American higher education. Beginning in the early 1900s, many administrators in higher education believed universities should either enhance their offerings by providing courses that are relevant to professionals, while other administrators thought it wise to split the curriculum between *junior* (first two years) and *senior* (second two years) students. By differentiating between two- and four-year colleges, as summarized by President Harper of the University of Chicago, "many students who might not have the courage to enter upon a course of four years' study would be willing to do the two years of work before entering business or the professional school."[lxii] Under President Harper in 1900, the University of Chicago became the first institution of higher learning in America to award an associate degree, which was conferred after two years of study.[lxiii] Most junior college proponents believed junior colleges should offer terminal programs (i.e., students would receive no further education upon completion) and provide instruction in agriculture, technical studies, manual training, and arts. With this curriculum in mind, two-year community colleges would offer a *middle ground* between manual labor and highly-trained professionals.[lxiv] As such, these colleges were generally career-oriented, with applicable terminology including *vocational, semiprofessional,* and *occupational.* Community colleges rapidly gained popularity, with the total number of two-year colleges increasing from eight in 1900 to 207 by 1922—and later, 719 in 1965.[lxv]

In 1965, the HEA directed states to create higher-education coordinating commissions in order to qualify for various grants. States responded by organizing commissions that were charged with creating uniform standards for curriculum, student access, and areas of focus. In addition, at this time, community college missions were defined to provide services for both pre-baccalaureate and occupational aspirants, meaning some students could attend community college for three clearly defined reasons: to earn an associate (2-year) degree, to gain occupational training without earning a degree, or to earn credits that they could transfer to other state universities in order to earn a bachelor's degree. Commissions ensured few barriers existed to entering a community college; most were open to students who hadn't finished high school while other state educational commissions focused on ensuring community colleges would be opened within reasonable commuting distance of population centers. State commissions further ensured community colleges were supported with state funding (usually around 50%).[lxvi] In the twenty years following the passage of the HEA of 1965, the number of public 2-year colleges grew from 452 to 1,067 while the number of private 2-year colleges fell from 267 to 155.[lxvii] As of 2022, there are 1,042 member institutions of the American Association of Community Colleges. 2019 fall enrollment included 10.3 million people, of which 60 percent of students were enrolled in classes that can be used for "credit" (i.e., credits can be used toward an associate or bachelor's degree). Community colleges remain heavily subsidized, with only 25 percent of their revenue coming from tuition. The balance is from federal (13%), state (34%), local (21%), and other (7%) sources.[lxviii]

Growth of Public and Private Colleges

In the years following the passage of the HEA, enrollment in institutions of higher learning swelled more rapidly than at any time in the history the United States. In 1969, fall enrollment reached 8.0 million—up from 3.6 million in 1959. Meanwhile, the number of institutions grew from 2,004 to 2,525.[lxix] This rapid growth created several problems for both the colleges and their students. Many college campus facilities became overcrowded, resulting in insufficient student housing and an increased use of large lecture halls.[lxx] Meanwhile, student satisfaction with their experience declined. Criticisms at the time included irrelevant or outdated course requirements, neglect of undergraduate teaching in favor of focusing on graduate education or research, and an increasingly *impersonal* nature of the college experience.

Other criticisms at the time were political in nature and mirrored general societal dissatisfaction with the United States' involvement in Vietnam. As a result, students increasingly looked to their institutions to enable broader societal change while simultaneously demanding that universities provide students with more autonomy and control.[lxxi] This confluence of forces led to many large antiwar protests on college campuses, which sometimes led to tragic results. In May 1970, four students at Kent State University were killed and nine seriously injured by the Ohio National Guard while they attended an antiwar protest. In response, student protests around the country erupted with over 900 campuses experiencing walkouts and millions of students participating in generally nonviolent demonstrations.[lxxii]

Following these demonstrations, governors and state legislators began to lose confidence in American colleges and universities. In less than ten years, colleges lost much of the luster they had gained the prior generation and were now seen less as a critical source of innovation and societal advancement and more a source of political liability. This change in attitude, combined with recessions in 1969–1970 and 1973–1975, led to a tapering of financial support for higher education. While university enrollment continued to expand, reaching 11.6 million by 1980, both the rate of enrollment growth as well as the founding of new institutions significantly slowed. By the early 1980s, on the heels of higher enrollment but less governmental support, many colleges found both their facilities and budgets stretched.[lxxiii] In response to these (and other) growing concerns, the Secretary of the U.S. Department of Education created the National Commission on Excellence in Education with the aim of evaluating primary through postsecondary education in the United States. In 1983, the committee produced the report titled *A Nation at Risk: The Imperative for Educational Reform*.

This scathing report identified over a dozen issues concerning proficiency in language and mathematics, declining standardized test scores, poor critical reasoning skills, increased remedial training requirements, and a lack of schooling in areas relevant to the growth of technology. The report also noted "the *average citizen* today is better educated and more knowledgeable than the average citizen of a generation ago—more literate, and exposed to more mathematics, literature, and science . . . . Nevertheless, the *average graduate* of our schools and colleges today is not as well educated as the average graduate of 25 or 35 years ago, when a much smaller proportion of our population completed high school and college."[lxxiv] Likely not lost on the drafters of this report was that the average fall college enrollment in the United States had grown from 3.6 million to 11.6 million (+222%) between 1959 and 1979;[lxxv] so, while the HEA had opened the floodgates to those interested in earning a bachelor's degree, the quality of the education had suffered as a result. So, while the *A Nation at Risk* report recommendations focus largely on secondary education, there was one notable recommendation for postsecondary institutions: *raise your standards.* The report specifically stated that colleges should "adopt more rigorous and measurable standards, and higher expectations, for academic performance and student conduct, and that 4-year colleges and universities raise their requirements for admission. This will help students do their best educationally with challenging materials in an environment that supports learning and authentic accomplishment."[lxxvi]

Following the report, enrollment in colleges and universities continued to increase, albeit at a slower pace. In response to student feedback and concerns among state and federal legislatures, college administrators spent the subsequent decades "upgrading." This included significant building projects, hiring more faculty and administrators (thereby improving the student-to-faculty ratio), expanding and modernizing their curriculums, investing in the "college experience," and raising the price of tuition. Established colleges and universities also became increasingly competitive with respect to freshman class SAT scores, high school GPAs, and other extracurricular activities. In short, colleges became what we know them to be today: a diverse body of institutions (some large, some small), generally competitive to enter and increasingly diverse with respect to their offerings, geography, and experience. And, most important, with respect to the focus on this book, they became increasingly expensive. In fact, for the first time in the history of postsecondary education in America, the cost of the education became the primary impediment to colleges achieving their objectives of advancing both students and society.

Growth of For-Profit Colleges

In 1970, for-profit colleges were fringe players in the arena of U.S. higher education. These institutions nationally enrolled fewer than 20,000[lxxvii] students and primarily offered vocational training. This changed following the 1972 reauthorization of the HEA, in which Congress substituted the word "postsecondary education" for "higher education" in Title IV (the section that details the conditions of federal grants to cover tuition expenses).[lxxviii] This change in language expanded the institutions that students could attend when qualifying for federal financial aid to include non-baccalaureate degree and vocational programs.[lxxix] This was a watershed moment for these institutions; many for-profit institutions raised tuition to coincide with the amount of available government aid. Meanwhile, for-profit institutions began sending recruiters to unemployment lines, welfare offices, and low-income housing projects in search of students. Successful enrollment led to a monetary reward for the recruiter. About half of the student enrollments were low-income individuals, which contributed to staggering default rates. However, as the for-profit institutions were insulated from the financial hardships attributed to student loan defaults, their economic incentive remained of maximizing their enrollment irrespective of students' outcomes.[lxxx]

Between 1970 and 1982, enrollment in for-profit institutions grew tenfold to 177,000, and then grew another elevenfold by 2010, reaching a maximum enrollment of 2 million students.[lxxxi] In 2014, the U.S. Department of Education (DOE) detailed new rules to protect students from enrolling in poor-performing for-profit programs. In their public statement, the DOE highlighted several concerns including: attending a two-year for-profit institution costs a student four times as much as attending a community college and more than 80 percent of students at for-profit institutions borrow while less than half of students at public institutions do. In addition, students at for-profit colleges represented only 11 percent of the total higher education population, but were responsible for 44 percent of all federal student loan defaults at the time.[lxxxii] Finally, as shown in Figure 1.3, graduates of for-profit institutions were more likely to borrow, borrowed larger amounts, and defaulted more regularly than students who had graduated from public or private non-profit institutions.[lxxxiii,lxxxiv]

> *". . . more than 80 percent of students at for-profit institutions borrow while less than half of students at public institutions do. Additionally, students at for-profit colleges represented only 11 percent of the total higher education population, but were responsible for 44 percent of all federal student loan defaults at the time."*

Beginning in 2015, the DOE required students from for-profit institutions to regularly achieve "gainful employment" upon graduation; otherwise, the for-profit institution would risk losing access to taxpayer-funded student aid programs. The DOE defined *gainful employment* as annual student loan payments of graduates would not exceed 20 percent of his or her discretionary income or eight percent of his or her total earnings. At the time, the DOE estimated that 99 percent of the for-profit institutions would fail this accountability standard.[lxxxv] Since then, enrollment in for-profit institutions has (fortunately) waned, with enrollment falling more than 50 percent to 982,410 in 2019.[lxxxvi] Possibly putting new wind into the sails of for-profits, in July 2019, Education Secretary Betsy DeVos issued a repeal of the Gainful Employment requirements, effective July 1, 2020.[lxxxvii] Following this announcement, the

College Type	Share of BA Recipients with Student Loan Debt at Graduation in 2016	Average Debt for BA Recipients with Loans at Graduation in 2016	Annual Default Rate in 2017
Public	66%	$26,900	9.3%
Private (Non-Profit)	68%	$31,450	6.7%
Private (For-Profit)	83%	$39,900	14.7%

Figure 1.3 Student debt at graduation and default following graduation, by college type. *Source*: https://ticas.org/files/pub_files/qf_about_student_debt .pdf. Per student debt figures: The Institute for College Access & Success. Annual default rate: U.S. Department of Education.

American Federation of Teachers (AFT) filed a lawsuit against Secretary DeVos (AFT v. Devos) in defense of the Gainful Employment regulation.[lxxxviii] In October 2021, Secretary of Education Miguel Cardona filed a brief stating that the Biden administration would not reinstate the Gainful Employment requirement. The primary reason he provides is the DOE no longer has the data and analytical systems needed to calculate the debt-to-earnings ratios; as such, the DOE couldn't administer the rule even if it wanted.[lxxxix]

FOUNDATIONAL QUESTIONS AND ANSWERS

At the beginning of this chapter, I posed this series of questions: what purpose do junior colleges, colleges, and universities serve? Do these institutions serve their students or their societies, and are students expected to utilize the knowledge they gain to advance themselves, serve society, both, or neither? Finally, are institutions of higher learning upholding their tacit societal contract, and if not, why? My proposed policy solutions address what I believe to be incentive misalignment among college stakeholders, which has led to an explosion in student debt. But, if we are to enact policies that align incentives among schools, banks, students, and others, we need to agree on the overarching goal of the postsecondary educational system. And to do that, let's start by answering these foundational questions.

What Purpose Do Junior Colleges, Colleges, and Universities Serve?

Since the founding of the first American college in 1636, state legislatures, faculty, administrators, and students have respectfully disagreed over the fundamental purpose of college. Should college offer training that would enable their students to better produce goods and services of monetary value, or should college offer training that would enable students to elevate society in a manner that can neither be measured nor taxed? Interestingly, while opinions regarding college and its role in society have evolved over the years, the diametrically opposed philosophies regarding the purpose of college have remained constant.

While there is no correct answer regarding what the primary purpose of college is, it is helpful to identify how the pendulum has swung over the centuries between the two dichotomous philosophies. In the pre-revolutionary war era, colleges educated two groups of people: future clergy and the sons of wealthy families. Most colleges at that time insisted their students should serve society, and there remained a tacit contract that graduates would carry the burden of elevating society—be that through work in the clergy or governmental administration. The religious revival of the early 19th century also saw a period of expansion of colleges with congregations heavily supporting these institutions. Meanwhile, in the post-revolutionary and civil war eras, a greater emphasis was placed on the accumulation of skills relevant to nation building. Following the 1944 GI Bill, the 1958 NDEA, and lastly the 1965 HEA, government support enabled the rapid expansion of higher education while also impacting its mission; right or wrong, taxpayer support brought with it the expectation that students would exit these institutions having acquired marketable skills. These skills would enable students to be able to better produce goods and services of value to the nation, thereby increasing the future tax base. As a result, government support of higher education could be rationalized not as an expense, but rather as an investment. So, *what purpose do junior colleges, colleges, and universities serve?* They exist to impart knowledge and skills that enable graduates to elevate both themselves and our society.

The next question was: *are students expected to utilize the knowledge they gain to advance themselves, serve society, both, or neither?* For much of their existence, colleges and universities were institutions that were available to only to the wealthiest of Americans. While their cost was not intended to be prohibitive, requirements of proficiency in Greek, Latin, and mathematics served as a barrier to entry for all but the most fortunate to have received a formal and complete secondary education. Therefore, all those who graced its halls of institutions of higher learning knew that they owed most, if not all, of their opportunity to attend college to their position at birth. For this reason, institutions regularly instilled in their students a sense that with their position came responsibility, both to God and their fellow Americans. Graduates were expected to become "public servants," serving in positions of authority within the government, and could therefore steer society from atop a political structure. Others were expected to serve society by spreading the gospel.

However, the confluence of three societal changes would erode both the purpose of college as well as the expectations that colleges placed upon their students. An increase in secularism as well as the eventual establishment of separate seminary schools caused colleges to drift away from both religious instruction and religious motivation. Separately, the growth of the American Republic and expansion of voting rights increased the inclusiveness of government, thereby reducing the need for colleges to produce "public servants." Finally, government support for higher education generated pressure for colleges to produce a "return" for the government "investment," otherwise, the support may wane. Taken together, colleges have always professed their expectations that students both advance themselves and serve society; however, the emphasis on public service has significantly waned. Rather, those who are considering college and the governmental representatives who support the institutions largely focus on the cost-benefit analysis of tuition and forgone earnings versus future income and tax receipts. Thus, college graduates and public officials today generally emphasize personal, and not societal, advancement following the completion of a postsecondary education. As noted by American Historian Frederick Rudolph in his book *The American College & University*: "In time colleges would be more concerned about the expectations of their students than about the expectations of society. In time going to college would come very close to being an experience in indulgence rather than an experience in obligation."[xc]

Finally, *are institutions of higher learning upholding their tacit societal contract, and if not, why?* Today, institutions of higher education are *not* upholding their societal contract[4] and are in dire need of reform. While the knowledge a student can acquire while earning an associate or bachelor's degree is of immense value, the fact remains that over 40 million adults have student debt and would be in a far better situation to advance themselves and society if that debt had not been assumed. There is no doubt that colleges would argue that this means states need to support the schools more; however, as will be shown in subsequent chapters, this isn't necessarily true. Instead, colleges and universities have been responding to perverse incentives, which has crushed a generation of students and impaired their ability to elevate themselves and their country. What are those incentives, and why is college so expensive? Let's find out.

---

[4] This is not to say that school administrators, trustees, and faculty are bad people, have committed a crime, or should be ashamed. The objective of this book is not to place blame on any group for the current state of affairs; rather, this book is intended to be an honest assessment of our system and offer solutions for improvement. No one group can be blamed for the crushing stock of student debt, and no one group can solve this issue.

FIGURE SOURCES

- *U.S. Population. 1650–1800.* Walter Crosby Eells: Baccalaureate Degrees Conferred by American Colleges in the 17th and 18th Centuries (Washington, 1958). Table 4: Ratio of Living Baccalaureate Graduates to Total Population 1650–1950.
- *U.S. population. 1810–2020.* U.S. Census Bureau.
- *U.S. population with bachelor's degrees. 1650–1950.* Walter Crosby Eells: Baccalaureate Degrees Conferred by American Colleges in the 17th and 18th Centuries (Washington, 1958). Table 4: Ratio of Living Baccalaureate Graduates to Total Population 1650–1950.
- *U.S. population (25y+) with bachelor's degree (%). 1910–2020.* National Center for Education Statistics (NCES). Table 104.10. Rates of high school completion and bachelor's degree attainment among persons age 25 and over, by race/ethnicity and sex: Selected years, 1910 through 2020.
- *Total postsecondary institutions. 1650–1780.* Walter Crosby Eells: Baccalaureate Degrees Conferred by American Colleges in the 17th and 18th Centuries (Washington, 1958). Table 4: Ratio of Living Baccalaureate Graduates to Total Population 1650–1950.
- *Total postsecondary institutions. 1800–1860.* Colin Burke (Author). American Collegiate Populations: A Test of the Traditional View (New York University Series in Education and Socialization).
- *Total postsecondary institutions. 1870–1940.* NCES. Table 23. Historical summary of higher education statistics: 1869–1870 to 1989–1990.
- *Total postsecondary institutions. 1950–2018.* NCES. Table 317.10. Degree-granting postsecondary institutions, by control and level of institution: selected years, 1949–1950 through 2020–2021.
- *Enrollment in degree-granting postsecondary institutions. 1870–1940.* NCES. Table 105.30. Enrollment in degree-granting postsecondary institutions.
- *Enrollment in degree-granting postsecondary institutions. 1947–1989.* NCES. Table 303.10. Total fall enrollment in degree-granting postsecondary institutions, by attendance status, sex of student, and control of institution: Selected years, 1947–2030 (forecasted). Data shown through 2020.
- *Enrollment in degree-granting postsecondary institutions. 1990–2020.* NCES. Table 105.30. Enrollment in degree-granting postsecondary institutions.
- *U.S. Population with bachelor's degree. 1959–2020.* Author's calculations.
- *U.S. Population with bachelor's degree (%). 1650–2020.* Author's calculations.

2

Why Is College so Damn Expensive?

In 1969, the average annual cost (including tuition, fees, room, and board) to attend a four-year college in the United States was $1,545, or 19 percent of the median U.S. household income. So, while college wasn't cheap, it was well within the realm of affordability for most households. In addition, students could work part-time (work-study) and during the summer, and they would generally graduate in four years without college debt. However, by 2020, the annual cost had increased to $28,775 or 42 percent of the median U.S. household income. The increase of a private four-year college education has grown even more dramatically, from $2,356 in 1969 to $45,932 in 2020,[i] which is 68 percent of the median U.S. household income in 2018.[ii]

The growth in college expenditures has forced students to rely on work-study, grants, and more recently, loans, to make ends meet. As we will learn in Chapter 3, while the objective value of a college degree has grown, not every college degree is equal nor has the financial benefit of a college degree grown at the same rate as the cost of college. Despite these inconvenient facts, administrators are increasingly competing for students—not by elevating the value of the education, but by elevating the college experience. This entails offering students access to grand amenities like luxurious apartments, ornate libraries and lecture halls, and spacious sports facilities. Colleges are engaged in an arms race and the end result is that students may enjoy country club-like amenities such as lazy rivers[iii] (see Figure 2.1) while in college, but find themselves increasingly burdened by debt following graduation.

No doubt, college administrators are acting in good faith when they approve projects and reprice tuition. But when setting their annual budgets, whose interests are of pinnacle importance at those universities—the school, the faculty, the students, the administrators themselves, or some combination of these groups? In addition, how do administrators gauge the relative

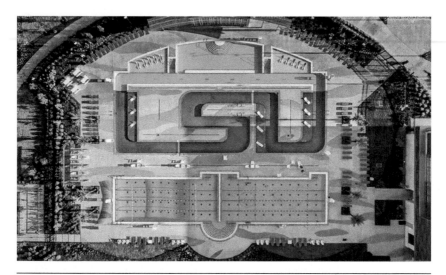

Figure 2.1   The LSU Lazy River. Completed in 2017.[1]

interests of these respective groups, and what happens when those interests conflict? Furthermore, why are students increasingly willing and able to pay for college despite the growing evidence that the value of a college education has waned relative to its cost?

In this chapter, I'll answer all of these questions. I'll detail the growing demand for a college degree and how postsecondary institutions have expanded (or have not expanded) their capacity in order to meet this rising demand. I'll also contextualize the growth in cost of a university education and explain how college tuition is spent by universities. I'll also review both the *academic* and *practical* explanations for rising tuition, and by doing so, I will demonstrate how universities' incentives are misaligned with those of their students. Specifically, because administrators are not incentivized to ensure that students graduate without debt and with degrees that ensure gainful employment, we may expect universities to continue to advance projects that lead to higher tuition but unchanged educational value. As a result, unless Congress

---

[1] The LSU lazy river was part of an $85 million renovation of the LSU recreation center. In 2008, a consultant ranked LSU at the bottom of the Southeastern Conference in terms of fitness space per student. In response, the student government passed a resolution in 2011 that authorized a $135 student fee increase to finance a new fitness center. By 2017, lazy rivers also existed on the college campuses of the Universities of Alabama, Iowa, Missouri, and Texas Tech. *Source: The Wall Street Journal.*

acts, we may expect more of the same: annual tuition increases that exceed inflation along with a growing stock of student debt. But before we figure out what we should do about this, let's figure out how we got here.

RISING DEMAND FOR ADVANCED DEGREES

From an economic perspective, the explanation for any development that involves an increase in price over time is relatively simple: the demand for a good or service must have grown faster than the supply of that service. As a result, prices rise in order for the quantity demanded (purchased) to equal the quantity supplied (sold). This overly simplistic explanation fits the data nicely. As shown in Figure 2.2, from 1950 to 2020, the number of undergraduate and graduate students has risen almost eightfold, increasing from 2.3 million to 19.9 million. At the same time, the number of institutions has grown roughly twofold, increasing from 1,851 in 1950 to 3,982 in 2020.[iv] Meanwhile, the growth in college expenses has far outpaced inflation.

While the increase in demand for a college is not the whole story, it does help us understand why generations of students (and their families) have both tolerated tuition increases and accepted this as normal. So why has demand for a college degree risen since at least the 1940s? There are several explanations—some benign and some harmful. I'll cover each.

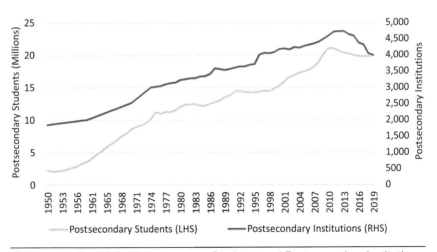

Figure 2.2 Growth in Postsecondary Students and Postsecondary Institutions. *Source*: National Center for Education Statistics.

Rising Demand: Benign Reasons

The growth in the U.S. population, the growth in household incomes (which leads to an increased ability to afford a college degree), and the real or perceived increase in the value of a degree (which leads to an increased willingness to pay for a college degree) have all contributed to an increase in the portion of the population who are aspiring to acquire a bachelor's degree. So, how much have each of these trends contributed to an increase in demand for college? Let's start by looking at population and income. As shown in Figure 2.3, in 1950 the U.S. population was 152.2 million, and by 2020 that population had grown 118 percent to 331.4 million.[v] Meanwhile, the resources available to a family to pay for a college education had also increased. From 1950 to 2020, the median family income in the United States (in 2020 dollars) increased 145 percent from $37,245 to $91,559.[vi]

While population and income are a good start, it's an incomplete explanation for the growth in postsecondary students. In 1950, approximately 1.5 percent of the population was enrolled in at least one postsecondary course, while the percentage of the U.S. population with a bachelor's degree was 3.5 percent. By 2020, those figures had grown to 6.0 and 25.8 percent, respectively. Similarly, in 1937, only 15 percent of recent high school graduates enrolled in a college;[vii] by 2018, that figure was about 63 percent. So, with a fourfold increase in the percentage of the population enrolled in postsecondary education and a nearly sevenfold increase in percentage of the population with a bachelor's degree between 1950 and 2018, clearly there was a societal shift in the appetite for college degrees. In addition, although the primary source of college students was people recently graduated from high school, older adults also obtained degrees in greater numbers, while more college students earned even higher designations and stayed in school longer.

Proponents of the current educational system like to attribute that shift in appetite (demand) for a college degree to the increase in the value of the degree. They do have a point. College graduates on average have higher income, lower unemployment, better health and lifestyles, and they benefit from collegiate networks. But, while all the aforementioned benefits are true *on average*, these statements ignore the distribution of educational value (some degrees offer higher salaries than others), educational outcome (a lot of students drop out), cost (some degrees are more expensive than others), and the potential for burdensome student debt. We'll cover all of those topics in Chapters 3 and 6.

Year	U.S. Population	Median Family Income in the U.S. (2020 dollars)	Postsecondary Students	Recent High School Graduates Enrolled in College (%)	Postsecondary Students (% Population)	U.S. Population with Bachelor's Degree (% Population)
1950	152,271,417	$37,245	2,281,298	No data	1.5%	3.5%
1959	177,829,628	$52,645	3,639,847	45.1*	2.0%	4.2%
1970	205,052,174	$73,399	8,580,887	51.7	4.2%	6.0%
1980	227,224,681	$75,988	12,096,895	49.3	5.3%	10.0%
1990	249,622,814	$78,174	13,818,637	60.1	5.5%	13.5%
2000	282,162,411	$84,483	15,312,289	63.3	5.4%	16.6%
2010	309,330,219	$78,085	21,019,438	68.1	6.8%	19.8%
2020	331,449,281	$91,559	19,744,000	62.7	6.0%	25.8%
1950–2020 Change	118%	146%	765%	39%**	298%	642%

* Figure as of 1960
** Figure shown is increase in the proportion of recent high school graduates entering college from 1960 to 2020

Figure 2.3 Growth in U.S. Population, Income, and Postsecondary Students. *Sources*: U.S. Census Bureau, National Center for Education Statistics, U.S. Federal Reserve, and author's calculations. For a more detailed description on each source, see the disclosure of sources at the end of Chapter 1.

Rising Demand: Harmful Reasons

So, there appear to be good reasons for people to aspire to earn and obtain a college degree. But, the growth in the stock of student debt, as well as the high percentage of underemployed college-educated adults, suggests that too many people are earning degrees. So, what could drive millions of people to make such poor financial decisions? The four areas I've identified are: (1) credential inflation (employers demanding higher credentials than are necessary), (2) societal pressure (politicians, teachers, friends, and family pressuring students to attend college), (3) the ability of universities to engage in price discrimination (like on an airplane, nobody pays the same fare), and (4) the accessibility of student loans.

The concerning trend by which employers require an advanced degree when one is not warranted was identified as early as 1979 by then University of Virginia Professor Randall Collins. In his prescient book titled *The Credential Society: An Historical Sociology of Education and Stratification*, Professor Collins argued over forty years ago that credential inflation hampers social mobility. Highly controversial at the time, he asserts "education is not associated with employee productivity on the individual level, and job skills are learned mainly through opportunities to practice them."[viii] He also claimed that the overuse of credentials has and will continue to provide "the means of building specialized professional and technical enclaves, elaborated bureaucratic staff divisions, and in general, has served to monopolize jobs for specialized groups of workers and thus insulate them from pressures for directly productive work."[ix]

Fast forward 35 years and in 2014, Burning Glass Technologies (a job market data and analytics firm) attempted to quantify the degree to which credential inflation is impacting workers' ability to find employment. In their white paper titled *Moving the Goalposts*, Burning Glass cross-referenced requirements for millions of job openings across 40,000 websites, and then compared those positions to their data on the existing workforce. They found employers are increasingly seeking bachelor's degrees for jobs that traditionally didn't require one; their metric is the *credential gap*, which is defined as the difference between postings requiring a bachelor's degree and the percentage of the existing workforce with a bachelor's degree. Positions with high credential gaps include production supervisor (26%), executive assistants (25%), employment and placement specialists (21%), computer network specialists (21%), and several more.[x] In 2017, researchers at Accenture, Grads of Life, and Harvard Business School came to the same conclusion. After analyzing 26 million job postings and surveying 600 businesses, these researchers found that several job titles experienced severe degree inflation; for example, 67 percent of the job postings required a bachelor's degree, but only 16 percent of workers already in that position held such a degree. As a result, these researchers estimated that as many as 6.2 million workers have been negatively impacted and are unable to secure a position for which they are otherwise qualified.[xi]

No doubt, millions of Americans have been motivated to earn a college degree simply because prospective employers require them, even if they are not necessary for that particular position. According to U.S. Federal Reserve estimates, as of September 2020, 33 percent of college graduates were working in a position that did not require a college degree; this figure has held steady between 31 and 35 percent from 1990 until today.[xii] Despite the apparent *over-education* of society, and the declining satisfaction with the receipt of a college degree (this is explored in detail in Chapter 6), American society continues to pressure young adults to enroll in college courses; this pressure can be attributed to fellow high school students, teachers, counselors, parents, and even the White House. In 2015, First Lady Michelle Obama and Jay Pharoah produced a rap video encouraging young adults to go to college; the video was uploaded to YouTube and Collegehumor.com.[xiii] Lyrics include:

If you wanna fly jets, you should go to college
Reach high and cash checks, fill your head with knowledge
If you wanna watch paint, don't go to college
But for everything else, you should go to college

Better make room! Better make room!
We comin'!
We applyin'!
That paper is not getting thrown in the garbage!
You go to college!

While the intent for this video was no doubt noble, the reality is that a one-size-fits-all prescription for postsecondary education is not appropriate. The value of a college degree varies dramatically by area of study and post-college employment. In addition, students that lack the cognitive acumen to advance in a college setting often fail to earn their degree but find themselves saddled with debt. Yet, you won't find that level of discussion in a video of this nature, nor do some parents or high school advisors appropriately dissuade select students from entering an expensive four-year program. Rather, as evidenced by the FLOTUS music video, the choice is simple: go to college and make money, or don't go to college and watch paint dry. The choice may seem simple, but for many, it's the wrong choice.

Another recent development that has heightened demand for college is the practice of price discrimination, particularly among private non-profit four-year colleges. Let me explain how it works. Colleges will post a *sticker price* for tuition, room, and board. This figure (say, $70,000 per year) is generally well out of reach for most applicants. Once accepted into a college, colleges that offer need-based aid will direct students to fill out a Free Application for Federal Student Aid (FAFSA) form. This form requires a complete disclosure to colleges of students' and parents' income and assets. From this information, colleges then determine each students' ability to afford college (say, $20,000 per year). Colleges will then offer a package to the student (say, $40,000 in grants and $10,000 in loans) thereby bringing down the effective price so that it is within reach of the student. By doing this, colleges can charge students with a higher willingness and ability to pay a higher rate for the same experience and degree. Proponents argue that this policy allows colleges to be increasingly progressive in their pricing; yet, this policy benefits students who deserve a spot at the college but whose financial situation might otherwise prevent them from attending the college.

According to the National Association of College and University Business Officers (NACUBO), the average tuition discount (sticker minus grants) at private non-profit colleges for the 2019–2020 academic school year among undergraduates was 47.6 percent, up from 36.4 percent in 2010. As a result, only 11 percent of first-year undergraduates paid the full sticker price.[xiv] Like the FLOTUS music video, we can assume this policy is well intentioned; but it ultimately creates three undesirable side effects. The first is that students may choose to attend the college with the largest financial aid package but not the lowest net cost. Many consumers believe there is a correlation between price and quality (higher price, better quality); thus, a $70,000/year private college (with a net cost of $30,000) may offer a better educational investment than a $20,000/year public college. In addition, $40,000 in grant money sure seems enticing. Second, this process increases the overall demand for colleges since some students apply to college not knowing if they can afford college. Once admitted and with a financial aid package in hand, students may choose to attend college even if they would have forgone the application process had they possessed complete information prior to the application process.

The final adverse impact of college price discrimination is that the value of education savings accounts (such as 529 plans or Coverdell savings accounts) is included in the disclosure of parental financial assets. This means colleges can (and often do) capture these savings in the form of a less generous financial aid package. Allow me to clarify how it works. Adam and Bob have been accepted into a private four-year college. Adam's parents and Bob's parents earn the same income, but Adam's parents have saved $100,000 in a 529 plan, whereas Bob's parents have not. The college will assess Adam's ability to pay for college to be higher than Bob's, and therefore Adam's financial aid package will be lower than Bob's. As a result, Adam's parents (who were the more fiscally responsible of the two) have ended up paying significantly more for the same education for their son, despite years of sacrifice and savings.[2,3]

> *"As a result, Adam's parents (who were the more fiscally responsible of the two) have ended up paying significantly more for the same education for their son, despite years of sacrifice and savings."*

The final source of increased demand for a college degree is the growth and maturation of the student loan market. The chartering of Sallie Mae in 1973 and its subsequent growth, as well as the expansion of other private lenders (see Chapter 6), has dramatically increased the financial resources available to students. Therefore, students who may have passed on attending college because they didn't have the cash on hand to afford tuition may now decide to attend a college. This is good. However, like all government policies, there are unintended consequences. In 1987, then Secretary of Education William Bennett penned a scathing opinion piece in the *New York Times* titled *Our Greedy Colleges*. In this piece, Secretary Bennett took colleges to task for decades of raising tuition at a rate that exceeded inflation. Secretary Bennett further took aim at government involvement in financing higher education, stating:

> *"If anything, increases in financial aid in recent years have enabled colleges and universities blithely to raise their tuitions, confident that Federal loan subsidies would help cushion the increase. In 1978, subsidies became available to a greatly expanded number of students. In 1980, college tuitions began rising year after year at a rate that exceeded inflation. Federal student aid policies do not cause college price inflation, but there is little doubt that they help make it possible."*[xv]

---

[2] The FAFSA form asks "what is the net worth of your parents' investments?" Later in the form it specifies that investments include qualified education savings accounts. While a 529 account is included in the aggregate value of all investments, education savings accounts are not a specific line item. As a result, some colleges assign a factor to the aggregate value of investments to assess ability to pay. For example, each $100,000 in financial assets increases the parents' ability to pay by $5,000 per year.

[3] In addition to a FAFSA form, around 240 mostly large, private institutions also require students to fill out a College Scholarship Service (CSS) profile. Universities utilize this profile to award non-federal (i.e., institution-specific) grants to students. This profile will include a complete disclosure of student and parent assets, including financial assets held in a 529 plan.

UNIVERSITIES' RESPONSE TO A SURGE IN DEMAND

As mentioned previously, demand for college and other postsecondary degrees increased dramatically following the second world war. In 1950 there were approximately 2.28 million postsecondary (undergraduate and graduate) students in the U.S.; this figure grew roughly ninefold to just under 20 million students in 2020. The supply-side response to this increase in demand included two components—more schools opened and existing schools got bigger. As shown in Figure 2.4, between 1950 and 2020 postsecondary accredited schools grew from 1,851 to 3,982, while the average institution size grew from 1,232 students to about 5,000 students.[xvi]

Interestingly, one category of schools did not meet this surge in demand by materially increasing the size of the student body—the largest, wealthiest, and most prestigious schools. I'll focus on just the Ivy League schools here. As shown in Figure 2.5, in fall 1987 there were 60,722 enrolled undergraduate students; this came to 0.55 percent of all undergraduate students in the U.S. By fall 2019, the total number of students enrolled in the U.S. had grown by 50 percent, from 11 million to 17 million. Meanwhile, the Ivy League schools enrolled a modest 8,000 more undergraduate students, growing this student body by only 13 percent. Harvard University actually enrolled slightly *fewer* students in 2020 than in 1987. As a result, the number of undergraduate students earning their education at Ivy League schools fell from 0.54 to 0.41 percent, indicating that the Ivy league schools had become even *more* prestigious, as measured by their selectiveness.

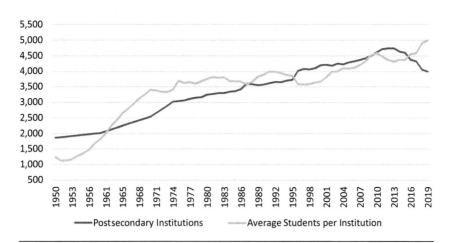

Figure 2.4   Growth in Postsecondary Students and Postsecondary Institutions. *Sources*: National Center for Education Statistics and author's calculations.

	1987	2020	33-Year Change (%)
Brown University	5,747	7,043	23%
Columbia University	5,790	8,216	42%
Cornell University	13,000	15,182	17%
Dartmouth College	3,583	4,418	23%
Harvard University	10,394	9,950	−4%
Princeton University	4,667	5,428	16%
University of Pennsylvania	11,722	11,851	1%
Yale University	5,291	5,964	13%
All Ivy League Colleges	60,194	68,052	13%
U.S. Undergraduate Population	11,046,235	16,692,000	51%
Ivy Enrollment % Total Undergraduate	0.54%	0.41%	

Figure 2.5   Growth in Ivy League Schools and Total U.S. Student Body. *Sources*: National Center for Education Statistics and Integrated Postsecondary Education Data System.

Full stop. So, for the past 33 years, the schools with the greatest means to expand their student body in response to a surge in demand, didn't? Correct! So why did they do that, and why is this relevant? Stick with me. The answer to both of these questions will shed further light on why college is so expensive and how thoughtful legislation can address this.

THE PRICE OF A COLLEGE DEGREE

As mentioned earlier in this chapter, there are two prices to college: a sticker price (posted on a college's website and found in marketing materials) and the actual (net) price paid by students. The latter price is highly variable and is equal to the sticker price minus scholarships, grants, and financial aid. Beginning in 2011, colleges were required to offer net price calculators on their websites whereby prospective students could enter financial information and the website would provide an estimate of awarded grants or scholarships. Then, in 2015 the Department of Education created an online portal called the *College Scorecard*. This comprehensive website includes information on each college's fields of study, costs, graduation rates, financial aid and debt, salary after completing a field of study, student body demographics, and test scores among accepted students. Most relevant to this discussion is a tool that provides an estimate to prospective students of each student's personal net price.[xvii] So, depending on family income and assets, this website can provide an estimate as to how much a student will likely pay after receipt of grants and other scholarships.[4] Once this information became publicly available, a couple of interesting patterns emerged. Public schools are generally cheaper than private schools. However, the *price curve* for private schools is steeper than public schools. Said another way, private schools tend to offer steeper discounts to low-income students than do public schools.[xviii] For the purpose of the following analysis, I utilize publicly available data concerning the net, and not the sticker, price of college.

How Much Has the Price of a Degree Risen?

At this point, we know that the cost of a bachelor's and other advanced degrees has risen; but, by how much, over what time period, and how has this cost risen relative to general inflation or to incomes? Utilizing data from the U.S. Bureau of Labor Statistics, we can compare the price inflation of college tuition and fees to other categories as well as general U.S. Consumer Price Index (CPI) inflation. In my analysis, I subdivide the data into three time periods (1977 to 1997, 1997 to 2019, and 1977 to 2019) because U.S. inflation was notably higher from 1977 to 1997; so, by splitting the data into two roughly equal periods, we can see how college prices rose in both low- and high-inflation periods.

What we find is that college tuition has risen more rapidly than any other category for all time periods. As shown in Figure 2.6, from 1977 to 1997, college tuition and fees rose an average of 8.6 percent per year, or 3.7 percent higher than the general inflation rate. Similarly, from 1997 to 2021, college tuition and fees rose an average of 4.6 percent per year, or 2.3 percent higher than the general inflation rate. The only other category that has experienced a significant increase in cost, above and beyond the general CPI, is medical care. Interestingly, goods that are manufactured (food, beverages, electricity, vehicles, and apparel) have all experienced relative price declines.[xix] This indicates that manufacturers have become increasingly efficient and passed cost

---

[4] More recently, there has been a proliferation of websites offering to help prospective students estimate their net college expense and identify colleges that will likely offer the most generous financial aid packages. These websites include CollegeRaptor, MeritMore, MyinTuition, Edmit, and TuitionFit. These sites vary in terms of the services they provide, their expense (prices range from $0 to $100), and their methodology for collecting data. For example, TuitionFit users upload their actual financial aid letters, which has allowed TuitionFit to build a database with more accurate estimates than what is normally available on the college's own website. Edmit also utilizes publicly available data along with user financial aid packages to refine their estimates of net college cost.

	Category Annual Inflation			Category Annual Inflation—General (CPI) Inflation		
	1977–1998	1998–2021	1977–2021	1977–1998	1998–2021	1977–2021
College Tuition and Fees	8.6%	4.6%	6.4%	3.7%	2.3%	2.9%
Medical Care	7.2%	3.4%	5.1%	2.3%	1.1%	1.6%
Services	5.9%	2.7%	4.2%	1.0%	0.4%	0.7%
Motor Fuel	3.6%	4.6%	4.2%	-1.2%	2.3%	0.7%
Housing	5.0%	2.5%	3.7%	0.1%	0.2%	0.2%
U.S. CPI	4.9%	2.3%	3.5%	–	–	–
Food and Beverages	4.4%	2.5%	3.3%	-0.5%	0.2%	-0.1%
Electricity	4.1%	2.4%	3.2%	-0.8%	0.1%	-0.3%
New Vehicles	3.4%	0.6%	1.9%	-1.5%	-1.7%	-1.6%
Apparel	2.6%	-0.3%	1.0%	-2.3%	-2.6%	-2.5%

Figure 2.6 Historical Category Annual Inflation Rates. *Sources:* U.S. Bureau of Labor Statistics and author's calculations.

savings on to their customers. However, because a college education is not a widget whereby production can be dramatically improved via automation, technological advances have not led to efficiencies that benefit consumers (students).

So, why does a cost increase of 2.9 percent per year, in excess of inflation, matter? It seems relatively benign. However, as shown in Figure 2.7, this is an annual increase in price that is cumulative. Thanks to the power of compounding, the cost of the increase in college tuition and fees between 1977 to 2019 is astounding. From 1977 to 2020, if $100 had been put in a bank account that grew at the rate of inflation, the bank account would have grown to $415. Thus, $100 in 1977 would have the same purchasing power as $450 in 2020. Conversely, $100 spent on college tuition and fees in 1977 would cost a whopping $1,547.81 in 2020. Therefore, the inflation adjusted cost of college has grown roughly fourfold from 1977 to 2020.

Thus, college tuition is far more expensive today when taking into account how the purchasing power of a dollar has changed (i.e., overall inflation). But, is college less affordable for the average adult or household today versus a generation ago? We know that salaries and household incomes have risen; so, what has been rising more quickly—college expenses or household incomes? Unfortunately, the answer is that college expenses have risen much more rapidly than household incomes, and as a result, college is significantly less affordable. As shown in Figure 2.8, there was a brief period between 1969 and 1979 when college became marginally more affordable; specifically, college tuition and fees rose at a rate slower than the rate at which household incomes grew. However, since that time, tuition and fee expense rates have far outpaced household income growth. This is true for all quintiles (household incomes divided into five groups based on salary).

As shown in Figure 2.9, in 1969 the cost of college tuition and fees was 19 percent of household income for the median (middle income) family. So, if the average family made $10,000 per year, the cost of sending a child to college was $1,900 per year. That's a nontrivial expense, but it was well within reach for most families. Meanwhile, the cost of college education was 80 percent of the bottom fifth's household income, meaning the poorest 20 percent of households would have to spend $8 on college tuition and fees for every $10 earned. This socioeconomic demographic had the lowest percentage of students attending college (for financial reasons), and were generally the most likely to receive aid and assume loans. Since 1969, what we find is that for every quintile of households, the cost of college tuition and fees has grown as a percentage of household income; as a result, the burden has been greatest for the lower income groups. In 2020, the median household would have to spend 42 percent of its income to send a single student to college (up

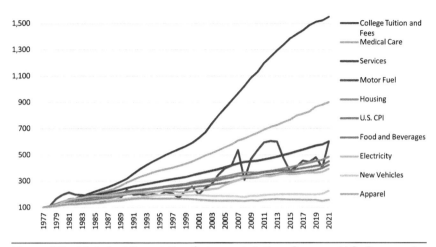

Figure 2.7 Historical Cumulative Category Inflation. *Sources*: U.S. Bureau of Labor Statistics and author's calculations.

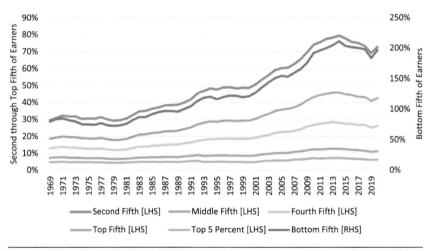

Figure 2.8 Cost of College Tuition and Fees as a Percentage of Household Income. *Sources*: U.S. Department of Education, National Center for Education Statistics, U.S. Census Bureau, and author's calculations.

from 19% in 1969). Meanwhile, the bottom fifth of households would need to work two years, and spend all income earned, to send a student to college for one year![xx,xxi] The critical takeaway from this analysis is that the growth rate in the cost of a college degree has far exceeded the growth rate of household income. As a result, college has become significantly less affordable for all but the most affluent.

	Bottom Fifth	Second Fifth	Middle Fifth	Fourth Fifth	Top Fifth	Top 5 Percent
1969	80%	30%	19%	13%	8%	5%
1979	73%	29%	18%	12%	7%	4%
1989	96%	39%	23%	15%	8%	5%
1999	120%	49%	29%	19%	9%	5%
2009	176%	70%	41%	26%	12%	7%
2020	197%	73%	42%	26%	11%	6%
Increase (1969–2020)	1.47	1.46	1.29	0.98	0.51	0.32

Figure 2.9 Cost of College Tuition and Fees as a Percentage of Household Income. *Sources*: U.S. Department of Education, National Center for Education Statistics, United States Census Bureau, and author's calculations.

What Does Tuition Support?

So, what is tuition spent on anyway? The following is an attempt to answer this question as well as show how priorities (i.e., spending habits) have shifted over time. University life today has dramatically evolved since the 18th century. No longer does a four-year college consist of a dormitory, a student union with a dining hall, a library, and a lecture hall with some adjacent faculty offices. Rather, universities are the size of small towns, and in some cases, large towns, while the services, education, and experiences offered are expansive. Whether or not this is a good thing can be debated later; however, it should be sufficient to state that the breadth of college expenditures echoes the breadth of the services being offered.

The single largest expense incurred by colleges and universities is instruction expenses. This includes faculty salaries, organized activities related to instruction (field trips), academic support, and materials related to classroom instruction. Utilizing data from the National Center for Education Statistics (NCES),[5] I estimate that from 1939 to 2019, between 59 and 46 percent of

---

[5] This analysis was challenging. The publicly available data includes time-varying classifications of expenses, different accounting methods, and different categories of universities (public, private, or an aggregation). Also, some expenses may be placed in different accounting categories, and this categorization may vary by school. For example, should the regulatory expenses that are associated with demonstrating compliance for a research grant fall into an administrative expense or a research expense? Should building expenses include annual depreciation or only the direct expenses incurred? How should we compare schools that do or do not operate hospitals? With that said, I attempt to normalize and recategorize the NCES data in order to ensure consistency across time periods and accounting methods. While the results presented in this chapter should be thematically accurate, the figures are estimates.

all university expenditures was spent on instruction; currently the figures stand at 52 percent for private and 49 percent for public universities. The next largest category of expenditures includes administration who are responsible for day-to-day operations of the campus. This category of people occupies a tremendous breadth of responsibilities. For example, administrators hire faculty and set budgets; engage directly with students and parents by addressing financial, academic, or other concerns; and work with government officials to secure financial support or demonstrate compliance with federal or state guidelines. Administrative expenses, like student instruction, have varied across time and by type of school (public or private). In general, these expenses were around 12 percent of total expenses in 1939 but grew to around 20 percent by 1995. Today, administrative expenses are likely in the 17 percent vicinity (but possibly lower for some public universities). In a 2013 survey conducted by Vanderbilt University, researchers learned that regulatory compliance expenses (not related to research grants) ranged from two to eight percent of an institution's non-research budgets.[xxii]

Another nontrivial university expense includes maintaining campus facilities (housing, libraries, lecture halls, sports facilities, etc.). Because of time-varying accounting approaches and changes in expense classification methodologies, it is difficult for us to ascertain how large an expense this constitutes; although, I would venture to guess that building expenses constitute around 10 percent of a typical university budget. Research is another material source of university expenditure; although, this varies highly by university or college, and has varied a lot by time period. Research budgets expanded significantly during and following WWII, peaking around 22 percent of all university expenditures by 1959. However, research expenditures have fallen in relative importance since then. *Public service* includes programs that are sponsored by entities that are separate from the university, while the *All Others* category includes student services like job placement, healthcare, counseling, or other general campus expenditures that do not fit into one of the other categories.

Most categories have experienced annual increases in expenditures in excess of inflation, over each decade since 1929, as shown in Figure 2.10.[6] For

---

[6] Figure 2.10 shows annual category inflation, per student, per period. What does that mean? By pulling several data sets together, and after consuming copious amounts of coffee, I estimate how per-student expenses changed over time, as related to inflation. Specifically, we have data on aggregate expenses from colleges for different categories, and we know how many students attended those institutions, so we can calculate per-student expenses on each category. We can then see how those expenses change over time, while adjusted for inflation. This gives us a sense of how incremental university revenue is being spent.

All Degree-Granting Institutions

Period	Inflation (Everything)	Annual Category Price Inflation in Excess of General Inflation						
		Student Instruction	Admin	Campus Facilities	Research	Public Service	All Others	Total
1930–1939	-2.0%	2.3%	2.9%	1.3%	3.1%	2.4%		2.2%
1940–1949	5.4%	0.6%	2.2%	1.4%	12.2%	-1.2%		1.8%
1950–1959	2.2%	1.0%	2.7%	0.2%	8.1%	1.2%		2.3%
1960–1969	2.5%	2.4%	4.8%	2.5%	-3.1%	0.1%	41.3%	2.2%
1970–1979	7.4%	0.8%	1.4%	1.3%	-0.8%	2.0%	-10.1%	0.5%
1980–1989	5.1%	2.0%	2.8%	0.5%	2.6%	3.1%	1.5%	2.1%
1990–1995	3.3%	1.2%	2.2%	0.3%	1.5%	2.8%	2.4%	1.4%
Private Non-Profit Institutions								
1998–2007	2.7%	2.2%	2.6%	-1.2%	2.5%	–	3.2%	2.5%
2008–2019	1.7%	0.7%	0.5%	5.4%	1.1%	0.3%	1.9%	1.0%
Public Institutions								
1998–2007	2.7%	15.1%	9.5%	17.2%	6.2%	7.5%	16.8%	12.5%
2008–2019	1.7%	2.0%	2.2%	Unknown	1.9%	1.4%	9.5%	1.6%

Figure 2.10   Annual Changes in University Expenditures by Category and by Decade. *Sources:* U.S. Department of Education, National Center for Education Statistics, United States Census Bureau, and author's calculations.

example, administrative expenses rose 2.8% per year from 1979 to 1989 while general inflation went up 5.1 percent. So, administrative expenses rose annually (for 10 years) at a rate of 7.9 percent between 1979 and 1989. Similarly, student instruction expenses rose at an annual rate of 4.5 percent between 1989 and 1995, which is 1.2 percent in excess of inflation.

WHY HAS TUITION RISEN? THE *ACADEMIC* EXPLANATIONS

So far, we've established that the demand for postsecondary degrees has risen dramatically in the post-WWII environment. Furthermore, while colleges have an implicit contract with both society and their students that *should* temper tuition inflation, the cost growth of a postsecondary education has far outpaced both inflation and income growth. In the words of American economist and Cornell professor Ronald Ehrenberg, colleges have become like "cookie monsters searching for cookies. They seek out all the resources that they can get their hands on and then devour them."[xxiii] So, the question is: why do colleges and universities continually raise tuition even if it is a detriment to society in general and their students in particular? A supply and demand analysis isn't sufficient; we know that since 1977, demand for apparel, vehicles, electricity, food, and beverages, has substantially grown. However, the cost of these goods has fallen relative to inflation, meaning they've become increasingly affordable. There must be other explanations for this growth in expense that is fundamental to our modern postsecondary education system. In this section, I'll cover the *academic* theories for rapid tuition inflation, which are not mutually exclusive and may all have elements of truth. The explanations (in order of what I believe to be most to least compelling) are: (1) the principal/agent problem, (2) the Bennett Hypothesis, (3) Bowen's Revenue Theory, (4) the Baumol Effect, (5) the Chivas Regal Effect, and (6) the Declining Public Support Hypothesis. After reviewing these theories, I'll then review other less academic explanations for the rise in tuition and the decline in affordability of postsecondary education in America.

The Principal/Agent Problem

Have you ever worried that an auto mechanic would repair something that wasn't broken, worried that an attorney would bill you for more hours than necessary, or worried that a doctor was ordering expensive tests even though the results wouldn't impact the treatment for an ailment? These are all examples of the principal/agent problem. In these examples, you are the *principal* (the owner or purchaser of an asset or service) and you have delegated control over that purchase to an *agent* (a mechanic, lawyer, or doctor). In all instances, your incentive is to control cost and ensure all goods and services purchased are necessary. In contrast, the agent's incentive is to maximize the amount you purchase; this is because the agent receives a commission or financial incentive when you purchase more. As a result, incentives between principals and agents are not fully aligned. While a vast majority of mechanics, doctors, and lawyers are honest, the unscrupulous ones (the agents) can take advantage of the situation to the detriment of you (the principal).

The principal/agent problem was first identified in the 1970s by Michael Jensen of Harvard Business School and William Meckling of the University of Rochester. In a paper published in 1976, these economists proposed methods for both quantifying as well as minimizing the *agency cost* borne by the shareholders of publicly traded companies.[xxiv] While the focus of this groundbreaking paper is on corporations, the foundational issue of the principal/agent problem is highly relevant to the university system. Specifically, students, parents, alumni, donors, and taxpayers are principals. Meanwhile, faculty members, administrators, and trustees are the agents. The objectives of the principals in general (and students in particular) is to maximize the economic value of their education. This involves cost controls and a continual cost-benefit analysis utilized by the agents who allocate resources at the universities. However, the interests of the agents are not to maximize the economic value of the education they provide, but to improve the schools' rankings, elevate reputation, and enhance prestige. Because of this, capping tuition increases does not factor prominently into their decision-making process. Later in this chapter, I'll further detail exactly what the motivations are of the colleges and universities, and how these agents' incentives may be diametrically opposed to their students' welfare.

The Bennett Hypothesis

This explanation for tuition inflation is named after Secretary of Education William Bennett, who served from 1985 to 1988 under President Reagan. As mentioned earlier in this chapter, Secretary Bennett penned a scathing *New York Times* piece in which he argued that "federal student aid policies help make it [tuition inflation] possible."[xxv] After this piece, the argument that universities captured most, if not all, of additional loans available to students (by raising their tuition) became known as the *Bennett Hypothesis*. In 2015, economists at the Federal Reserve Bank of New York tested this hypothesis and published their results in a paper titled *Credit Supply and the Rise in College Tuition: Evidence from the Expansion in Federal Student Aid Programs*. These

> *"For every dollar of federally subsidized loans made available to students, the colleges increased their sticker prices for tuition by roughly 60 cents while simultaneously decreasing the grants awarded to students by roughly 20 cents."*

economists used data from 1999 through 2012 and merged data from a variety of datasets to ascertain if there was a causal link between financing availability, college tuition, and extension of grants. The results of their study were both enlightening and disappointing. For every dollar of federally subsidized loans made available to students, the colleges increased their sticker prices for tuition by roughly 60 cents while simultaneously decreasing the grants awarded to students by roughly 20 cents. Taken together, the economists concluded that colleges were capturing most of the value of federal loans made available to students and the Bennett Hypothesis was generally accurate. The authors were silent on whether making federally subsidized loans available to students was good economic policy, but they did opine that a complete analysis of existing programs should weigh both "tuition effects and increased participation (college enrollment)." Said another way, increasing the amount of loans available to students increases the size of the student body, but it puts a lot more students in debt as well (and the authors didn't want to opine as to whether or not that was a good thing).

Bowen's Revenue Theory

Also known as *Bowen's Law*, Bowen's Revenue Theory was named after Howard Bowen, an economist and former president of Grinnell College, the University of Iowa, and Claremont Graduate University. Bowen released a scathing assessment of cost control in higher education in 1980 (he had retired from academia nine years prior). In his book titled *The Costs of Higher Education*, Bowen asserted, "unit cost [i.e., the cost of education] is determined by hard dollars of revenue and only indirectly and distantly by considerations of need, technology, efficiency, and market wages and prices." Bowen further elaborates on runaway tuition inflation with his five rules of thumb: (1) "The dominant goals of institutions are educational excellence, prestige, and influence," (2) "There is virtually no limit to the amount of money an institution could spend for seemingly fruitful educational ends," (3) "Each institution raises all the money it can," (4) "Each institution spends all it raises," and (5) "The cumulative effect of the preceding four laws is toward ever increasing expenditure."[xxvi] In 2006, two economists from the

College of William and Mary attempted to test Bowen's Law by examining the yearly price increases for college tuition and comparing them with other service-based industries between 1929 and 1995. The assumption was that if Bowen's Law was the primary driver of education expense increases, it's path of annual price increases would be idiosyncratic (i.e., unique to that industry). However, economists found other industries also experienced a similar path of price increases.[xxvii] So, while Bowen's Revenue Theory was not necessarily incorrect, it was likely incomplete.

The Baumol Effect

The "effect" or the "cost disease theory" (depending on the literature) is named after William Jack Baumol, an American economist who, prior to his death, taught at NYU and Princeton University. In 1966, he and William Bowen (another economist and former president of Princeton University) published an article that is seemingly unrelated to higher education titled *Performing Arts, The Economic Dilemma*.[xxviii] The paper explained why the salaries of live performers had continued to increase even though their productivity hadn't increased. For example, in 1826 it took four people 40 minutes each to perform Beethoven's String Quartet No. 14 (or 160 minutes total); in 2026, it will still take 160 minutes split evenly between four people to perform String Quartet No. 14. So, there has been no productivity growth associated with an enhancement in skills or technology; yet, the salaries for live performers have risen. Why? The answer (as unintuitive as this sounds) is that other jobs have experienced labor productivity growth.

Imagine in 1826 London, a moderately skilled laborer could earn £5 in a single day, and with that £5 she could purchase a concert ticket to hear Beethoven's String Quartet No 14. Two hundred years later, that same laborer could earn £150 in a day, meaning that laborer is now 30 times more productive. The cost of a concert ticket may now be £150, meaning the price of a string quartet performance has also risen 30 times, but it is equally affordable to a moderately skilled laborer because it still costs a single day of labor to attend the concert. This is relevant because other types of labor have become more productive, so the cost of industries without the benefit of productivity growth has also risen; but its affordability remains unchanged.[xxix] We can draw a parallel between college educators and classically trained musicians. It takes the same number of hours to grade a paper or lecture in front of a class today as it did in 1950. Thus, we would expect the cost of college to rise as peoples' income rises following enhancements in labor productivity in noneducation-related fields. Where this explanation falls short is that while this hypothesis may explain some of the cost increases in a college education, it does not explain the subsequent decline in affordability. Returning briefly to Figure 2.9, we see that in 1969, the average annual cost of a college degree for the median household was 19 percent of its annual income; by 2020, that figure had increased to 42 percent. So, unlike the string quartet example where the price has increased but the affordability is unchanged, with higher education we know that the price has increased while the affordability has decreased. Therefore, the Baumol Effect, while not necessarily incorrect, is also likely incomplete.

The Chivas Regal Effect

The *Chivas Regal Effect* is known in marketing as the phenomenon whereby consumers associate value with price. In other words, if a consumer is ignorant of the product (other than its price), they will assign a higher value to a product if it has a higher price. So, the price becomes a signal of the product's desirability or value, including the product's desirability vis-à-vis its peers. The name of the effect comes from the urban legend surrounding the increase in sales and desirability of the Chivas Regal blended Scotch whisky. As the story goes, in the 1940s, the whisky was selling poorly in the United States. So, the owners had a brilliant idea—they would double the price! Supposedly, unit sales rose (not fell) as demand rose and consumers began believing it was a premium product.[7]

The Chivas Regal Effect was first cited by *Time Magazine* in 1989 in an article about runaway tuition inflation at prestigious universities. Between 1987 and 1989, college tuition increased by 16 percent; the student who was interviewed in the *Time* article described how her total educational expenses had jumped to $16,100—how outlandish! Meanwhile, the consultant in the article noted that "It's Chivas Regal pricing—schools can afford to charge what they want because they've got lines out the door."[xxx] Since that time, the Chivas Regal Effect and tuition inflation have been largely synonymous as people annually assign higher value to a college education in lockstep with the higher price tag.

Declining Public Support Hypothesis

This hypothesis states that the primary reason for increasing tuition and fees can be directly attributed to declining public support. In other words, as federal and state governments redirect funds away from public universities in

---

[7] The more likely contributor to the change in sales was that Seagrams purchased Chivas Regal in 1949, and Seagrams increased both the marketing and distribution of the product.

favor of other programs, these public schools must raise tuition and fees in order to plug a hole in their budget. To be fair, since revenue and expenditures must equal each other, there is some validity to this argument. In 2019, the Pew Charitable Trust (a District of Columbia-based public policy nongovernmental organization) released a study showing a steady decline in public support for colleges and universities between 2000 and 2015. In inflation-adjusted dollars, researchers estimated total state and federal revenue per full-time student fell $1,378 (−12.5 percent) to $9,634 between 2000 and 2015.[xxxi] Separately, in 2017 Professor Douglass Webber at Temple University released a study demonstrating that since 2000, students will pay an average of $318 more in tuition and fees for every $1,000 cut in state budgets.[xxxii]

The declining public support hypothesis is generally utilized by administrators and public officials who are clamoring for additional public support for higher education. The reduction in support must be made up somehow; but this hypothesis speaks nothing to the way in which universities spend money or how they do (or do not) establish cost controls or utilize a cost-benefit analysis. Furthermore, as shown in Figure 2.10, tuition has increased in the U.S. in every 10-year period, which also includes periods of both increasing and decreasing public support for postsecondary institutions. Finally, remember the LSU lazy river that was mentioned at the beginning of this chapter (which was completed in 2017)? In 2015, in response to a $1.6 billion fiscal deficit, the Louisiana legislature proposed cutting LSU's funding from $110 million to $58 million.[xxxiii] School administrators and government officials later agreed to a smaller budget cut, but this was only after the Louisiana governor threatened to cancel the 2016 football season if a compromise wasn't reached.[xxxiv] Meanwhile, the construction of the lazy river moved forward despite budget concerns and was completed on time. Clearly, there is not a strong causal link between tuition expenses, college amenities, and state support.

WHY HAS TUITION RISEN? THE *PRACTICAL* EXPLANATIONS

While colleges and universities are unique in terms of the services they provide, they are not unique when it comes to responding to incentives. In fact, one of the foundational principles of economics is that all rational actors respond to incentives and act in a manner that is in their own self-interest. For this reason, legislatures tax items that they deem to be harmful to society and subsidize items they deem to be beneficial to society. These taxes and subsidies will incentivize behavior and (hopefully) lead to an outcome that will be better than it would have been if the legislature had neither taxed nor subsidized. With respect to postsecondary institutions, there are undoubtedly many incentives to which their administrators respond when reviewing and approving projects, hiring staff, and setting class sizes, among other items of consideration. So, with over 70 years of tuition rising at a rate that exceeds inflation and household income, clearly there is no incentive to control costs. So, what are the incentives to which universities are most sensitive? In my opinion, they are: maximize rankings, maximize financial security, and maximize the happiness of all constituents.

Incentive 1: Maximize Rankings

In 1983, *U.S. News and World Report* sent a survey to 1,308 university and college presidents and asked them to rank colleges in the United States based on their reputation. The published results were popular among readers; so, the editors sent surveys again in 1985—this time asking presidents to select the top five undergraduate colleges similar to their own, and again in 1987—this time, presidents were asked to rank their top 10 institutions. Beginning in 1988, these rankings were published annually, and the ranking methodology was updated in three ways: (1) reputation as a contributor of rankings was reduced from 100 percent to 25 percent; (2) academic deans and admissions officers were also surveyed; (3) objective data, such as admissions selectivity, educational resources, and graduation rates, were included.[xxxv] While surveys of universities with an attempt to establish a hierarchy had been published prior to 1983, the *U.S. News and World Report* annual survey became a lightning rod. The annual publishing was quickly lauded by prospective students and their parents for its comprehensiveness and insight, and the rankings were panned by school administrators who objected to the ranking methodology and feared a seemingly objective metric could negatively impact the schools as well as reflect negatively on the administrators. Over the years the *U.S. News and World Report*'s methodology has evolved as the publisher has responded to requests by administrators and readers to enhance its utility by including or giving greater weight to specific inputs.

From the 1990s until today, school administrators and trustees have cared deeply about their respective ranks and the changes of those ranks. There is good reason for them to care about their ranks—it is critical input that is utilized by applicants. As early as 1999, economists had identified that there was a strong correlation between school rankings and applications; however, the earliest studies didn't distinguish between rank and school quality. This leads to the question: do more students apply to schools that are higher quality, higher ranked, or both? In 2011, economists figured that out. Harvard

Business School Professor Michael Luca and a Ph.D. student at Boston University named Jonathan Smith gathered data on the *U.S. News and World Report* rankings and found something interesting: often, the number of university applications increased or decreased because of changes in the *U.S. News and World Report* methodology and not because of a change in the quality of the school. For example, applications jumped in 1999 to the California Institute of Technology after its rank jumped from ninth to first following a *U.S. News and World Report* methodology change—but why would applications rise even though each of the criteria by which the school is evaluated was unchanged? It turns out, even if a school's reputation rank, selectivity rank, graduation rank, financial resource rank, or several other ranks remained unchanged, as long as the school's overall rank rose (fell), it's applications rose (fell). In fact, a one-rank improvement (decline) in a school would increase (reduce) applications by about one percent![xxxvi]

Because administrators care about rankings (and they should), they also care about the metrics that are utilized to determine their rankings. And what metrics are those? As of 2021, *U.S. News and World Report* assigned weights to nine different dimensions on college evaluation. These dimensions (percent weight) are:

- Graduation and retention rates (22%)
- Social mobility (5%), which is the percent of students receiving Pell Grants
- Graduation rate performance (8%), which is actual versus forecast graduation rates
- Undergraduate academic reputation (20%)
- Faculty resources including class size and faculty compensation (20%)
- Student selectivity (7%)
- Financial resources (10%), which is per-student spending
- Alumni giving rate (3%)
- Graduate indebtedness (5%)

The metric for graduate indebtedness was added in 2020. When explaining why this metric was added, *U.S. News and World Report* stated: "Affordability of college and the value of that degree after graduation, in terms of being able to earn enough money to be able to make the loan payments, are prime concerns of prospective students and their families. Those vital issues are accounted for in graduate indebtedness."[xxxvii]

These all seem like reasonable inputs for determining university metrics. So, the question is: what is the link connecting university rankings to tuition inflation? The answer is that these metrics indirectly reward administrators for spending, and charging, more! Consider the following hypothetical situation. Administrators are considering their 2024 budget and have the following four proposals. Note: the figures within the parentheses are the weights assigned by *U.S. News and World Report* to school ratings:

1. Raise tuition to hire several well-respected and well-published faculty members. *Pro*: this will improve academic reputation (20%) and increase the financial resources utilized per student (10%), thereby improving rankings. *Con*: the school is marginally less affordable (5%).

2. Raise tuition and build lavish apartments. *Pro*: this will increase applications and allow the school to increase student selectivity (7%) and increase the financial resources utilized per student (10%), thereby improving rankings. *Con*: the school is marginally less affordable (5%).

3. Raise tuition and spend more on academic support and mental health support. *Pro*: this will improve graduation and retention rates (22%) and increase the financial resources utilized per student (10%), thereby improving rankings. *Con*: the school is marginally less affordable (5%).

4. Reduce tuition and increase school affordability. *Pro*: the school is marginally more affordable (5%). *Con*: cuts to programs may lead to faculty losses and a fall in academic reputation (20%), a decline in retention (22%), and a fall in financial resources per student (10%). As a result, rankings will fall.

When filtered through the lens of maximizing rankings, it is clear that each of the first three proposals will be approved while the fourth proposal will fail. In fact, because only five percent of student rankings are given to an affordability metric, affordability (cost) is a secondary or tertiary consideration among those setting budgets. Thus, as well intentioned as the rankings are, they have nevertheless contributed to an arms race among colleges and universities that has led to a drastic increase in cost and a decline in affordability.

Finally, you may recall that earlier in this chapter, I noted that between 1987 and 2019, Ivy League colleges collectively enrolled a smaller percentage of the U.S. undergraduate population (see Figure 2.5). Let's revisit the question—why? In order to maximize rankings, schools are not incentivized to grow, but to contract; considering how rankings are calculated. Admitting fewer students improves the student selectivity metric, thereby improving rankings. Admitting fewer students increases financial resources per student (as the size of the endowment is unchanged), thereby improving rankings. Finally, admitting fewer students improves the student-to-faculty ratio,

"Because of the way in which rankings are calculated, elite universities are generally penalized by expanding and rewarded for contracting." thereby—you guessed it—improving rankings. Because of the way in which rankings are calculated, elite universities are generally penalized by expanding and rewarded for contracting. This is a tragic misalignment of incentives because the most elite schools with the largest endowments are better able to expand than any other postsecondary institution.

Incentive 2: Maximize Financial Security

University endowments are an important source of financial security. Specifically, the income that is generated by these stores of wealth can ensure that universities remain solvent even during an extended period of decline in other sources of revenue. So, what are the sources of university income? There are four sources: student tuition and fees, alumni donations, endowment income, and miscellaneous goods and services including ticket sales, food sales, and others. Because university income must equal expenditures, administrators are mindful of how an increase or decrease in one source of income impacts the need to either raise income elsewhere or cut expenses.

With respect to alumni donations and other miscellaneous sources of income, administrators have little control over these sources. Alumni donations correlate to recent stock market moves, while ticket sales may be driven by the recent successes or failures of a sports team. In addition, administrators have only moderate control over expenses in any given year, as most financial commitments such as professor salaries, building maintenance, and student grants, are medium- to long-term commitments. Therefore, whenever administrators find they need to increase revenue in order to not run a deficit, there are two natural outlets: student tuition and endowment income.

Consider then for a moment, if administrators find they need to raise revenue by $10 million the following year and are presented with two options: (1) increase tuition by four percent (or 2% higher than inflation), or (2) increase the endowment payout from three percent to four percent. Which option will an administrator choose? Many schools will choose option one, raise tuition. We've already established that raising tuition does little to penalize schools with respect to rankings. In addition, students' access to loans means the increase in tuition and fees are unlikely to materially impact applications or cause an increase in attrition. Finally, ensuring an endowment payout remains modest (i.e., avoiding an increase in its payout) will allow an endowment to continue to compound, thereby improving the long-term financial security of the school. For these reasons, when university finances deteriorate, raising tuition is often the primary lever being pulled by administrators to balance budgets.

Incentive 3: Keep All Constituents Happy

There are no fewer than six stakeholders at universities and colleges, and each constituent has his/her own independent (albeit not mutually exclusive) set of objectives. These constituents are: trustees, administrators, faculty, non-faculty employees, alumni, and students. In short, there are no proposals that will satisfy all objectives simultaneously. Since financial resources are finite, any increase in expenditures to satisfy the objective of one (or more) group of constituents necessitates either reducing expenditures or raising tuition, which will then disappoint another constituency. Since students are only one of the six constituencies, and since tuition minimization is but one of several items of importance to students, cost minimization is not a primary consideration during budgeting. As a result, raising tuition is generally the *least bad* option when evaluating a plethora of proposals.

RECENT DEVELOPMENTS

In 1997, a National Commission on the Cost of Higher Education was established as a public advisory commission under the U.S. Department of Education (DOE). This commission was charged with evaluating 11 factors related to the increases in the cost of postsecondary education. These factors included: tuition inflation vis-à-vis other goods and services, ways to moderate future tuition increases, trends in university expenditures including salaries and facilities, and the extent to which government policies have contributed to tuition inflation. The accompanying report included 330 pages of analysis, convictions, and recommendations. If implemented, the commission believed their policy recommendations would (ideally): "(1) strengthen institutional cost control; (2) improve market information and public accountability; (3) deregulate higher education; (4) rethink accreditation; and (5) enhance and simplify federal student aid."

Focusing only on the first item—cost control—the report stated, "The Commission has found no conclusive evidence that loans have contributed to rising costs and prices." Rather, more recent increases in spending could be attributed to increased facility expenses; increased utilization and expenditures on technology; costs associated with maintaining regulatory compliance; and increased expectations for specialized curriculum, additional on campus facilities, and other student amenities and activities. Prior to listing its recommendations, the Commission stated that it "believes it is impossible to formulate an effective single set of directives on cost control applicable to the diverse institutional settings and missions of American colleges and universities." The Commission then lists 10 voluntary steps that colleges and universities could take in order to operate more efficiently and better manage costs. Finally, the Commission asserts that "price controls and federal monitoring of college charges are inappropriate mechanisms for dealing with the issue of college costs." It asserted that price controls would lead to rapid deterioration of the quality of a university education. But no analysis is presented to substantiate that claim.[xxxviii]

Unfortunately, this detailed and thoughtful analysis fell mostly on deaf ears. As shown previously in Figure 2.6, in the 22 years following this Commission report, college tuition and fees have risen at a rate of 4.6 percent per year, or at a rate exceeding inflation by 2.3 percent per year. Meanwhile, tuition and fees as a percentage of median household income has risen from 29 percent in 1998 to 42 percent in 2020.[xxxix,xl] It is with this hindsight bias that we may conclude that, despite the Commission's best intentions, their analysis was flawed in two respects: first, former Secretary of Education William Bennett was correct when he asserted that the availability of student loans enabled colleges and universities to raise tuition without concern of pricing out their clientele (the members of the National Commission on the Cost of Higher Education rejected this premise). Second, anything less than a powerful policy response by the federal government, which includes price control, will not succeed in improving the affordability of postsecondary education. The Commission believed that price controls would damage the quality of education; but, as I will discuss in Chapter 8, that need not be the case.

In a tacit admission that the 1997 National Commission on the Cost of Higher Education had failed to facilitate an improvement regarding the affordability of higher education, President George W. Bush, in 2007, signed the College Cost Reduction and Access Act into law. This law was most known for two things: increasing Pell Grants and creating the Public Service Loan Forgiveness (PSLF) program. With respect to Pell Grants, which are awarded to low-income students, the Act increased the maximum Pell Grant award from $4,310 in 2007 to $5,400 by 2012, at a cost of $11.4 billion. With respect to the PSLF program, general terms are that if a person makes 120 payments (10 years' worth) on their federally issued student loans, and that person worked for a qualifying employer, then the person may have their federal student loans fully discharged irrespective of the remaining balance. Qualifying employers include federal, state, or local governments, or non-profits such as schools, hospitals, libraries, or the military.[xli] Despite initial optimism for this program, the PSLF loan program is now considered a "broken promise."

According to data from the DOE, fewer than two percent of applications for student loan forgiveness are accepted, with most applicants rejected because the agency believes the borrower has not yet made 120 loan payments.[xlii]

Despite the growth in college tuition and student debt associated with the various degrees, policy discussions in the 2020s have generally focused on expanding and improving existing student debt forgiveness programs. But, if former Secretary of Education William Bennett is correct, and the accessibility of student loans enable and encourage tuition inflation, then debt forgiveness will not address tuition inflation. Rather, large-scale debt forgiveness will only encourage colleges and universities to charge more, and prospective students to borrow more, thereby making the situation worse for future generations of students.

". . . large-scale debt forgiveness will only encourage colleges and universities to charge more . . ."

CONCLUSION

Since the mid-1940s, the United States has experienced a dramatic surge in people seeking and earning postsecondary degrees. The drivers for this demand in education are both benign and concerning. Benign reasons for this surge in demand include a growing population, the greater value of a degree, and a general increase in population affluence. By contrast, concerning reasons for the increase in demand for an advanced degree include credential inflation, excessive societal pressure to earn a degree, university price discrimination, and the accessibility of student loans. Universities have responded to this rise in demand by growing larger and becoming more numerous. Unfortunately, the largest, wealthiest, and most prestigious universities did not expand. Why? These schools, like all universities, were responding to incentives that do not necessarily include either expanding or minimizing expenditures.

What are the incentives to which colleges and universities are responding? These incentives include improving rankings, improving prestige, becoming wealthier (as defined as the size of an endowment per student), and attracting and retaining the best and brightest students. For the past seventy years, cost control has not been top of mind for university administrators and trustees. No doubt the presumption was that if universities and colleges ever became too expensive, students would choose to not enroll and universities would be forced to reign in expenses and tuition. However, as long as society pressures young adults to go to college—at whatever the price—and Congress makes loans available to students, students will continue to enroll. As a result, there has been no market-correcting mechanism for tuition inflation, thus, tuition and university expenditures have spiraled out of control. College is now well beyond affordability for all but the most affluent families in the United States, which is in direct contradiction to higher educations' societal contract. But, going to college is still *worth it* in terms of the greater earnings potential that a bachelor's degree confers. Right? Let's find out.

3

The Value of a Degree:
Why Go to College?

Why should people go to college? What benefits are conferred to both individuals and society by the obtainment of a postsecondary education? And most important, should you or your kids go to college? The answer to that last question is . . . maybe. The *value proposition* of going to college—elevate oneself by acquiring knowledge—has remained unchanged since the first postsecondary institutions were established in the United States. However, the *value of that proposition* has varied dramatically over time. Since at least the 1970s, most Americans have considered it self-evident that college is an investment and not an expense. Specifically, this combination of investment in time, lost wages during study, and explicit financial cost of attending a college pays for itself in the form of higher income to the individual and a more well-rounded and civically minded society. While this is true on average, it is not true for everybody; as a result, this reasoning is tragically naïve.

One problem with the aforementioned line of logic is that it is exceptionally difficult to disentangle correlation from causation. Specifically, we know that highly educated individuals earn more; however, does this mean that the education is responsible for the higher earnings, or do the people who have the potential for greater lifetime earnings choose to earn college degrees early in life? We also know that college-educated people are more likely to vote in elections; does this mean that a college degree is responsible for that increase in civic engagement, or do people who are civically minded self-select and attend college when they are young adults?

Another problem with the notion that a college degree is only an investment and not also an expense is that this assertion fails to take a nuanced view on the distribution of outcomes among students. While the average students' income rises following graduation, perhaps we should also focus on the change in student income for the bottom 25 percent of graduates; do they earn more than their less-educated peers? Maybe there are certain fields of study that students should be discouraged from focusing their efforts on if their employment opportunities are no better after they earn their degree than they were before. In other words, perhaps we should ask if spending $200,000 for a degree in performing arts or social services makes economic sense. What about students who enroll in college but fail to earn a college degree; was the decision to attend college still worthwhile, and do they (or we) receive any return from their investment? The final problem with the belief that a college degree is always a worthwhile investment is that this assertion doesn't simultaneously consider both the cost and benefit of a degree. Perhaps in 1974 the earning of a sociology degree was a wise investment in time and resources, but the same may not be true in 2024.

In this chapter I'll demonstrate that while a college education undoubtedly has value, it is not appropriate to assume that value is the same for all potential students. In addition, I'll show that the economic benefits of a college degree have not outpaced the rise in expense of earning that degree. With that in mind, we can conclude that the value of a college degree has declined, and in some cases, the value of a college education may now be negative. If that's the case, there are significant implications for prospective students and their parents (see Chapter 9) as well as for policymakers (see Chapter 8).

BENEFITS OF A COLLEGE DEGREE TO THE INDIVIDUAL

Without considering the explicit (tuition) and implicit (not working) costs of a college education, or the risks of noncompletion, we may conclude that it is a wise decision to earn a bachelor's degree—there are a lot of perks to that degree! The benefits of a college education include better economic prospects, such as higher income, lower unemployment, and greater upward economic mobility. Other benefits include having the satisfaction of the college experience, enjoying a healthier lifestyle later in life, and a lower likelihood of living below the poverty line. So, how significant are those benefits, and how have those benefits changed over time? Let's find out.

"The benefits of a college education include better economic prospects, such as higher income, lower unemployment, and greater upward economic mobility."

Higher Income

The first and most commonly cited benefit of higher education comes in the form of higher lifetime earnings. In the 2019 College Board[1] report titled *Education Pays: the Benefits of Higher Education for Individuals and Society*,[i] researchers estimated that the recipient of a bachelor's degree would have sufficiently higher earnings by the age of 33, which would help to compensate for the cost of their education as well as the opportunity cost of not working while earning their degree. This study highlights a plethora of other compelling data that points to the strong correlation between higher income and greater education. For example, the authors note: "In 2018, median earnings of female 4-year college graduates were $56,700. This exceeded median earnings of female high school graduates by 74 percent ($24,100). Median earnings of male bachelor's degree recipients were $75,200. This exceeded median earnings of male high school graduates by 65 percent ($29,600)."

Researchers at the College Board also demonstrate that among people working in the same sector or industry, people with a bachelor's degree consistently earn more than people without a bachelor's degree. For example, "retail salespersons" with and without a bachelor's degree earn $48,500 and $31,400 per year, respectively. Similarly, "general and operations managers" with and without a bachelor's degree earn $89,200 and $60,100 per year, respectively. The authors of the Education Pays report further calculated earnings by level of education, by gender, and by year. By combining data from the National Center for Education Statistics (NCES), the U.S. Census Bureau, and the Bureau of Labor Statistics (BLS), the authors were able to demonstrate how inflation-adjusted earnings by cohort (gender and education level) have varied for the past 40 years. As shown in Figure 3.1, in every year from 1978 through 2018, the median income of a person with a bachelor's degree was higher than that of a person with only some college or an associate degree, while a person with only a high school diploma was consistently the lowest earning of these cohorts.[2]

---

[1] The College Board, formerly known as the College Entrance Examination Board, is a non-profit organization. Its membership includes over 6,000 schools, colleges, universities, and other educational organizations. The College Board administers standardized tests used in the college admission process, generating over $1 billion per year in revenue. While I don't doubt that the College Board's data concerning earnings and employment is accurate, I think it is worth noting that this organization has a vested interest in promoting college attendance.

[2] While this is outside the scope of this chapter (and book), I find it fascinating (and concerning) that the inflation-adjusted wages of all earning cohorts have been steady or slightly declined over the given period. This suggests the ability to save and consume of all groups are at or below that of their parents for any given level of education. Stagnant real wages often correlate to social unrest, and policy solutions should be considered to address this.

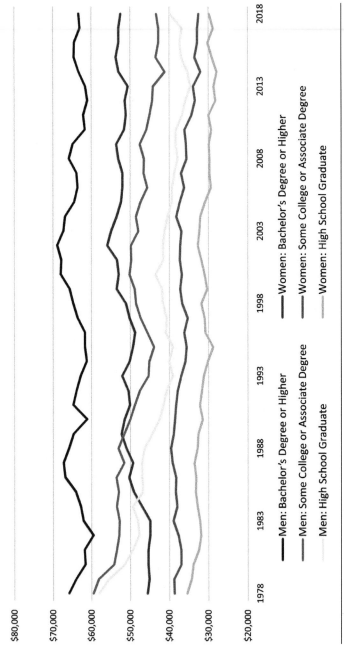

Figure 3.1   Inflation Adjusted Annual Income by Gender and Educational Achievement. *Source:* College Board.[ii]

Lower Unemployment

In addition to earning more, those with greater education have consistently lower unemployment rates. This is true both during times of economic expansion and during recessions, as shown in Figure 3.2. For the 30-year period ending 12/30/2021, the average unemployment rate for people with a bachelor's degree (or higher) was 2.8 percent. By comparison, the average unemployment rates for people with some college or an associate degree, or a high school diploma, was 4.7 and 5.7 percent, respectively. Meanwhile, people with less than a high school diploma had an average unemployment rate of 9.0 percent. Interestingly (and if you squint your eyes enough), people with higher levels of education generally experience lower spikes in unemployment during a recession, and as was the case in 2000–2001, they were the first to be rehired during the subsequent expansion. For example, during the 2008–2009 Great Recession, the unemployment rate for people with a bachelor's degree and higher peaked at 5.0 percent, up from 2.0 percent the previous year. Meanwhile, people with a high school diploma reached an unemployment rate of 15.2 percent, up from 6.5 percent two years prior.[iii]

Little is written about why people who have achieved a higher level of education experience lower levels of unemployment. Thus, we are left to assume that it is the *education itself* that confers the marketable skills that offer a higher demand for services in all economic environments—and for some, that's probably the case. For example, in 2019, according to data from the Federal Reserve Bank of New York, college students who majored in Elementary Education and Medical Technology (Medical Technician) had unemployment rates of 1.2 and 1.3 percent, respectively. By contrast, people with college majors of Physics and Social Sciences had unemployment rates of 8.0 and 8.5 percent, respectively.[iv] So, we can infer that the demand for medical technicians and teachers was higher than for physicists, thereby leading to reduced unemployment among certain professionals with advanced degrees.

As can be inferred by higher income and lower levels of unemployment, the level of education is strongly correlated with socioeconomic mobility. For example, in the United States, the poverty rate[3,vi] is 11.8 percent among all households. That percentage jumps to 25.9 and 12.7 percent for those without a high school diploma or those who earned a high school diploma but did not attend college, respectively. Among people who attended some college, only

---

[3] On an annual basis, the U.S. Department of Health and Human Services updates guidelines regarding what is considered the *poverty line*. In 2020, the annual income that would qualify as living below the poverty line for a single person living in their own household was $14,820; for a family of four, that figure was $30,480.

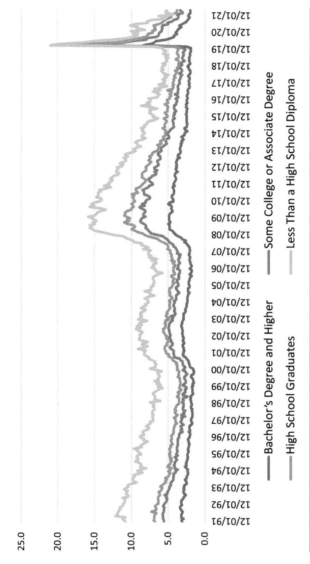

Figure 3.2 Unemployment Rates of Individuals Age 25 and Older by Education Level 1991–2021.
Sources: U.S. BLS and Federal Reserve Bank of St. Louis.[v]

8.4 percent live below the poverty line, while only 4.4 percent of people with a bachelor's degree live below the poverty line.[vii] In a similar vein, people with a bachelor's degree are less likely to need and utilize public assistance programs than people whose highest level of education was high school. These programs include the Supplemental Nutrition Assistance Program (38.3% high school diploma to 7.6% bachelor's degree), Supplemental Security Income (38.7% high school diploma to 7.9% bachelor's degree), Special Supplemental Nutrition Program for Women, Infants, and Children (36.4% high school diploma to 10.0% bachelor's degree), and the Temporary Assistance for Needy Families program (31.0% high school diploma to 5.5% bachelor's degree).[viii]

Better Health and Lifestyle

Seemingly, the economic benefits of higher education have been well established; but, are there other benefits conferred to individuals following the receipt of higher education? The answer is a resounding yes. Since the early 1970s it has been understood that greater education correlates with a variety of health benefits and lower mortality rates. In 1973, two University of Chicago Professors of Sociology, Evelyn M. Kitagawa and Philip Hauser, collaborated and published a seminal piece titled *Differential Mortality in the United States*. With large data-set statistical analysis still in its infancy, and because researchers were limited by computing power and little publicly available data, a causal relationship between education and health hadn't been established prior to that publication. That changed with their study. In their piece, Professors Katagawa and Hauser highlight different investigations studying the correlations between economic, demographic, and mortality characteristics. The professors first established the relationship between education and income or occupation; the authors then demonstrated how that level of education correlates with mortality and longevity. For example, around the year 1960, White men and women between the ages of 25 and 64 with less education had higher death rates than those with more education, all other things equal. The authors then demonstrated that when controlling for race, death rates among low-income people were statistically higher than those in higher-income categories.[ix]

Since the publication of *Differential Mortality in the United States*, dozens of studies have replicated the authors' methodology, reaffirmed their findings, and expanded the range of health-related items that correlate with higher education. Interestingly, starting in the early 1990s, statisticians began producing annual reports confirming the statistically significant correlation between educational attainment and mortality rates. In 1989, death certificates in the

United States were mandated to include the educational attainment of the decedent.[x] This allowed the National Center for Health Statistics and the U.S. Center for Disease Control and Prevention to incorporate educational data in their annual statistical analysis of mortality in the United States. In their most recent report detailing the causes of mortality in the United States (charmingly titled *Deaths: Final Data for 2018*), we can compare the mortality rate of people with a high school diploma versus people with some college or a college degree. Among both sexes in the age 25–64 category, the annual mortality rate is 397.6 per 100,000 (0.40%). That figure rises to 687.4 per 100,000 (0.69%) among people whose highest educational attainment was high school or a GED. Conversely, that figure falls to 222.9 per 100,000 (0.22%) for people with some college or a college degree. Comparing those with and without college, we find that the mortality rate among those without college is 3.1 times (0.69%/0.22%) higher than the mortality rate among those with a college degree![xi]

So, why do college graduates have a lower annual fatality rate—or in other words, why do college graduates live longer? One contributing factor is the type of jobs that people with and without college degrees generally hold. While the annual fatality rate among U.S. employees is fairly low (3.5 per 100,000), it is far higher among certain professions. Using data produced by the U.S. BLS, we can identify the most dangerous jobs and infer who is typically employed in those fields.[xii] Using 2019 data, nine of the ten most dangerous jobs are held by people who generally do not have college degrees.[4] Some of those occupations are fishing and hunting workers (145.0 deaths per 100,000), logging workers (68.9 per 100,000), roofers (54.0 per 100,000), construction trade helpers (40.0 per 100,000), refuse material collectors (35.2 per 100,000), and truck drivers (26.8 per 100,000).[5] While these figures are material, they're insufficient to explain the differential in annual fatality rates among people with and without college degrees. So, what other factors contribute to the disparity in life expectancy among those who have and have not earned a bachelor's degree? In general, college graduates make healthier lifestyle choices: they're less likely to smoke, more likely to exercise, and are less likely to be obese.

---

[4] The third most dangerous job category is aircraft pilots and flight engineers (61.8 per 100,000). While a college degree is often not a prerequisite to work at a regional airline, most of the major airlines in the United States require a college degree, making this occupation the most dangerous among holders of a bachelor's degree.

[5] What are the least dangerous jobs? Those include legal occupations (0.5 per 100,000), business and financial operations (0.4 per 100,000), computer and mathematical operations (0.3 per 100,000), and educational instruction and library occupations (0.3 per 100,000).

The earliest literature linking smoking habits to disease was published in the 1950s. Since then, it has become increasingly well understood that smoking is a major contributor to mortality and lower life expectancy. Today in the United States, it is estimated that illnesses linked to smoking habits are a contributing factor to more than 480,000 deaths per year, or roughly 17 percent of all deaths.[xiii,6] When it comes to smoking-related diseases, on average, smokers die 10 years earlier than nonsmokers.[xiv] So, with these lovely statistics in mind, we can imagine that a lower rate of smoking among any subgroup of the population would lead to better health outcomes. In 2004, a recently minted University of Chicago Ph.D., Damien de Walque, published a paper linking smoking rates to attributes including age, race, and education level; he then demonstrated how the smoking rate among various cohorts of people had changed over time. Using National Health Interview Survey data that began including both smoking habits and education in 1966, combined with multivariate regression analysis, de Walque's research provided several interesting insights. First, smoking rates among adults peaked in the 1950s. Prior to this, smoking rates among those with and without a bachelor's degree were quite similar. Since the 1960s, the smoking rate among people with a bachelor's degree declined more quickly than those without a bachelor's degree. Separately, de Walque's analysis showed that even when controlling for age, race, income, and veteran status, the rate of smoking declined by about four percent per year of education above high school.[xv] That is to say, someone with four years of post-high school education has an average smoking rate (4 times 4%) 16 percent lower than someone with only a high school diploma. That rate has remained steady since the publication of his paper, and as of 2017, in the United States, the smoking rate among college graduates and nongraduates was 10 and 26 percent, respectively.[xvi]

In addition to smoking less, college graduates exercise more. The degree (no pun intended) to which educational obtainment correlates with the amount of physical exercise can be found in each year's National Health Interview Survey. For example, survey participants are asked if they engage in aerobic physical activity of at least moderate intensity for more than 300 minutes/week, or more than 150 minutes/week of vigorous intensity. Results from the 2018 survey show that the percentage of respondents that meet this level of activity is 29.3 and 42.6 percent among holders of a high school diploma and bachelor's degree, respectively.[xvii] But, can we attribute the higher amount of exercise to the additional years of education, or are there cultural,

---

[6] The leading causes of death in the United States in 2019 were heart disease (659,041), cancer (599,601), and accidents (173,040). Smoking isn't listed as a cause of death, because it is the effect of smoking (a smoking-related illness) that is ultimately fatal.

racial, and other socioeconomic forces at work? To answer that question, in 2004, two faculty members at Feinberg School of Medicine of Northwestern University published a paper titled *Differences in Leisure-time, Household, and Work-related Physical Activity by Race, Ethnicity, and Education*. At the time, it was already documented that ethnic minority groups have lower levels of exercise (called *leisure-time physical activity*) than Whites, but it was unclear as to the degree to which this can be attributed to Whites' higher average educational attainment, higher income, or anything else. So, the faculty members gathered data from the 1992 Health and Retirement Study, which was a survey of 7,702 households conducted by the Institute for Social Research at the University of Michigan. After crunching the numbers, the authors concluded that educational attainment is a two to three times more relevant predictor of level of exercise than race. Said another way, a Black or White person with a similar level of education will allocate a similar amount of their week to exercise.[xviii]

Okay, so people with a bachelor's degree exercise more and smoke less; but, does that translate into a longer lifespan? Unsurprisingly, the answer is yes. To figure out just how much we can attribute obtaining a bachelor's degree to extending life expectancy, two faculty members at the School of Public and International Affairs at Princeton University started analyzing data—a lot of data. Using information found in the National Vital Statistical System, the researchers analyzed records for all 48.9 million deaths of people aged 25 through 84 between 1990 and 2018. Rather than calculate average life expectancy by subcategory (race, education, etc.), the authors chose a more actuarial measurement of life; specifically, the *expected years of life from age 25 to 74*. So, if the answer is *49*, then a 25-year-old would expect to live to be at least age 74. The researchers found a few interesting things when crunching all this data. First, in 2018, people who have earned a bachelor's degree live an average of 3.1 years longer than those who have not; that figure is up from 1.9 years in 1990. Second, while White people on average live longer than Black people, the interracial gap in life expectancy significantly narrows when accounting for educational attainment. In other words, people who have earned a college diploma have more similar life expectancies irrespective of race than people of the same race that have different levels of educational attainment.[xix]

> *". . . people who have earned a bachelor's degree live an average of 3.1 years longer than those who have not . . ."*

All of this data and statistical analysis begs one final question regarding education, health, and life expectancy. Why do more highly educated people live more healthy lifestyles and longer lives? This question, which borders on the philosophical, has three competing explanations. One explanation put forward by Nobel Prize winning economist Gary Becker states that because more highly educated people will earn a higher income, their lives are of greater financial value. Therefore, they are less likely to engage in activity that doesn't offer sufficient compensation for the risk that is inherent to that activity.[xx,7] A second explanation is offered by economists at Harvard and UCLA. It states that higher education changes people's resources (income and health care accessibility), their knowledge (understanding of risks of behavior), impacts their social groups (being around fewer smokers leads to less smoking), and raises people's general cognitive ability (school makes people smarter). As a result of all of the aforementioned items, more educated people live healthier lifestyles.[xxi] A third and final explanation is that we cannot draw causal relationships between education and lifestyle. Rather, people who are likely to live healthier lifestyles also self-select into attending college and earning higher-wage jobs. So, attempting to attribute years of education to longer lifespans is an erroneous use of statistics.[xxii]

The Signal

An additional benefit to earning an advanced degree can be attributed to the *signal* that this degree sends to future employers. What does that mean? Well, all things being equal, an associate, bachelor's, master's, or Ph.D. degree signals to employers a future employee's ability. An advanced degree is an imperfect signal, for sure. But, more highly educated people tend to be hired for higher value-add jobs, and this translates into more highly educated people being more highly compensated.

This phenomenon is called *The Signaling Model* and is attributed to Michael Spence, who is also the 2001 recipient of the Nobel Memorial Prize in Economic Sciences. In his landmark 1973 paper titled *Job Market Signaling*, Dr. Spence describes his signaling theory. It includes four assumptions. First, not all individuals are the same. Rather, some people are innately more

---

[7] I vividly remember a lecture with Professor Becker in 2009 where he described this theory. In the classroom, he put forward the following hypothetical: two people are offered a job for $10,000; but, there is a one percent chance the job will be fatal. What is the implicit value of a person's life in this instance? The answer is $1,000,000 (1% times $1 million = $10,000). So, who might take the job? Consider that one person is uneducated and earns a modest wage per year; this person may assess all their future earnings as approximately $500,000. If the other person is an investment banker, that person may assess all their future earnings as $5,000,000. Therefore, the poorer person, with a lower level of education, will take the job. As a result, we can link less education and lower income expectations with risky behavior that lowers life expectancy. I was uncomfortable with the example; but I couldn't disagree with it.

productive and some are less productive. Interestingly, this innate ability for production is initially unrelated to education. Second, education is costly—but, not just in the traditional sense of a monetary cost. Rather, the cost *also* includes the mental and psychological strain that earning an advanced degree entails. Time in a library, studying, researching, and forgoing other activities places a *cost* on students. In addition, Dr. Spence assumes that highly productive future employees (current students) have an easier time at school because they learn more quickly and retain information longer. Thus, the cost for an education is lowest for the most productive employees (i.e., the best students). As a result, the higher productive future workers often earn advanced degrees because the cost of an advanced degree is lowest for these students. The third and fourth assumptions in Dr. Spence's model are that there is an "information asymmetry" among employees and employers. Specifically, employees know if they are highly productive and can handle a difficult job, but employers do not know that. So, employers can use *level of education* as a reasonable proxy for estimating the productivity of prospective employees. Thus, employers can match jobs with employee skills simply by observing their level of education.[xxiii]

It's difficult to argue with the logic presented by Dr. Spence. But, while this model was highly descriptive in 1973 (when his seminal paper was first published), we now live in a different era, and this model may need updating. Specifically, this model assumes that prospective students earn degrees if the *signaling cost* (time, money, and mental strain) is lower than the value of that education. But in 1973, the annual expense of attending a four-year college was about 20 percent of the annual median household income. By contrast, today the expense is about 44 percent of the annual median household income. So, from the time Dr. Spence developed his model until today, the financial cost of a college degree has more than doubled. Why is this relevant? If his model is accurate, the value of an education has become less a signal of a person's innate ability and more an indication of a person's financial situation. To put it another way, whereas in the past a highly skilled but financially poor person might still earn a degree, today a poorly skilled but financially secure person (i.e., they have rich parents) might earn that degree instead. Thus, as the financial cost of a degree rises, the degree becomes less a signal of ability of a future employee and more a signal of financial status of an applicant's parents.

". . . as the financial cost of a degree rises, the degree becomes less a signal of ability of a future employee and more a signal of financial status of an applicant's parents."

The College Experience

One final rationale for entering college that should be addressed for thoroughness is the pervasive notion that there is value in the college experience itself. Game days, fight songs, lecture halls, beautiful libraries, freshman dorms, parties, campus life, lifelong friends, and other extracurriculars are experiences that many parents want their kids to have. This has lent itself to the notion that for many, college is the "best four years of my life." To state the obvious, the *college experience* requires students to attend college on campus; so, what happened during and after the 2020 and 2021 COVID-related lockdowns and cancellation of on-campus classes across the country? As expected, current and prospective college students reassessed their enrollment decisions in light of their inability to enjoy on-campus life. To better ascertain how the changing on-campus dynamic impacted student enrollment decisions, management consulting company McKinsey & Company surveyed 2,094 U.S.-based, mostly college-bound high school seniors between April 21 and 28 of 2020. Their responses shed much light on the importance that students place on being able to attend college in-person. Specifically, in light of COVID-19 restrictions, 21 percent of surveyed students stated that they had changed their top choice of college institution. Of the students that indicated their top choice had changed, cost and distance from home (too far) were the most commonly cited reasons for their change of heart. More striking, when asked how students would respond to learning that their fall classes would be *remote only*, 48 percent of students indicated they would defer enrollment or look to attend a different school.[xxiv]

Not surprising, some pushed back against college lockdowns and remote learning. For a brief time, Florida Governor Ron DeSantis indicated that he was considering a students' "bill of rights," which would protect students from "draconian" measures and encourage state-funded campuses to reopen.[xxv] Meanwhile, more than 70 lawsuits were filed by students and their parents against universities, generally demanding refunds for a lack of on-campus learning.[xxvi] While some would argue that the students' inability to take class in person is a trivial inconvenience that shouldn't impair the value of their education and experience, the employment data related to personal networks suggests otherwise. In a 2016 survey by LinkedIn, an online employment service, 62 percent of people who are currently employed responded that they got their job by "networking." The second most popular response (23%) was that they got their job via an internal application. There is no doubt that the ability for students to network and form connections that might lead to future career opportunities was impaired by an inability to socialize on campus. To put additional weight behind the LinkedIn survey, a Ph.D. student from Duke

University in 2019 gathered data on student networks and how those networks impacted job prospects. Her findings suggest that people who obtain jobs through classmate referrals earn more at the start of their jobs and are less likely to leave the firm.[xxviii]

SOCIETAL BENEFITS

A common theme among those who have crafted legislation in support of higher education is that education is an investment and not an expense. Furthermore, it is rational for the public to financially support higher education because the public benefits from a highly educated population. Some of those benefits are easier to quantify, such as higher tax revenue for the state, while others are more challenging to quantify but no less important, such as greater civic engagement and more stable nuclear families. Let's dive into some of those benefits and see how material they are.

Higher Tax Revenue

Because college graduates earn more (on average) than those without a college degree, college graduates are a larger source of tax revenue than those without a college degree. In addition, thanks to the progressive tax rates in the United States, college graduates pay a higher share of their income than those without college degrees. How much more? According to the Tax Foundation, a Washington, D.C.-based think tank, quite a lot. In their 2021 *Summary of the Latest Federal Income Tax Data*, researchers made the following observations: Earners in the top five percent have an adjusted gross income (AGI) of $217,913 and pay an average of 17.3 percent of their income in the form of federal income taxes. Meanwhile, earners in the top one percent have an AGI of $540,009 and pay an average of 25.4 percent of their income in the form of federal income taxes. By contrast, the bottom 50 percentile of earners (i.e., an annual income of $43,614 or less) pay an average of 3.4 percent of their income in the form of federal income taxes. When taken together, the top five percent of earners (including the top one percent of earners) are responsible for 60.3 percent of federal income tax receipts, while the bottom 50 percent of earners are responsible for 2.9 percent of federal income tax receipts.[xxix] With this in mind, the logic follows: to increase federal income tax receipts, develop a population of high earners; and to develop a population of high earners, encourage people to earn a college degree with public dollars. There is a compelling rationale to this.

Higher Civic Engagement

Interestingly, level of education correlates to greater civic engagement as measured by volunteer hours and voting rates. The U.S. Census Bureau's Volunteering and Civic Life Supplement, published every one to two years, includes data on the number of people who performed unpaid volunteer activities. This data is subdivided by both age and educational attainment. While 19 percent of people with a high school diploma volunteered in 2017, 42 percent of people with a bachelor's degree volunteered. The percentage was even higher among people with an advanced degree (master's or Ph.D.). The pattern was the same by age group and for both men and women. That is, both men and women, as well as young and old adults, volunteer more hours per year the more years of education they have received.[xxx] A similar pattern emerges when analyzing voting rates. According to data found in the U.S. Census Bureau Voting and Registration Tables, in every presidential election since 1964, the more highly educated citizens had higher voting rates. For example, in 1964, 88 percent of citizens with a bachelor's degree voted versus 76 percent with a high school diploma. In 2016, the voting rates were 76 for those with a bachelor's degree and 52 percent for those with just a high school diploma.[xxxi]

More Involved Parents

The final societal benefit, to which we can partially attribute to the earning of a bachelor's degree, is that more educated parents tend to be more involved parents. In fact, we can quantify this by examining the annual survey results produced by the NCES, part of the U.S Department of Education (DOE). These survey results are a gold mine for data covering schools (elementary through postsecondary), students, parents, and education outcomes. So, what do the surveys show? Parents with a bachelor's degree are (on average) more engaged and place a greater emphasis on their children's education. For simplicity, I will focus on the children where the highest level of education obtained by a parent is either a bachelor's degree or a high school diploma.[8]

For example, more educated parents enroll their kids in preschool (55% bachelor's versus 39% high school). In addition, they read more to their kids (89% versus 80%) and visit libraries on a monthly basis (43% versus 29%).[xxxii] More educated parents also tend to engage in more "enrichment" activities with their children. These activities include attending a play or live show (36% versus 26%), visiting a museum or historical site (31% versus

---

[8] Percentages are self-reported activities over the prior month.

21%), or attending an event sponsored by a community, religious, or ethnic group (56% versus 47%).[xxxiii] Last, more educated parents tend to be more engaged in their kids' schools as measured by the percentage who attend school or PTA meetings (93% versus 82%), attend parent-teacher conference meetings (82% versus 73%), attend class events (87% versus 70%), and volunteer at school (54% versus 27%).[xxxiv] This is great, but it also begs the question—why? How does a parent's decision to earn a bachelor's degree in journalism or fine arts lead to greater engagement and emphasis on their children's education? The answer is a mix of several reasons. The more educated parents tend to have greater resources available to them (both time and money), which enables this greater engagement. There are also cultural and social pressures that go along with working and living in a more affluent area and associating with other highly educated adults. So, it's difficult to disentangle how the process of earning a bachelor's degree impacts that person's future desire to read to his/her children, but it is nevertheless impossible to deny the correlation.

RISKS AND HARMS OF EARNING A COLLEGE DEGREE

Imagine you were offered a deal: You have a 66.5 percent[9] chance to receive $253,351,[10] along with a 33.5 percent chance to be assigned $13,930[11] in debt, lose $41,194[12] in savings, lose $81,952[13] in current income, and possibly incur other damages that may impair your ability to get married, buy a house, start

---

[9] 66.5 percent is the average completion rate for students who entered a public four-year bachelor's program in 2011. *Source*: NCES, Beginning Postsecondary Students 2012/2017.

[10] $253,351 is the estimated present value net increase in lifetime earnings following the earning of a bachelor's degree. *Source*: Kim et al., 2015. Table 4.

[11] $13,929.65 is the average student loan debt at the time of a student's dropout, according to a survey conducted by LendEDU. *Source*: College Dropouts and Student Debt. February 17, 2021. Mike Brown. Accessed 12/12/2021. https://lendedu.com/blog/college-dropouts-student-loan-debt/.

[12] $20,598 is the estimated average annual undergraduate tuition, fees, room, and board rate charged for full-time students in degree-granting postsecondary institutions during the 2018–2019 academic year. I assume here that the student drops out after two full years of a four-year program. *Source*: NCES. Table 330.10.

[13] The median weekly income for a high school graduate is $788, according to the U.S. BLS. I assume here that the student forgoes 104 weeks (2 years) of income while attending college. *Source*: BLS. Usual Weekly Earnings of Wage and Salary Workers News Release. Table 5. Accessed 12/12/2021.

a family, or start a business.[14] Would you take the deal?[15] Unclear. So why is attending college considered self-evident when this hypothetical situation is commensurate with the current value-proposition of attending college? To be frank, attending college shouldn't be taken as a given because the distribution of peoples' outcomes are wide and there is a significant downside should someone drop out of the program. I would argue that the decision to attend college should be made after a thoughtful and wholistic analysis of the costs and benefits of enrolling. And as the aforementioned hypothetical suggests, only people who are comfortable with high-risk propositions, or students who are highly confident in their ability to complete a college program, should apply.

College Dropouts

The first consideration in attending a two- or four-year program should be the likelihood of completing the program. Depending on the degree, it's not great. As shown in Figure 3.3, the dropout rates vary from 22.8 percent for a private four-year program at a non-profit university,

". . . dropout rates vary from 22.8 percent for a private four-year program at a non-profit university, to 76.5 percent (!) at a for-profit college."

to 76.5 percent (!) at a for-profit college. Having a non-zero dropout rate for college isn't inherently a bad thing. College is difficult, and for those who earn a degree, simply having the degree signals to future employers that the candidate has sufficient mental acumen and drive to overcome college-related obstacles. But, when evaluating the utility of attending college in the first place, knowing all potential outcomes (including not finishing the program) should be considered. In other words, a high school guidance counselor with 100 students probably shouldn't tell each student that they should attend college, especially if that counselor knows in advance that 35 to 40 of those students will fail to complete the program. Rather, a nuanced and student-specific recommendation is likely more appropriate.

---

[14] See Chapter 6 for a detailed discussion on the ways student debt may negatively impact a person's economic and psychological health.

[15] This hypothetical situation has a positive probability-adjusted value of $122,558, suggesting a rational actor that has no concerns of the potential other damages would still take the deal (i.e., attend college). Calculation: $0.665 \times \$253,351 - 0.335 \times (\$13,930 + \$41,194 + \$81,952) = \$122,558$.

Program	1972	1992	2011
Public Four-Year	35.7	36.5	33.5
Private Non-Profit Four-Year	35.9	23.4	22.8
Public Two-Year	79.8	82.4	68.4
For-Profit			76.5

Figure 3.3   Bachelor's and Associate Degree Dropout Rates.
Sources: National Bureau of Economic Research[xxxv] (1972 and 1992) and
NCES (2011).[xxxvi]

Separately, whether we are considering policies to improve educational outcomes, or are considering college for ourselves or our children, we should consider why students drop out. According to a poll of college dropouts conducted by LendEDU, an online marketplace that connects student borrowers and lenders, only 5.4 percent of respondents reported that they dropped out of college due to "academic reasons."[xxxvii] In fact, according to a poll conducted by Education Data Initiative, a small team of researchers who collect and aggregate education-related data, 40 percent of college dropouts have a 3.0 GPA or higher.[xxxviii,16] So, why do students usually drop out? The most common reason (35.3% of respondents in a LendEDU poll and 38% in an EducationData poll) was related to financial situations—that is, the cost of attending college was simply too high. Of those respondents who cited financial reasons, 74.2 percent of respondents in the LendEDU poll indicated that they dropped out because they didn't want to assume additional student debt. Other reasons regularly cited for dropping out include the need to support their family, mental or physical health issues, legal issues, and poor fit. So, what happens when a person drops out, as it relates to their income potential? According to the U.S. BLS, the median annual income of someone with "some college, no degree" is $45,604, which is higher than those with a "high school diploma, no college" ($40,612), yet lower than those with a bachelor's degree ($67,860).[xxxix] So, those who attended college but failed to earn a degree do have a modest increase in annual income versus those that did not attend college. Although, it is unclear if the higher income of college dropouts can be attributed to their time attending a college. Said another way, it's quite possible that the people who entered

---

[16] Interestingly, in the EducationData poll, 28 percent of students indicated that they dropped out due to "academic disqualification," significantly higher than the 5.4 percent of students that was reported by the LendEDU poll.

college but dropped out would have earned more than the average person who graduated high school but chose not to attend college. What we can say with high confidence is that the act of dropping out of college materially impairs future earnings potential.

Declining Economic Benefits

My three children are ages 6, 8, and 9. As I write this, I cannot say with certainty that when my children graduate high school, they will be better off financially whether they (or I) spend the money on college or if I simply give them a lump sum equal to the amount of their college education. But didn't I just spend 20 pages discussing the economic benefits of entering college? Well, yes. *Today*, and *on average*, people are better off going to college than not. In economic speak, net of all expenses (tuition, room, board, and forgone earnings) and risks (failing to earn a degree), entering college is still a positive net present value proposition as of 2022. But, if the current trajectory of the increase in annual college expenses remains unchanged and the incremental earning power of a holder of a bachelor's degree remains unchanged, my children may be better off not going to college in ten years' time. Here's why.

Let's return for a moment to Figure 3.1, which is the College Board estimate of the inflation-adjusted

". . . my children may be better off not going to college in ten years' time."

annual income by gender and educational achievement. The data does look compelling as holders of a bachelor's degree consistently earn materially more than people who have only a high school diploma. But, how much more (i.e., what is the *bachelor's degree premium*)? I calculate this amount by subtracting the annual income for the "High School Graduate" from the "Bachelor's Degree or Higher" category for both men and women. In addition to simply charting this in Figure 3.4, I also overlay the estimate of a bachelor's degree premium versus the average annual college expense, calculated by the NCES. All data is inflation-adjusted.

That all sounds a bit academic, so what does all this show? Well, the economic value for earning a bachelor's degree was significant in 1978. Specifically, after spending about $2,725 per year (for four years), male and female recipients of a bachelor's degree could expect to earn around $7,900 and $10,100 more per year (for the rest of their careers). That's a sweet deal! From 1978 until around 1992, the incremental income earned by the recipient of a bachelor's degree increased at around the same rate as the annual expense

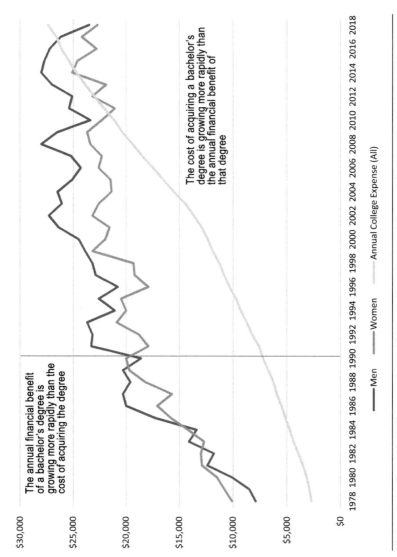

Figure 3.4   Bachelor's Degree Annual Income Premium and Annual College Expense.
Sources: College Board,[xl] NCES,[xli] and author's calculations.

> *". . . starting around 1992, the incremental income*
> *associated with earning a bachelor's degree largely*
> *flatlined while the cost of a college education continued*
> *to increase exponentially."*

for that degree. But starting around 1992, the incremental income associated with earning a bachelor's degree largely flatlined while the cost of a college education continued to increase exponentially. Currently, college-bound students (on average) will spend about $28,000 per year (for four years), and male and female recipients of a bachelor's degree can expect to earn around $20,500 and $21,100 more per year (for the rest of their careers). That's an okay deal, I suppose.

Another way of thinking about this is: how many years does somebody need to work in order to *cover* the expense of college? We can calculate this by dividing the annual incremental income pickup of a bachelor's degree recipient by the annual expense of college. As shown in Figure 3.5, both men and women need to work at least five years after graduating college just to cover the cost of college; this calculation doesn't include forgone earnings while in college. So, is that a lot? Well, that depends. This highly conservative estimate is that a person needs to work until they're at least age 27 to cover the cost of their degree; and that's assuming they graduate after four years, immediately have gainful employment, and that they wouldn't have earned a dime for four years had they not gone to college. The College Board offers us a more robust estimate of break-even time, as they included in their 2019 report an analysis that includes the opportunity of not working while earning a degree. Their analysis suggests the age at which cumulative earnings of college graduates exceeds those of high school graduates is between age 33 and 36 (depending on how long it takes to earn the degree).[xlii] Both these analyses assume the individual completes their program (i.e., it excludes the third of students that drop out). While these figures may not seem so bad, of concern is the general trajectory of the time it will take for the program to *pay for itself*. For example, an 18-year-old woman entering college today may not be better off financially unless she works into her mid-30s. By the time my daughter enters college, if trajectories remain unchanged, she may have to work well into her 40s before she financially *breaks even*. While some might argue that this isn't inherently bad, as people are living and working longer, women's fertility remains unchanged (*peak* fertility is in their 20s).[xliii] That's a bit of a left-hand turn. More on that in Chapter 6.

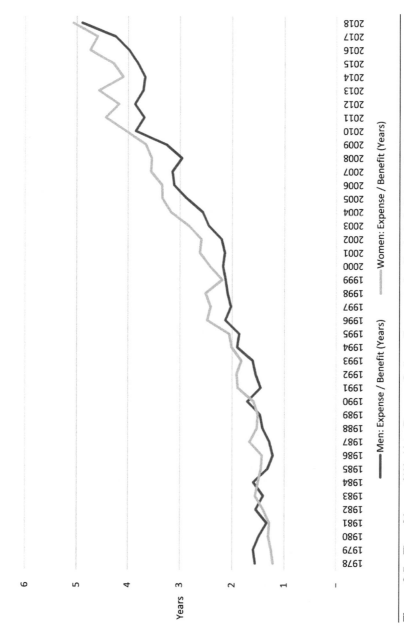

Figure 3.5   Time (Years of Work) to Recoup College Expenses for Bachelor's Degree Recipients. *Sources:* College Board, NCES, and author's calculations.

Variation of Outcomes

A major problem with much of the previously mentioned analysis is that it focuses on the average or median outcome.[17] But this significantly understates the distribution of outcomes. And why is this important? Well, we know that the benefits (on average) of going to college have been roughly unchanged for over 30 years, while the costs have been growing exponentially. Even though attending college and earning a degree is still the right financial decision for the typical earner of a degree, statistically there is a growing minority of people who are worse off for having earned a college degree. And who is in this minority? We can gain some insight by looking at data provided to us by the Federal Reserve Bank of New York (FRBNY) and the U.S. Census Bureau. Each year, the FRBNY publishes its findings in an online report titled *The Labor Market for Recent College Graduates.* In their 2021 report, the FRBNY included earnings data for college graduates, by major, for workers both early- (ages 22–27) and mid-career (ages 35–45). Their data shows that of the 73 majors identified by the FRBNY, only students with 26 majors (36% of students)[18] make more at graduation than the average high school graduate ($40,612). By mid-career, all college graduates earn more than high school graduates (again, on average) when grouped by major. However, there is a significant dispersion within this data. For example, recipients of a bachelor's degree in early childhood education earn $35,000 at graduation and $42,000 mid-career, while recipients of a bachelor's degree in performing arts earn $34,600 at graduation and $56,000 mid-career. Meanwhile, earnings of people with bachelor's degrees in chemical or computer engineering earn $74,000 at graduation and over $110,000 mid-career.[xliv]

To further sharpen our understanding of how the college student's field of study impacts his/her lifetime earnings, in 2015, researchers from the University of Kansas, Texas A&M, and the U.S. Office of Retirement Policy collaborated and published their findings. In their paper titled *Field of Study in College and Lifetime Earnings in the United States,*[xlv] the authors demonstrate exactly which fields of study and corresponding degrees influence lifetime earnings. The researchers began with data from the U.S. Census Bureau's *Survey of Income and Program Participation,* which provides detailed educational information by household; the authors then matched this household data with earnings data compiled by the U.S. Social Security Administration.

---

[17] In other words, the 50th percentile or the middle. Imagine you have a data set of nine outcomes—when listed in numerical order, the median is the 5th outcome.

[18] This assumes an equal number of students earn a degree in each major. Unfortunately, the FRBNY doesn't provide the data stating how many people majored in each field of study.

For simplicity, researchers grouped college fields of study into eight categories, including: business; science, technology, engineering, and mathematics (STEM); social sciences; education; liberal arts; and all others. The authors then calculated the net present value of 40 years of earnings, using a four percent discount rate, by field of study and education level. The results? The field of study in college is as impactful to earnings—and in some cases more so—than the decision to attend college at all. This is true for both men and women.[19] For example, researchers estimate that the net present value of a lifetime of earnings for a male high school graduate is $679,885. Meanwhile, the present value earnings of someone who graduated with a STEM degree increases to $1,149,086, while that figure for someone with a degree in education is $650,920. That's less than someone with only a high school diploma! There is a similarly wide dispersion among graduate degrees; the present value of lifetime earnings for men graduating with a degree in medicine or dentistry is $1,962,536, while the lifetime earnings for men graduating with a graduate degree in liberal arts is $740,359.

In 2021, three faculty members at Georgetown University conducted a similar study and also concluded that a person's income earning potential is both highly variable and materially impacted by his/her field of study. Using data from the U.S. Census Bureau's American Community Survey, these researchers constructed an earnings profile that was unique to cohorts of people considering their undergraduate major, occupation, race, gender, industry, and state of residence. Unlike in the previous study, the authors did not calculate the present value of earnings (so their earnings estimates seem significantly higher). In their white paper titled *The College Payoff—More Education Doesn't Always Mean More Earnings*,[xlvi] the authors state: "Even though workers with more education tend to earn more, there is substantial variation in earnings at each level of education." To demonstrate this variation, the authors calculated both the median (middle or average income) of each cohort of people, as well as the range of earnings for those cohorts. So how is that relevant? Well, over a lifetime the average high school graduate earns $1.6 million, someone with some college or an associate degree earns $1.9 million, and the holder of a bachelor's degree earns $3.0 million. But, what about the high-earning, and not the *average* high school graduates? Researchers found that 31 percent of high school graduates earn more than the average holder of

---

[19] For the sake of brevity, in this paragraph I included only the results discussing men's lifetime earnings because men have a higher labor force participation in the United States. However, I encourage people to review the data concerning women's employment outlook as well (they are similar to the men). This data can be found in Table 4 of the referenced paper.

an associate degree, and 16 percent of high school graduates earn more than the average holder of a bachelor's degree.

Building off of others' work, in 2021, researchers from the Austin-based right-leaning Foundation for Research on Equal Opportunity (FREOPP) published a report called *Is College Worth It? A Comprehensive Return on Investment Analysis*. Utilizing a DOE dataset and Census Bureau surveys, researchers estimated the return on investment (ROI) for roughly 30,000 bachelor's degree programs in the U.S.; making their study the most comprehensive evaluation of the economic value of a degree to date. The author selected ROI because this metric includes an estimate of the present value of future earnings as well as the upfront direct (tuition, books, and fees) and indirect (lost income) costs of earning a degree. Researchers found the median ROI for earning a college degree is $306,000 for students who graduate on time. But this conceals the variation of ROI by field of study, it assumes that students graduate in four years, and it assumes that no students drop out or take longer than four years to complete their degree. When adjusting for the number of students who take longer than four years to complete the program, or who drop out entirely, the median ROI drops to only $129,000. Even more astonishingly, 37 percent of degrees have a negative ROI when accounting for all direct and indirect expenses and the risk of non-completion! That finding deserves more attention, so I'll say it again: researchers at FREOPP have estimated that 37 out of 100 graduating high school students who enter a four-year program will be worse off financially for having made the decision to go to college.[20,xlvii]

> *". . . 37 out of 100 graduating high school students who enter a four-year program will be worse off financially for having made the decision to go to college."*

Long-Term Risks of Enrolling in a College Program

As will be discussed in greater detail in Chapter 6, there are nontrivial numbers of potential harms that are associated with attending college in general—and with assuming student debt in particular. The significant up-front cost of attending college, and for some the burden of ongoing student loan payments, has significant long-term implications. For example,

---

[20] There is one caveat to this statement; the authors calculate that 37 percent of roughly 30,000 bachelor's degree programs offered at 1,775 U.S. colleges and universities have a negative return on investment. So, the statement that 37 out of 100 students are worse off financially assumes each program has the same proportional representation of students.

debt-laden college graduates experience delayed household formation, delayed home purchases, and delayed marriage. Other consequences include fewer people starting their own businesses, people pursuing careers that have greater personal meaning but less financial reward, and even people suffering with poorer mental health. It's difficult, if not impossible, to place a monetary value on all of these implications. However, for the purpose of a comprehensive review, considering these risks is essential to both personal and public policy decisions.

CONCLUSION

So now that you've waded through this entire chapter, looked at the data, and glossed over dozens of footnotes and references, what's the answer to the most important questions: should you or your kids go to college, and is it worth it? The frustrating answer is: it depends on the likelihood of having a positive outcome.

Here's a profile of a prospective student who is unlikely to have a positive outcome:

- Was an academically poor student in high school with poor standard assessment scores
- Requires remedial classes if they attend college
- Doesn't like studying, researching, or writing
- Doesn't know what they want to study
- Wants to study something with a very low likelihood of conferring a marketable skill[21]
- Will be forced to assume significant student debt
- Wants to learn a trade that doesn't require a college degree

By contrast, here's the profile of a person who will likely benefit from attending college:

- Was a good student in high school with high marks and strong test scores
- Enjoys studying and has sufficient self-discipline to focus on and complete tasks, even those that are not enjoyable
- Wants to study something that is likely to confer marketable skills[21]
- Will not be forced to assume significant student debt

---

[21] So, what degrees confer marketable skills and what degrees do not, as measured by income and employment rates? See Appendices 3.1 and 3.2 at the end of this chapter.

To be fair, these are all generalizations, and there will always be exceptions to such rules of thumb. But the point must be made—the exceptionally high (and growing) expense of college, along with the dramatic variability of outcomes, means that attending college is not a "golden ticket." Perhaps a third or more of high school students who enter college would have been better off had they not chosen to attend. This wasn't always true. In the 1970s and 1980s, the explicit and implicit costs of college were sufficiently low and the economic benefits of earning a degree were sufficiently high so that most (if not all) people entering a college program found that program worthwhile. But that's no longer the case. Failure to complete the college program, failure to develop a marketable skill,[21] and the assumption of oppressive student debt are real risks that must be weighed heavily. But don't take my word for it. In a 2019 online survey conducted by PayScale (a compensation consultancy firm), 71.3 percent of millennials indicated they have regrets regarding their college decisions, including assuming debt or simply in their selection of a major.[xlviii]

These statistics are both frustrating and tragic. However, if we hope to improve the outcomes of future students or to craft legislation leading to more positive outcomes, it is important to take stock of our current state of affairs. So, while the College Board may proclaim in their triennial[22] (every third year) study *Education Pays*, a more honest assessment would include the caveats "but not for everybody," and "not as much as in prior generations." We can do better, and so we should.

---

[22] The most recent reports were produced in 2019, 2016, 2013, 2010, 2007, 2006, 2005, and 2004.

Major	Unemployment Rate	Underemployment Rate	Median Wage Early Career	Median Wage Mid-Career	Share with Graduate Degree
Accounting	2.9	23.2	$52,000	$75,000	30.3
Advertising and Public Relations	6.2	48.1	$45,000	$78,000	20.4
Aerospace Engineering	4.5	23.6	$70,000	$110,000	51.8
Agriculture	4.5	56.6	$44,000	$66,000	21.6
Animal and Plant Sciences	4.3	58.1	$40,000	$64,000	35.0
Anthropology	8.3	61.3	$36,000	$60,000	48.8
Architecture	5.2	22.2	$50,000	$81,000	41.0
Art History	7.8	54.5	$40,000	$80,000	44.2
Biochemistry	1.7	41.7	$40,000	$86,000	71.6
Biology	4.4	48.3	$40,000	$70,000	63.1
Business Analytics	3.3	30.8	$60,000	$95,000	23.5
Business Management	4.7	56.0	$45,000	$70,000	24.0
Chemical Engineering	6.7	20.5	$70,000	$111,000	49.8
Chemistry	3.9	37.2	$45,800	$75,000	64.3
Civil Engineering	3.6	15.6	$63,000	$100,000	37.0
Commercial Art & Graphic Design	7.7	34.5	$40,000	$70,000	12.0
Communications	5.7	51.0	$43,100	$74,000	23.3
Computer Engineering	4.1	14.2	$74,000	$110,000	41.4
Computer Science	5.3	16.2	$70,000	$100,000	31.8

Appendix 3.1   Employment and Salary Data Sorted Alphabetically by Major. *Sources:* U.S. Census Bureau, American Community Survey (IPUMS); U.S. Department of Labor, O*NET.

Major	Unemployment Rate	Underemployment Rate	Median Wage Early Career	Median Wage Mid-Career	Share with Graduate Degree
Construction Services	1.6	24.5	$60,000	$94,000	9.8
Criminal Justice	4.6	71.1	$40,000	$65,000	22.5
Early Childhood Education	1.4	22.0	$36,000	$43,700	38.8
Earth Sciences	3.0	40.8	$42,000	$75,000	44.1
Economics	4.1	33.9	$60,000	$91,000	41.3
Electrical Engineering	3.5	18.2	$70,000	$107,000	47.4
Elementary Education	1.7	15.1	$39,000	$45,400	47.4
Engineering Technologies	3.2	42.2	$55,000	$85,000	24.8
English Language	6.8	49.1	$38,000	$65,000	46.4
Environmental Studies	5.5	49.9	$40,000	$70,000	31.5
Ethnic Studies	8.5	48.0	$40,000	$70,000	49.5
Family and Consumer Sciences	4.5	44.0	$32,000	$51,000	33.5
Finance	3.6	30.4	$60,000	$95,000	30.2
Fine Arts	9.2	58.0	$38,000	$60,000	22.7
Foreign Language	8.0	54.8	$38,000	$67,000	50.9
General Business	5.6	52.0	$45,000	$75,000	24.7
General Education	2.1	25.9	$40,000	$50,000	49.1
General Engineering	2.1	27.8	$62,000	$90,000	37.3
General Social Sciences	11.4	56.3	$34,000	$65,000	38.3

Appendix 3.1 *(continued)*

Major	Unemployment Rate	Underemployment Rate	Median Wage Early-Career	Median Wage Mid-Career	Share with Graduate Degree
Geography	5.2	47.5	$46,000	$74,000	34.0
Health Services	4.6	47.6	$40,000	$58,000	51.1
History	8.0	52.8	$40,000	$65,000	50.2
Industrial Engineering	2.9	24.9	$69,000	$93,000	39.4
Information Systems & Management	6.1	28.9	$52,000	$81,000	25.0
Interdisciplinary Studies	4.1	48.7	$40,900	$65,000	37.5
International Affairs	5.4	47.5	$48,000	$82,000	45.0
Journalism	3.9	44.2	$40,000	$68,000	26.2
Leisure and Hospitality	5.8	59.0	$38,000	$63,000	32.8
Liberal Arts	8.8	52.6	$37,400	$60,000	30.4
Marketing	5.8	53.3	$47,000	$80,000	17.6
Mass Media	6.9	49.9	$41,500	$69,000	18.6
Mathematics	7.6	25.9	$53,000	$85,000	51.7
Mechanical Engineering	4.4	19.4	$68,000	$104,000	40.1
Medical Technicians	0.7	56.0	$48,000	$65,000	22.4
Miscellaneous Biological Science	4.9	48.9	$38,000	$65,000	58.7
Miscellaneous Education	3.2	25.3	$41,000	$53,000	57.4
Miscellaneous Engineering	4.4	27.7	$65,000	$100,000	45.5
Miscellaneous Physical Sciences	4.8	43.6	$52,000	$82,000	55.4

Appendix 3.1 *(continued)*

Major	Unemployment Rate	Underemployment Rate	Median Wage Early Career	Median Wage Mid-Career	Share with Graduate Degree
Miscellaneous Technologies	6.7	59.0	$42,000	$80,000	17.6
Nursing	2.0	11.8	$55,000	$71,000	28.3
Nutrition Sciences	3.1	42.8	$44,600	$60,000	43.7
Performing Arts	9.1	70.2	$34,000	$60,000	38.5
Pharmacy	5.0	23.4	$45,000	$100,000	62.2
Philosophy	5.1	51.8	$44,000	$65,000	55.7
Physics	5.4	27.1	$55,000	$80,000	68.3
Political Science	6.2	49.7	$46,000	$80,000	52.2
Psychology	5.3	48.3	$37,000	$60,000	50.4
Public Policy and Law	7.0	47.8	$50,000	$66,000	43.7
Secondary Education	3.6	24.9	$40,000	$52,000	49.6
Social Services	2.1	34.4	$35,000	$50,000	50.5
Sociology	4.9	53.8	$40,000	$61,000	37.7
Special Education	3.5	15.8	$40,000	$52,000	61.8
Theology and Religion	4.4	44.6	$36,600	$55,000	43.5
Treatment Therapy	3.1	43.2	$39,000	$70,000	50.1

Appendix 3.1 (continued)

Major	Unemployment Rate	Underemployment Rate	Median Wage Early Career	Median Wage Mid-Career	Share with Graduate Degree
Chemical Engineering	6.7	20.5	$70,000	$111,000	49.8
Aerospace Engineering	4.5	23.6	$70,000	$110,000	51.8
Computer Engineering	4.1	14.2	$74,000	$110,000	41.4
Electrical Engineering	3.5	18.2	$70,000	$107,000	47.4
Mechanical Engineering	4.4	19.4	$68,000	$104,000	40.1
Civil Engineering	3.6	15.6	$63,000	$100,000	37.0
Computer Science	5.3	16.2	$70,000	$100,000	31.8
Miscellaneous Engineering	4.4	27.7	$65,000	$100,000	45.5
Pharmacy	5.0	23.4	$45,000	$100,000	62.2
Business Analytics	3.3	30.8	$60,000	$95,000	23.5
Finance	3.6	30.4	$60,000	$95,000	30.2
Construction Services	1.6	24.5	$60,000	$94,000	9.8
Industrial Engineering	2.9	24.9	$69,000	$93,000	39.4
Economics	4.1	33.9	$60,000	$91,000	41.3
General Engineering	2.1	27.8	$62,000	$90,000	37.3
Biochemistry	1.7	41.7	$40,000	$86,000	71.6
Engineering Technologies	3.2	42.2	$55,000	$85,000	24.8
Mathematics	7.6	25.9	$53,000	$85,000	51.7
International Affairs	5.4	47.5	$48,000	$82,000	45.0

Appendix 3.2 Employment and Salary Data Sorted by Median Wage Mid-Career (High to Low). *Sources:* U.S. Census Bureau, American Community Survey (IPUMS); U.S. Department of Labor, O*NET.

Major	Unemployment Rate	Underemployment Rate	Median Wage Early Career	Median Wage Mid-Career	Share with Graduate Degree
Miscellaneous Physical Sciences	4.8	43.6	$52,000	$82,000	55.4
Architecture	5.2	22.2	$50,000	$81,000	41.0
Information Systems & Management	6.1	28.9	$52,000	$81,000	25.0
Art History	7.8	54.5	$40,000	$80,000	44.2
Marketing	5.8	53.3	$47,000	$80,000	17.6
Miscellaneous Technologies	6.7	59.0	$42,000	$80,000	17.6
Physics	5.4	27.1	$55,000	$80,000	68.3
Political Science	6.2	49.7	$46,000	$80,000	52.2
Advertising and Public Relations	6.2	48.1	$45,000	$78,000	20.4
Accounting	2.9	23.2	$52,000	$75,000	30.3
Chemistry	3.9	37.2	$45,800	$75,000	64.3
Earth Sciences	3.0	40.8	$42,000	$75,000	44.1
General Business	5.6	52.0	$45,000	$75,000	24.7
Communications	5.7	51.0	$43,100	$74,000	23.3
Geography	5.2	47.5	$46,000	$74,000	34.0
Nursing	2.0	11.8	$55,000	$71,000	28.3
Biology	4.4	48.3	$40,000	$70,000	63.1
Business Management	4.7	56.0	$45,000	$70,000	24.0
Commercial Art & Graphic Design	7.7	34.5	$40,000	$70,000	12.0
Environmental Studies	5.5	49.9	$40,000	$70,000	31.5

Appendix 3.2 (continued)

Major	Unemployment Rate	Underemployment Rate	Median Wage Early Career	Median Wage Mid-Career	Share with Graduate Degree
Ethnic Studies	8.5	48.0	$40,000	$70,000	49.5
Treatment Therapy	3.1	43.2	$39,000	$70,000	50.1
Mass Media	6.9	49.9	$41,500	$69,000	18.6
Journalism	3.9	44.2	$40,000	$68,000	26.2
Foreign Language	8.0	54.8	$38,000	$67,000	50.9
Agriculture	4.5	56.6	$44,000	$66,000	21.6
Public Policy and Law	7.0	47.8	$50,000	$66,000	43.7
Criminal Justice	4.6	71.1	$40,000	$65,000	22.5
English Language	6.8	49.1	$38,000	$65,000	46.4
General Social Sciences	11.4	56.3	$34,000	$65,000	38.3
History	8.0	52.8	$40,000	$65,000	50.2
Interdisciplinary Studies	4.1	48.7	$40,900	$65,000	37.5
Medical Technicians	0.7	56.0	$48,000	$65,000	22.4
Miscellaneous Biological Science	4.9	48.9	$38,000	$65,000	58.7
Philosophy	5.1	51.8	$44,000	$65,000	55.7
Animal and Plant Sciences	4.3	58.1	$40,000	$64,000	35.0
Leisure and Hospitality	5.8	59.0	$38,000	$63,000	32.8
Sociology	4.9	53.8	$40,000	$61,000	37.7
Anthropology	8.3	61.3	$36,000	$60,000	48.8
Fine Arts	9.2	58.0	$38,000	$60,000	22.7

Appendix 3.2   *(continued)*

Major	Unemployment Rate	Underemployment Rate	Median Wage Early Career	Median Wage Mid-Career	Share with Graduate Degree
Liberal Arts	8.8	52.6	$37,400	$60,000	30.4
Nutrition Sciences	3.1	42.8	$44,600	$60,000	43.7
Performing Arts	9.1	70.2	$34,000	$60,000	38.5
Psychology	5.3	48.3	$37,000	$60,000	50.4
Health Services	4.6	47.6	$40,000	$58,000	51.1
Theology and Religion	4.4	44.6	$36,600	$55,000	43.5
Miscellaneous Education	3.2	25.3	$41,000	$53,000	57.4
Secondary Education	3.6	24.9	$40,000	$52,000	49.6
Special Education	3.5	15.8	$40,000	$52,000	61.8
Family and Consumer Sciences	4.5	44.0	$32,000	$51,000	33.5
General Education	2.1	25.9	$40,000	$50,000	49.1
Social Services	2.1	34.4	$35,000	$50,000	50.5
Elementary Education	1.7	15.1	$39,000	$45,400	47.4
Early Childhood Education	1.4	22.0	$36,000	$43,700	38.8

Notes: Figures represent a 2018–2019 average. Unemployment and underemployment rates are for recent college graduates (that is, those aged 22 to 27 with a bachelor's degree or higher), and median wages are for full-time workers with a bachelor's degree only. Early career graduates are those aged 22 to 27, and mid-career graduates are those aged 35 to 45. Graduate degree share is based on the adult working-age population (that is, those aged 25 to 65) with a bachelor's degree or higher. All figures exclude those currently enrolled in school. Data are updated annually at the beginning of each calendar year. Source: U.S. Census Bureau, American Community Survey (IPUMS), Federal Reserve Bank of New York. Website: https://www.newyorkfed.org/research/college-labor-market/college -labor-market_compare-majors.html. Accessed 6/26/22.

Appendix 3.2   (*continued*)

4

The University Endowment: What Is It and Why Should We Care?

A common quip about elite universities like Harvard, Yale, and Princeton is that they're hedge funds with schools attached to them. The joke is meant to relay that these three schools (whose endowments collectively hold around $100 billion in assets) and others like them are in the business of generating investment returns, and as a side hustle, also educate students. Of greater concern than the institutional focus on asset management (in lieu of education) is that these endowments have preferential tax treatment, are highly concentrated among the most elite schools, and are not utilized to maximize the educational value of either students or society. In a viral 2015 *New York Times* op-ed, UCI Law Professor Victor Fleischer pointed out that in 2014, Yale paid $480 million to private equity managers but only $170 million for tuition assistance.[i] In response, five-time best-selling author Malcolm Gladwell tweeted (among other jabs), "I was going to donate money to Yale. But maybe it makes more sense to mail a check directly to the hedge fund of my choice."[ii] So what are these enormous pools of capital attached to universities, known as endowment funds? And are they really so bad?

> *". . . in 2014, Yale paid $480 million to private equity managers but only $170 million for tuition assistance."*

University endowment funds are permanent pools of capital that are intended to assist a university. These endowment funds regularly generate both income and capital appreciation, and this income and capital appreciation allow a university to pay for operations, grants, and other expenses. Endowments enjoy a tax advantage, meaning there are no taxes applied to endowments' income or capital gains, while the donors also receive a tax deduction for donations. With the exception of the colleges that were beneficiaries of the Morrill Act of 1862 (see Chapter 1), most endowments were seeded by alumni and other private donors. The National Association of College and University Business Officers (NACUBO) in 2021, collected data from 720 colleges and universities and reported aggregate university endowment assets were $821 billion,[iii] while the median university endowment was $144.4 million in 2019. These data were from colleges and universities that voluntarily participated in an annual NACUBO survey, meaning the aggregate university endowment funds are likely even larger since thousands of (mostly small) colleges did not participate in the survey.[iv] The size of university endowments is heavily skewed and the ten largest endowments (including Harvard, Yale, University of Texas, Stanford, and Princeton) collectively control approximately $230 billion in assets.[v]

There are two reasons why public policy toward endowments is highly relevant to our discussion of college expenses and student debt. First, the income generated by endowments is critically important to select universities. Therefore, any change to public policy or regulation of endowments will have a material impact on the operations of these universities. Second, endowments receive special tax treatment since income and capital gains are not taxed. Endowments (and colleges and universities by extension) may not receive explicit taxpayer support in the form of strings-free transfer payments. However, the preferential treatment enjoyed by an endowment means that a university is the beneficiary of an implicit taxpayer subsidy in the form of forgone taxes. In some cases, this taxpayer subsidy is enormous. Therefore, it is sensible to ask if taxpayers (or students) are benefiting from this tax policy. With this in mind, in this chapter we'll dive deep into this topic by discussing the theoretical and practical purpose of endowments, how they support universities, and problems with current policy endowment tax policy. In Chapter 8, I'll explain how thoughtful endowment legislative reforms may both alleviate the student debt crisis, as well as ensure that endowment wealth may become more equitably distributed among a breadth of schools.

ENDOWMENT HISTORY AND OBJECTIVES

Philanthropy supporting universities is as old as the university system itself. Two years after Harvard College was established in 1638, John Harvard left his library collection and half of his estate to the institution that bears his name.[vi] Fourteen years after the Collegiate School of Connecticut was established, Elihu Yale made a large donation to the fledgling institution, after which the school changed its name.[vii] Yet, these (and others' subsequent) gifts generally supported the immediate needs of the universities; while donations in the form of books would benefit future students, financial support was often spent shortly after receipt of the gift. Thus, permanent pools of capital that would support the financial needs of the university were not widely utilized until the passage of the Morrill Act of 1862. Following the passage of this act, U.S. states received federal land which would be sold and the proceeds used to support colleges. In addition, the proceeds of these sales would seed college endowments, which would fund the college in perpetuity at a rate of five percent.[viii]

The notion that wealthy private citizens should directly contribute to these endowments became more generally accepted after Andrew Carnegie wrote *The Gospel of Wealth* in 1889. In his essay, Carnegie argued that it was the moral responsibility of the wealthiest to redistribute their wealth to society in the form of philanthropy. While the means of this wealth redistribution may occur through an estate tax or large one-time donations to charities, Carnegie's preferred method of philanthropy involved the establishment of permanent programs that would continue to benefit society. By the time the *Gospel of Wealth* was published, Carnegie had already begun building libraries in both the United States and Scotland. Receipt of a Carnegie library had several stipulations including requiring that the municipality establish a tax to fund the ongoing operations of the library, thereby ensuring the library would be free for all.[ix] By the time of his death, Carnegie had donated over $56 million to build 2,509 libraries across the world.[x] In addition to libraries, Carnegie established six endowments, the largest, last, and most famous of which was the Carnegie Corporation of New York. Established in 1911 with $145 million,[xi] the philanthropic foundation continues to operate and has grown to $4.7 billion as of 2021.[xii]

Following Andrew Carnegie's example, wealthy alumni of universities donated generously to endowments in the early 1900s. As shown in Figure 4.1, the aggregate size of university endowments grew from $195 million in 1900 to $1.4 billion by 1930. After a period of modest growth between 1930 and 1940, university endowments resumed a rapid upward trajectory, growing roughly tenfold every 30 years. As of 2020, endowment funds of the largest 120 degree-granting postsecondary institutions aggregate to nearly $515 billion while the average endowment is over $176 million.[1] Separately, as shown in Figure 4.2, the size of university endowments (per student) grew from only

---

[1] The National Center for Education Statistics provides data for the largest 120 degree-granting institutions and the smallest endowment disclosed was $912 million; these institutions collectively hold $515 billion in assets. Meanwhile, there are 3,931 degree-granting institutions in the United States as of 2020, which collectively held roughly $691 billion in assets. As a result, there is a heavy skew of assets to the largest endowments, which means the median (or middle) endowment is significantly smaller than the average of $176 million per school.

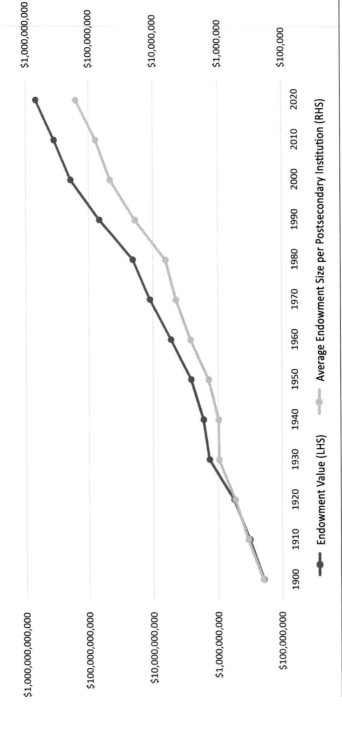

Figure 4.1 Aggregate Endowment Size per U.S. Postsecondary Institutions (LHS) vs Average Endowment Size per Postsecondary Institution (RHS). *Sources:* See end of chapter.

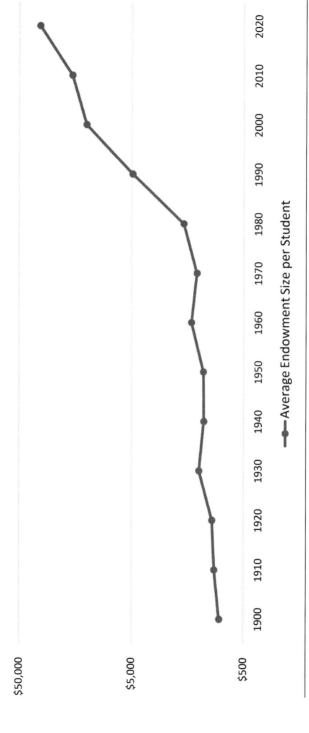

Figure 4.2 Average Endowment Size per Student. *Sources:* See end of chapter.

$821 to $1,246 between 1900 and 1930. By 1970, the average university endowment was only $1,306 per student. However, since 1980, growth in postsecondary enrollment has slowed while the size of endowments per student has drastically risen to roughly $33,000 in 2020.

Endowment Objective 1: Maintain University Independence

As explained by David Swenson, former Chief Investment Officer of Yale University and author of *Pioneering Portfolio Management*: "Greater institutional needs for current income correspond to greater degrees of external influence."[xiii] The sources of current income to which Swenson refers includes government grants, donor gifts, and student tuition; however, each of these sources generally comes with some *strings attached*. Government grants are usually provided for specific projects and not general university operations. Similarly, donor gifts usually have stipulations regarding how and for whom the gifts are spent; a donor might specify a gift is for construction of a new building, whereas the university may have a need to hire additional faculty. Finally, dependence on student tuition requires universities to ensure that the offered courses are constantly evolving to attract and retain students in sufficient numbers to maintain operations. When a university aspires to maintain its operations without being beholden to the government, their donors, or their students, the means by which it can achieve its independence is to grow and maintain a large endowment. Should the income generated by a university endowment be sufficient to maintain its operations, universities would be unfettered from most, if not all, external forces that would guide its operations.

The obvious question we should ask ourselves would be: is a university being completely independent from external forces a good thing? We established in Chapter 1 that universities have a tacit obligation to enable the advancement of their students' abilities to contribute both to society and to their own financial future. So, is breaking the link between the success of the students, society, and the ongoing operations of universities an appropriate aspiration? Mr. Swenson sadly passed away in 2021, so we can only speculate that he would argue that universities (unfettered from external forces) would still be responsible for both advancing society as well as benefiting the students that grace their halls. However, in practice, a university that is free from all external financial influences has no explicit checks ensuring that the university is effectively operating for the benefit of its stakeholders.

Endowment Objective 2: Provide the University with Financial Stability

The second objective of a university endowment is to provide financial stability. As noted by Mr. Swenson, nonpermanent funding sources can be highly variable. These nonpermanent sources include government grants (which often have set time frames), donor generosity (which is correlated to economic growth and stock market returns), and student enrollment. A stable revenue stream enhances operational efficiency and enables long-term planning. It can also insulate the school from sudden shocks in declining enrollment or loss of another source of income. Therefore, a well-endowed university has the ability to maintain operational efficiency in all economic conditions and can evolve and adapt to new circumstances without the risk of draconian cuts or pivots that would disrupt students' educational experiences.

A university highlighted by Mr. Swenson that could have benefited from the financial stability provided by a large endowment is the University of Bridgeport in Connecticut; this university's undergraduate enrollment declined from 9,000 in the 1970s to 4,400 in 1991. As a result of the loss of student enrollment and the corresponding decline in tuition receipts, the school cut nearly one-third of its degree programs but still struggled to meet payroll costs.[xiv] Further adding to the trustee's desperation, in 1992 the law school seceded and joined Quinnipiac College, becoming the Bridgeport School of Law at Quinnipiac College. Having initially resisted an offer of financial support, the trustees begrudgingly accepted a $50 million infusion of cash from the Professors World Peace Academy, an affiliate of the Reverend Sun Myung Moon's Unification Church. In return for the capital infusion, the board appointed 16 members of the Professors World Peace Academy as trustees, giving the academy a majority.[xv] Students and faculty were right to be concerned that the university was largely controlled by the Unification Church; the church was known for mass weddings in Madison Square where its leader, Sun Moon, would introduce the bride and groom. Parents of recent converts reported needing to deprogram their children to break them from church influences, and in the 1980s, Mr. Moon was found guilty in the United States of tax evasion and sentenced to 18 months in prison.[xvi] In 2019, the Board of Trustees successfully voted to cut all ties with Professors World Peace Academy and the Unification Church.[xvii]

A large endowment at the University of Bridgeport clearly would have alleviated the need to affiliate with the Unification Church. However, it is difficult to conclude from this single anecdote that the financial stability offered by university endowments only leads to positive outcomes. Consider the case of Evergreen State College in the state of Washington. In 2017, students with administrative support organized a "Day of Absence" in which White people were discouraged and coerced into not coming on campus; in previous years, the Day of Absence involved students of color meeting off campus to discuss racial issues. In response to this, Professor Bret Weinstein, a biology professor, posted a message on a campus email list in which he objected to the proposal. He stated, "There is a huge difference between a group or coalition deciding to voluntarily absent themselves from a shared space in order to highlight their vital and underappreciated roles (the theme of the Douglas Turner Ward play *Day of Absence*, as well as the recent Women's Day walkout), and a group encouraging another group to go away . . . The first is a forceful call to consciousness, which is, of course, crippling to the logic of oppression. The second is a show of force, and an act of oppression in and of itself . . . On a college campus, one's right to speak—or to be—must never be based on skin color."[xviii] In response to Professor Weinstein's note, on the day of the event, students interrupted Professor Weinstein's class, called him racist, and demanded his resignation. Students then barricaded themselves in the library and began issuing demands of the administration. For the next three days, the campus was largely shut down, students occupied the president's office, and some students were rumored to be searching cars for Professor Weinstein.[xix] Professor Weinstein was advised by police not to come on campus. Following a return to normalcy on campus, the president of Evergreen State, George Bridges, did not fire Professor Weinstein; however, the president did praise protestors and made concessions to several of their demands.[xx]

From 2017 to 2019, enrollment at Evergreen State College fell by roughly 1,000 to 2,900, despite having an acceptance rate of 97 percent. The administration responded by cutting 34 positions and revising their curriculum to have more formalized paths of study.[xxi] While administrators have asserted that the loosely defined curriculum was an impediment to attracting and retaining students, one might argue that the collapse in enrollment can be attributed to the reputational damage to the institution following the 2017 protests. In 2018, the Evergreen State College Foundation held a modest $20.8 million in net assets which generated $162,121 in unrestricted income.[xxii] This income is far too small to offset a nearly 26 percent decline in enrollment. However, if Evergreen State College was significantly endowed, it's entirely possible neither its administrators nor students would have faced either consequence or been motivated to alter course following these events.

Endowment Objective 3: Enable the Creation of an Excellent Institution and Student Experience

The income generated from an endowment has the potential to produce a superior educational environment. As noted by Mr. Swenson, at the very least, endowment income enables the hiring of superior scholars and faculty, provides funds for superior facilities, and enables pioneering research. Mr. Swenson goes on to demonstrate that there is a strong correlation between the annual college and university rankings by the *U.S. News and World Report* and the size of the respective institutions' endowment.[xxiii] As shown in Figure 4.3, the most heavily endowed universities are generally at the top of the national university rankings. While the correlation between endowment size and university rank is clear, the causal link is debatable. Do high-quality institutions generate high-income alumni, who later in their careers donate generously to their school enabling the growth of the endowment? Or, does the large endowment provide the resources required to create high-quality institutions that are later identified as such by college rankings? Regardless, we can conclude that there is a somewhat virtuous cycle associated with this process.

My undergraduate alma mater, the University of Southern California (USC), has a sizable $5.9 billion endowment. However, with a full-time enrollment between all programs of over 46,000, this comes to an endowment of only $128,000 per student. By contrast, the combined full-time enrollment of Harvard, Yale, and Princeton is 50,304 students (marginally larger than USC's enrollment). However, the combined endowments of these schools are a whopping $99 billion—or nearly $2.0 million per student! If we are to assume that a university's primary mission is to elevate both society and the individual student by transferring knowledge and skills to their students, then USC is doing the work of Harvard, Yale, and Princeton, combined. But it's doing it with significantly less support from its endowment, and by extension, less support from the government.

The discrepancy between school endowment sizes becomes particularly notable when we compare the income that each university's endowment generates per student. Harvard University has the largest university endowment with $42 billion in assets; this equates to $4.9 million per undergraduate or $1.4 million per student.[2] Assuming the endowment generates a modest return of five percent per year, this endowment generates roughly

---

[2] As of 2021, Harvard had roughly 8,500 undergraduate students and another 21,900 graduate students; combined, the full-time enrolled study body was roughly 30,400.

Endowment 2020 Assets ($1,000s)	2020 U.S. News National University Rank	2020 Fulltime Undergraduate Enrollment	2020 Fulltime Enrollment (All Programs)	Endowment Assets per Undergrad ($1,000s)	Endowment Assets per All Students ($1,000s)	Annual Per Undergrad Student Income (at 5%)
$41,894,380	2	8,527	30,391	$4,913	$1,379	$245,657
$31,201,686	4	4,703	12,060	$6,634	$2,587	$331,721
$28,948,111	6	6,366	15,953	$4,547	$1,815	$227,365
$25,944,283	1	4,774	7,853	$5,434	$3,304	$271,725
$18,381,518	4	4,361	11,254	$4,215	$1,633	$210,749
$11,257,021	3	8,148	30,135	$1,382	$374	$69,078
$9,169,028	21	8,101	15,398	$1,132	$595	$56,592
$5,914,358	24	19,786	46,287	$299	$128	$14,946
$4,151,994	58	23,157	32,277	$179	$129	$8,965
$2,530,872	88	22,304	30,318	$113	$83	$5,674
$2,169,707	35	16,561	39,771	$131	$55	$6,551
$1,830,892	124	19,135	26,744	$96	$68	$4,784
$1,458,648	41	8,537	13,927	$171	$105	$8,543
$1,350,187	28	5,441	8,789	$248	$154	$12,408
$1,150,827	63	35,844	50,411	$32	$23	$1,605
$1,071,908	97	24,643	33,081	$43	$32	$2,175

Figure 4.3 Select University Endowment Asset Size, National Rank, and Assets per Student. *Sources: U.S. News and World Report* Rankings, Endowment Rank and Size: National Center for Education Statistics, and Enrollment: Various college websites.

$246,000 per undergraduate or $69,000 per student, per year. Princeton, with its significantly smaller student body, has an endowment equal to $3.3 million per student ($5.4 million per undergraduate), generating $139,000 per student, per year ($271,000 per undergraduate). By contrast, Rutgers University has an endowment equal to $23,000 per student ($32,000 per undergraduate), generating $1,100 per student, per year ($1,600 per undergraduate).

No doubt the Harvard, Yale, and Stanford endowments enable these universities to hire better faculty, maintain nicer buildings, and ensure a better student experience than most universities; as a result, these institutions will attract higher quality students who can donate to these endowments later in life. If this is a virtuous cycle, then isn't the comparative disadvantage that is experienced by institutions such as the University of Kansas, Rutgers University, or the University of Utah a vicious cycle? Specifically, if these universities are efficiently run but are unable to afford high-profile faculty or maintain luxurious facilities, these schools will be unlikely to attract and retain the highest quality students. As a result, the poorly endowed schools will be unable to compete with Harvard, Yale, and Stanford because of the starting conditions of their school's respective endowment sizes and not the respective quality of their educational instruction. Therefore, the *richest* schools are likely to remain the *richest* owing to financial inertia alone. We might question whether this is an appropriate system; in any other private industry, should a company no longer create a high-quality product, it will lose customers and sales. Thus, healthy competition ensures that the poorly run organizations falter and are replaced by superior organizations with better products. But, the largest endowments at select universities may be sufficiently large to ensure that a poorly run university will continue as an ongoing concern in perpetuity. Similarly, smaller endowments may act as an impediment to the ability of these schools to offer a better product vis-à-vis the better-endowed schools. As a result, the creative destruction that is inherent in a capitalist system is less present in the university system.

So, is the current system optimal? We may assume that because universities and their respective endowments are private entities, we have no say in the matter. However, endowments, and by extension the universities they support, are the beneficiary of an enormous tax subsidy—so we can, and should, have a say in the matter.

> *". . . endowments, and by extension the universities they support, are the beneficiary of an enormous tax subsidy . . ."*

HOW ARE ENDOWMENTS MANAGED?

Regardless of the size of a university endowment, its trustees must evaluate a plethora of factors when setting policy for an endowment's management. Considerations include current spend rates, investment return targets, alumni and donor stipulations, and legal guidelines.[3,xxiv] By far the most contentious objective set by the trustees is the rate at which an endowment spends its current assets. High current spending rates provide more generously for the university today, while low current spending rates allow for long-term asset accumulation thereby benefiting the university in the future. A second and equally important objective is the investment return target. A high return target enables both a faster growth of the endowment as well as a higher current spend rate; however, with this higher return target comes additional volatility including the risk of principal loss and prolonged periods during which the endowments' payout must be curtailed or suspended. It is ultimately the trustee's obligation to ensure both spending and investment return targets are prudent given the perpetual nature of a university.

Endowment Investment Objective

Due to the perpetual nature of an endowment, its spending rate is connected with its investment objective. Specifically, since one objective of trustees is to grow the endowment, the endowment investment return must exceed its spending rate; therefore, the first question an endowment's board must define is what determines a realistic and achievable investment return objective. A board of trustees may arrive at an investment objective by utilizing either a *top-down* or *bottom-up* approach. From a top-down perspective, the board may first assess what specific assets have historically returned and how comfortable the board is holding those assets. For example, between 1928 and 2019, equities (a high-risk asset) have returned an average of +9.7 percent per annum with an annual volatility of 19.5 percent. This means that 95 percent of the time, equities returned between −29.2 and +48.7 percent in

---

[3] With the exception of Pennsylvania, all U.S. states have adopted a version of the Uniform Prudent Management of Institutional Funds Act (UPMIFA). The preceding law to the UPMIFA, the Uniform Management of Institutional Funds Act (UMIFA), was written in 1972 to provide both guidance and guardrails to trustees who were managing endowments affiliated with nonprofits. The act was updated in 2006, becoming the UPMIFA. Current standards involve a *prudent* management of assets, discourage high levels of current spending to ensure the endowment remains a perpetual consideration, and ensure that endowments are spent in accordance with donors' wishes.

a year. Alternatively, less-risky BAA-rated corporate bonds turned an average of 7 percent per year with an annual volatility of 7.5 percent. Therefore, 95 percent of the time, BAA-bonds returned between −8.1 and +22.0 percent in a year. These are pretty wide ranges and these figures may not be entirely applicable to an endowment with a perpetual horizon. Specifically, since endowments set budgets over multiyear periods, a multiyear range of potential investment outcomes is more relevant. So, its trustees may consider that between 1939 and 2019, U.S. stocks generated a 10-year annualized return between +20.1 and −1.7 percent, whereas BAA-rated bonds generated a 10-year annualized return between +16.1 and +2.3 percent.[xxv]

A bottom-up approach would include trustees constructing an estimate of inflation and then determining what constitutes a reasonable portfolio return in excess of inflation. An endowment generating a return equal to inflation would neither grow nor shrink on an inflation-adjusted valuation. While a return target equal to the inflation rate would satisfy the need to ensure capital preservation, such a portfolio return would not provide the endowment with the ability to either grow or generate distributions to benefit a university. Therefore, the long-term endowment return target must be in excess of inflation in order to satisfy both the goals of creating a meaningful distribution stream while also growing the endowment for the benefit of future generations. The return in excess of riskless assets (such as three-month U.S. Treasury bills) is known in finance as a *risk premium*, and this premium has also varied throughout time. It is impossible to know in advance (or ex-ante) what this premium will be; therefore, trustees must again turn to history.

There is no right answer regarding the optimal endowment portfolio target, but there is a general consensus. The NACUBO conducts an annual survey of all college endowments and has found that the average return target among university endowments is 7.9 percent per year as of 2021. As shown in Figure 4.4, this return target has remained between 7 and 7.9 percent since 2010.[xxvi,xxvii,xxviii] The downward pressure on return targets from 2009 to 2019 can be attributed to two phenomena: first, the 10-year average return (as represented by the blue line) has generally failed to meet the trustees' long-term objective, meaning the investment objective was either too high or endowment portfolios not sufficiently risky. Second, interest rates were lower in 2019 than in 2009; assuming the previously mentioned risk premiums are unchanged, it will be more difficult to generate higher returns for future 10-year periods than prior 10-year periods. However, strong equity returns of roughly 30 percent (U.S. large-cap equities) in both 2019 and 2021 led to a notable increase in return expectations.

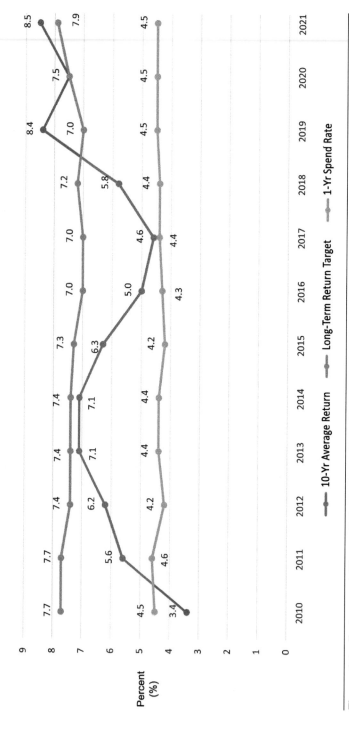

Figure 4.4   Endowment 10-year Returns, Long-Term Return Target, and 1-year Spend Rate. *Source:* NACUBO.

Endowment Spending Target

Trustees must establish a spending target that is consistent with the trade-off between current budgetary support and asset growth. The trustees are fiduciaries and stewards of capital, and each has their own preference for current versus future spending. For an endowment with a perpetual horizon, this trade-off will ultimately translate into a specific spending target of current assets. If an endowment is $1 billion in size, will the trustees authorize $1 million (0.1%), $10 million (1.0%), or $100 million (10.0%) in annual distributions? As shown in Figure 4.4, universities generally target an annual spend rate of between 4.2 to 4.5 percent of their annual assets. Interestingly, we can look to endowment investment targets and spend rates to ascertain their trustee's relative preference for current spending versus asset appreciation and future spending. For example, in 2019, the average return target was 7 percent and the average spend rate was 4.5 percent. The difference between the targeted spend rate and return target is 2.5 percent; this 2.5 percent is set aside and is expected to continue to grow into the future. So, trustees target an average spend rate of 64 percent (4.5 to 7%) and set aside 36 percent (2.5 to 7%) for capital preservation and growth of the endowment.

Once an average spend rate (say, 4.5%) is established, how should this be applied to a dollar amount spent from the endowment each fiscal year? If the portfolio appreciates in a year by 20 percent, does this mean that the total spend amount increases by 20 percent as well?[4] What if the value of the endowment falls? Should spending from the endowment also fall, and if so, by how much? Trustees have developed several formulaic approaches to addressing the desire for a steady and predictable contribution to the operating budget, but also the necessity of adjusting the spend rate to account for endowment value fluctuations. Most approaches involve some sort of *smoothing*. For example, rather than spending 4.5 percent of the endowment after valuing the endowment at a single point in time (such as the beginning of the year), a spend policy might involve spending 4.5 percent of the *average* value of the endowment, as measured over the last four years. Alternatively, Yale's spending policy involves spending an amount equal to 80 percent of the spending in the previous year plus 20 percent of the long-term spending rate

---

[4] Imagine an endowment is $100 million and the spend target is 4.5 percent. In year one, the total budgetary contribution from the endowment is $4.5 million (4.5% × 100 million). If the endowment appreciates (after any spending) by 20 percent that year, its closing value is $120 million. If the spending target remains at 4.5 percent, the total budgetary contribution is $5.4 million (4.5% × $120 million). Thus, the annual spend from the endowment has risen by 20 percent as well (5.4 × 4.5% = 1.2).

applied to the endowment's market value in the previous year. This method also ensures that year-over-year spend rates are sensitive to changing valuations of the endowment while also being smoothed.[xxix]

Endowment Spending Uses

Income generated by endowments makes a meaningful contribution to many university operating budgets. On average, endowments fund roughly 10 percent of universities' operating budgets; however, this figure is skewed by a few large endowments. For example, Harvard and Yale use endowment income to cover more than one third of their budgets.[xxx] In aggregate, the 774 American universities that responded to the 2019 NACUBO survey collectively withdrew and spent $22.6 billion from their endowments that year. So, how is this money spent? The largest component of endowment spending is student financial aid (49%); this financial aid may include scholarships, grants, loans, or contributions to a work-study program. The support of academic programs (17%), faculty positions (11%), operations including maintenance of campus facilities (7%), and all other purposes (16%) together constitute the remaining half of endowment expenditures.[xxxi]

It is interesting to note that roughly half of endowment expenditures is for student financial aid; we should have some ambivalence when considering this. On the one hand, directly supporting students in their educational endeavors is an excellent use for these funds since it enables recipients to receive an education that would otherwise have been financially out of reach. On the other hand, the availability of student aid enables administrators to charge more for their services, placing education out of reach for others. How does this work? As mentioned in Chapter 2, the greater the availability of financial resources—whether those resources be derived from income, grants, or loans—the greater the ability for students to spend money on their college education. Administrators respond to this increased ability (and unchanged willingness) to spend by increasing tuition and other expenses. No doubt some of the marginal revenue generated by higher tuition adds to the students' educational experience—nicer labs, larger libraries, etc. However, there are likely diminishing marginal returns to these expenditures. Does an upgraded student union, dormitories with central air conditioning, and elaborate sports facilities really enhance a student's ability to apply their education once they leave the campus? Probably not; but, the availability of funds enables students to pay and administrators to charge higher tuition, some of which is spent in a plethora of areas that while nice, may not lead to better educational or student outcomes.

ENDOWMENT CRITIQUES

The eye-popping size of university endowments, many in the billions controlled by the largest and wealthiest endowments, have increasingly become popular targets across the political spectrum. On the left, endowments embody multigenerational wealth and power hoarded by those who need it least. Furthermore, those that donate to endowments are making errors in judgment as their donations should be given to charities that can better use the funds. Taking issue with John Paulson for his $400 million donation to Harvard, Malcolm Gladwell tweeted, "Harvard's pitch to Paulson: not all privileged people are equally privileged!" and "It came down to helping the poor or giving the world's richest university $400 mil it doesn't need. Wise choice John!"[xxxii] Meanwhile on the right, critics charge that endowments enable universities to operate without regard to their classical roots, foster anti-American sentiment, and possibly engage in indoctrination. In 2020, then President Trump tweeted, "Too many Universities and School Systems are about Radical Left Indoctrination, not Education. Therefore, I am telling the Treasury Department to re-examine their Tax-Exempt Status and/or Funding, which will be taken away if this Propaganda or Act Against Public Policy continues. Our children must be Educated, not Indoctrinated!"[xxxiii]

Regardless of where one lies on the political spectrum, the largest endowments are easy targets for criticism because they're both enormous and egregiously concentrated. As of 2020, the six largest university endowments (0.1% of degree-granting institutions) control 21 percent of total endowment assets, while the 40 largest endowments (1% of degree-granting institutions) control 67 percent of total endowment assets.[xxxiv] Most of these endowments

> *". . . the six largest university endowments (0.1%*
> *of degree-granting institutions) control 21 percent of*
> *total endowment assets, while the 40 largest endowments*
> *(1% of degree-granting institutions) control 67 percent*
> *of total endowment assets."*

are connected with large private universities. In addition, as noted by Sandy Baum, Senior Fellow at the Urban Institute, endowments connected to public universities are also highly concentrated. She finds five state universities and systems, which enroll one percent of the state university population, hold a quarter of all the endowment assets. As a result of this concentration, the ability of most university endowments to meaningfully offset educational expenses is limited. Ms. Baum calculates that half of the students studying at private non-profit colleges attend institutions with endowments that can provide less than $1,300 per student per year.[xxxv]

So, because our principal concern is student debt and the adverse effect it has on students and society, endowment reform will not offer a panacea. University endowments are not a primary cause of the dramatic increase in college expenses and corresponding student debt, and the ability of endowments to reduce tuition expenses is limited. However, we can argue the egregious concentration of endowment assets among a small group of universities is still problematic. So, perhaps thoughtful legislation can, over time, level the playing field among universities and ensure endowment assets are more evenly distributed among institutions. An even distribution of endowment assets among postsecondary institutions would lead to a greater ability among endowments to collectively reduce tuition expenses regardless of the institution. Furthermore, if endowment tax breaks are tied to student outcomes and the number of students educated, no doubt universities will take more care to educate more students and ensure that students graduate with little debt and are gainfully employed at graduation. But, before we can propose policy solutions, we must first identify what has led to the problems of excessive accumulation of endowment funds at a small percentage of universities. I'll address four here: (1) tax laws do not sufficiently differentiate between large (rich) and small (poor) endowments, (2) there are tax benefits without taxpayer accountability, (3) there is no direct link between tax benefits and educational outcome, and (4) heavily endowed schools are not incentivized to grow their student bodies.

Problem 1: Tax Laws Do Not Sufficiently Differentiate Between Large (Rich) and Small (Poor) Endowments

Exemption from income or capital gains tax is critical to endowments; this tax exemption allows endowments to grow more rapidly and it motivates individuals to donate more generously. The tax-exempt status enjoyed by endowments was first codified by law in the Wilson-Gorman Tariff Act of 1894. This law included the passage, "nothing herein contained [taxes] shall apply to corporations, companies, or associations organized and conducted solely for charitable, religious, or educational purposes, including fraternal beneficiary associations." While the law was ruled unconstitutional, similar language would reappear in the Revenue Act of 1909.[xxxvi] Meanwhile, the War Revenue Act of 1917 introduced the individual income tax deduction for charitable donations.[xxxvii] When these laws were written, the state of higher education looked far different from today. As we reviewed in Chapter 1, in

1910 only 0.7 percent of the U.S. population had a bachelor's degree and less than 0.4 percent of the population was enrolled in postsecondary institutions. In addition, the average endowment per institution at the time was $340,000. So, the tax exemption for some 950 institutions was a relatively trivial, albeit well-intended concession. By contrast, at the end of 2021, 110 institutions had an endowment greater than $1 billion,[xxxviii] while the total educational endowments in the country exceeded $0.82 trillion.[xxxix]

Separate from those two tax exemptions, universities today regularly utilize an unintended loophole in current tax policy when raising funds for large capital projects. Imagine a university will spend $100 million on a new facility; it can either spend that money from its endowment or issue a tax-exempt municipal bond to fund the project. Universities regularly choose the latter option because the interest paid on the municipal debt is far lower than the interest earned on their endowment portfolio. As a result, since the late 1960s and early 1970s when states began exempting interest on debt issued by universities, the public has been subsidizing campus facilities.[xl]

Until 2017, tax laws that were applicable to endowments made no differentiation between large and small endowments, whether measured in aggregate or per full-time enrolled student. As a result, the endowment tax benefits were proportional to the initial size of the endowment. How big was this tax benefit? *Big*. Professor Charlie Eaton of the Haas Institute for Fair and Inclusive Society estimated the 2012 tax benefit to endowments equaled $19.6 billion.[xli] While not exactly apples to apples, assuming this tax benefit has grown in lockstep with endowments (which have grown over 63% between 2012 and 2021), the annual tax benefit as of 2021 is likely in excess of $31 billion. And who are the recipients of this tax benefit? The schools that need it the least: Harvard, Yale, Stanford, Princeton, etc. Recognizing the serious need in tax policy reform, in 2017, Congress made a small change to the tax law to begin to address this inequity. The 2017 Tax Cuts and Jobs Act (TCJA) imposes a 1.4 percent tax on investment income; this tax applies to institutions with greater than 500 students and an endowment equal to at least $500,000 per student. The U.S. Treasury estimated about 40 institutions met these criteria at the time the law was passed, and the law was expected to generate about $200 million per year.[xlii]

While a modest 1.4 percent tax is a good start, the current tax policy still disproportionately benefits the largest endowments and wealthiest schools; 1.4 percent is far less than the current long-term capital gains tax rate (20%) and

". . . the current tax policy still disproportionately benefits the largest endowments and wealthiest schools . . ."

top income tax rate (37%). Returning to the schools previously highlighted, Figure 4.5 provides a *rough* estimate of the tax benefit received by a university per full-time enrolled student. With some simplistic assumptions (footnoted below), I estimate that even with the recently passed TCJA, each of the top five endowments still receive an annual tax benefit of between $30k and $62k per student! Meanwhile, Rutgers University and the University of Utah each receive less than a $700 per student tax benefit.

Problem 2: Endowments Include Tax Benefits but Have No Taxpayer Obligation

The next problem I'll cover with current tax policy toward endowments is that the tax benefits received by universities do not obligate the universities to act in a manner commensurate with their public support. By contrast, if universities want their students to be eligible for grants, the universities must adhere to all nondiscrimination guidelines codified in the Civil Rights Act of 1964, title IX of the Higher Education Act (as amended in 1972), and a litany of other nondiscrimination laws. Similarly, in the event that a university receives grant money for a research project, that university must adhere to a variety of stipulations upon receipt of the grant money. However, a university and its endowment are under no obligation to the taxpayer or government to produce goods or services of similar value to uncollected income and capital gains taxes. Rather, universities and their endowments are unfettered when it comes to pursuing whatever activities are in the best interest of those universities, regardless of the degree to which they are benefiting from current tax policy.

---

[5] (see Figure 4.5) The numbers shown here are a rough estimate and should be considered a guide and not an exact amount. Assumptions are:
- Net investment income tax per student: portfolio return is 8 percent; tax rate is 1.4 percent. This tax applies to universities with endowments in excess of $500,000 per student (Harvard, Yale, Stanford, Princeton, and MIT).
- Estimated tax without preferential treatment per student: portfolio return is 8 percent; tax rate is 25 percent. This is an approximation and a blend of the long-term capital gains tax rate (20%) and the top marginal federal income tax rate (37%); it applies to all endowments.
- Estimated annual tax benefit per student: this is the difference between the estimated tax without preferential treatment per student and the net investment income tax per student columns.

Institution	Endowment Size Rank	Endowment 2020 Assets ($1,000s)	Estimated Annual Tax Benefit ($1,000s)	2020 Fulltime Enrollment (All Programs)	Estimated Annual Tax Benefit per Student
Harvard University	1	$41,894,380	$790,966	30,391	$26,026
Yale University	2	$31,201,686	$589,088	12,060	$48,846
Stanford University	4	$28,948,111	$546,540	15,953	$34,259
Princeton University	5	$25,944,283	$489,828	7,853	$62,375
Massachusetts Institute of Technology	6	$18,381,518	$347,043	11,254	$30,837
Columbia University	12	$11,257,021	$225,140	30,135	$7,471
Emory University	13	$9,169,028	$183,381	15,398	$11,909
University of Southern California	24	$5,914,358	$118,287	46,287	$2,556
University of Pittsburgh	30	$4,151,994	$83,040	32,277	$2,573
University of Iowa	40	$2,530,872	$50,617	30,318	$1,670
Georgia Institute of Technology	50	$2,169,707	$43,394	39,771	$1,091
University of Kansas	60	$1,830,892	$36,618	26,744	$1,369
Tulane University	70	$1,458,648	$29,173	13,927	$2,095
Wake Forest University	80	$1,350,187	$27,004	8,789	$3,072
Rutgers University	90	$1,150,827	$23,017	50,411	$457
University of Utah	100	$1,071,908	$21,438	33,081	$648

Figure 4.5 Endowment Sizes and Estimated Annual Tax Benefits per Student by University. *Sources:* Endowment rank and size: National Center for Education Statistics, Enrollment: various college websites, Estimated Annual Tax Benefit per Student: author's estimates.[5]

So, have the wealthiest universities responded to this strings-free tax policy by growing their student bodies, thereby benefiting society to the greatest extent possible? Nope. In fact, they haven't increased their undergraduate student body despite their significantly larger endowments and the public subsidy associated with those endowments. We can speculate that the motivations for this are twofold. First, low admissions rates (high selectivity) tend to improve university rankings;[xliii] thus, a university that is motivated toward prioritizing ranking would want to shrink its student body, not grow it. Second, if the university is attempting to maximize its endowment income per student, and by extension its implicit tax benefit per student, again, the university would be motivated to shrink its enrollment. We can observe how the most heavily endowed universities have responded to these perverse incentives by returning for the moment to Charlie Eaton of the Haas Institute for Fair and Inclusive Society. He calculates that the wealthiest five percent of private schools awarded 8,816 bachelor's degrees in 1976, grew that figure to 10,496 by 1988, and since that time, the annual number of bachelor's degree awards from these institutions is unchanged. In contrast, from 1976 to 2012, the number of bachelor's degree awards grew from 203,343 to 428,208 at public research university systems with campuses that are members of the Association of American Universities. Because endowments among the wealthiest institutions have grown but their student bodies have not, the estimated revenue per student attributable to endowments has grown from under $20,000 in 1986 to roughly $55,000 in 2012. As described by Professor Eaton, current tax policy toward endowments has created an "Ivory Tower Tax Haven."[xliv]

Problem 3: There Is No Direct Link Between Tax Benefits and Educational Outcome

In a similar vein to Problem 2, whereby universities have no direct accountability to the *taxpayers*, universities also do not have direct accountability to their *students*. Specifically, endowments enjoy their tax-exempt status irrespective of the educational outcome or employment status of their graduates. Because of that lack of accountability to either students or taxpayers, universities regularly pursue policies in their own best interests, even if those policies are not ideal for either the taxpayers or the students. As detailed in Chapter 1, the most egregious examples of educational institutions operating in their own best interests came from the for-profit education sector. In 2014, attending a two-year, for-profit institution cost four times as much as attending a community college, while students at for-profit colleges represented 11 percent of the total higher education population but 44 percent of all federal student loan defaults.[xlv] In response, the Department of Education implemented "gainful-employment" metrics and applied these metrics to for-profit colleges. The intent was to ensure that for-profit alumni graduated with student loan debt that was manageable upon graduation; otherwise, the for-profit college would lose access to federally subsidized loans. Unfortunately, despite their success in drastically reducing enrollment in unsuccessful for-profit programs, many of the gainful-employment guidelines were repealed in July 2020.[xlvi]

To be fair, for-profit colleges generally do not have endowments, so why is this relevant to a discussion of endowment tax policy? The answer is that as many as 60 percent of private non-profit institutions and 70 percent of public colleges and universities would also fail the gainful-employment test if it was applied to them.[xlvii] An online tool created by the Texas Public Policy Foundation uses all publicly available information and found that a surprising number of colleges and universities are not producing students that are able to earn a sufficient income upon graduation in order to service and repay their student loans. While the causes and solutions to this problem will be discussed in subsequent chapters, it's worth noting that many of these institutions do have sizable endowments and therefore are the beneficiaries of current tax policy.[xlviii]

Problem 4: Heavily Endowed Schools Are Not Incentivized to Grow Their Student Bodies

An unintended but highly perverse incentive of the endowment tax policy is that the universities that are beneficiaries of the largest implicit tax subsidy are not incentivized to grow their student bodies. In fact, they're incentivized to maintain or even *shrink* them! Think that's absurd? Then take a look at Figure 4.6. This table shows the total undergraduate population for the 1986 and 2020 school years, as well as the average endowment (in millions) per student. The last two columns show the change in the size of the student body and size of the endowment. The results? In the past 33 years, the most heavily endowed schools' student body population is largely unchanged, while their endowments collectively grew by a factor of 11.6. Yale, Harvard, and the University of Pennsylvania even managed to slightly reduce their student bodies while growing their endowment ten- to twenty-fold!

So, why does tax policy incentivize universities to maintain or shrink their student bodies? The answer is that the implicit tax policy break has no explicit limit on a per student basis.[6] Said another way, a school with a $1 billion

---

[6] The limit is now $500,000 per student. But, as mentioned previously, the 1.4 percent tax on investment income is insufficient to materially impact endowment and school policy.

	Undergraduate Students		Endowment ($Million)		Change (%)	
	1986–1987	2020–2021	1986–1987	2020–2021	Students	Endowment
Brown University	5,747	6,792	$357	$4,377	18%	1127%
Columbia University	5,790	8,148	$1,387	$11,257	41%	712%
Cornell University	12,622	14,743	$540	$6,883	17%	1174%
Dartmouth College	3,583	4,170	$535	$5,975	16%	1017%
Harvard University	10,394	8,527	$3,850	$41,894	–18%	988%
Princeton University	4,667	4,774	$1,892	$25,944	2%	1271%
University of Pennsylvania	11,722	11,155	$649	$14,877	–5%	2194%
Yale University	5,291	4,703	$2,111	$31,202	–11%	1378%
All Ivy League Colleges	59,816	63,012	$11,321	$142,410	5%	1158%

Figure 4.6 Ivy League Undergraduate Student Body, Endowment Size, and 33-Year Change. *Sources:* National Center for Education Statistics, Integrated Postsecondary Education Data System, Digest of Education Statistics, univstats.com, https://irp.dpb.cornell.edu/, author's calculations.

endowment and 50,000 students gets the same tax break as a school with a $1 billion endowment and 5,000 students. So, if the objective of university administrators is to maximize endowment income and the endowment tax subsidy on a per student basis, then universities should admit fewer students. Therefore, is this a problem? Yes! People and organizations respond to incentives, and a failure to link the implicit tax subsidy is incentivizing policies that run counter to the objective of maximizing the educational opportunities of citizens. Properly incentivized tax policy should incentivize the most heavily endowed schools to educate more, not fewer, people. Otherwise, the most elite schools with the largest endowments will continue to receive the largest aggregate and per-student tax subsidy.

CONCLUSION

Endowments, like the universities to which they are affiliated, have benefited students for generations. These stores of wealth have the ability to enable universities to remain independent, financially stable and secure, and create an environment that offers educational excellence. Early benefactors like Andrew Carnegie realized the intergenerational potential of foundations and endowments while legislatures in the early 20th century also recognized the benefit of allowing endowments to grow without tax liabilities.

But, as with all legislation if given enough time, there will be unintended consequences. Specifically, endowments have become incredibly concentrated into a small percentage of degree-granting institutions. As a result, preferential tax treatment now most heavily favors the universities with the largest endowments per full-time student; which is to say, tax laws favor the endowments and universities that need the least support. Some universities have responded to their enviable position by eliminating tuition for students whose parents earn below a certain income, while others have pledged that their students will graduate debt-free. While these developments are certainly welcome, and I applaud the administrators at schools who have made these decisions, much more can be done.

". . . tax laws favor the endowments and universities that need the least support."

To be fair, endowment tax policy is not the primary cause of our current student debt crisis. Rather, tuition is far too expensive, dropout rates are too high, and students are regularly graduating with degrees that do not confer sufficient earning power to service and repay debt. However, this reality does not mean that the endowment tax policy should not be a part of a legislative basket of solutions to our student debt crisis. On the contrary, endowments are important sources of revenue for colleges and universities, and so these institutions will no doubt respond to incentives that impact their endowments. Therefore, when considering the legislative solutions that might alleviate the student debt crisis, I believe it is wise to also include endowment tax reform as one of the many tools that will address misaligned incentives and educational inequities. Feel free to skip ahead to Chapter 8 if you'd like to read about what the legislative solutions are to align endowment incentives with the students (and taxpayers), reduce endowment concentration to a few elite universities, and improve educational outcomes.

FIGURE SOURCES FOR FIGURES 4.1 AND 4.2

- *Total Postsecondary Institutions.* 1900–1940. NCES. Table 23. Historical summary of higher education statistics: 1869–1870 to 1989–1990.
- *Total Postsecondary Institutions.* 1950–2020. NCES. Table 317.10. Degree-granting postsecondary institutions, by control and level of institution: Selected years, 1949–1950 through 2020–2021.
- *Enrollment in degree-granting postsecondary institutions. 1900–1940.* NCES. Table 105.30. Enrollment in degree-granting postsecondary institutions.
- *Enrollment in degree-granting postsecondary institutions. 1947–1989.* NCES. Table 303.10. Total fall enrollment in degree-granting postsecondary institutions, by attendance status, sex of student, and control of institution: Selected years, 1947–2029.
- *Enrollment in degree-granting postsecondary institutions. 1990–2020.* NCES. Table 105.30. Enrollment in degree-granting postsecondary institutions.
- *Endowment Value.* 1900–1960. Figure shown is estimated endowment book value. National Center for Education Statistics (1993). 120 Years of American Education: A Statistical Portrait. U.S. Department of Education Office of Educational Research and Improvement. Editor: Thomas D. Snyder. Table 35.
- *Endowment Value.* 1970–1990. Figure shown is estimated endowment market value. National Center for Education Statistics (1993). 120 Years of American Education: A Statistical Portrait. U.S. Department of Education Office of Educational Research and Improvement. Editor: Thomas D. Snyder. Table 35.

- *Endowment Value.* 2000–2020. National Center for Education Statistics. Endowment funds of the 120 colleges and universities with the largest amounts: 1999 and 2000, Table 357; Endowment funds of the 120 colleges and universities with the largest endowments, by rank order: 2009 and 2010. Table 376; Endowment funds of the 120 degree-granting postsecondary institutions with the largest endowments, by rank order: Fiscal year 2020. Table 333.90.
- *Average Endowment Size per Postsecondary Institution*: Author's calculations.
- *Average Endowment Size per Student*: Author's calculations.

Part II

Student Debt

5

The Student Loan Industry: How Debt Grew and Consumer Protections Shrank

As of 2021, recent college graduates from non-profit institutions borrow (on average and depending on the source) $26,627[i] to $30,030[ii] to attend a public institution, and $32,029[iii] to $33,900[iv] to attend a private institution. Unless you, a close friend, or family member have been directly impacted by student debt, it is difficult to grasp the magnitude of the current student debt crisis. Both its breadth (over 45 million debtors)[v] and depth (nearing $1.8 trillion in debt outstanding)[vi,vii] is unlike anything this country has witnessed before. In other words, never have so many people borrowed so much with so few chances of repayment in full. The economic, psychological, and sociological toll of this debt burden is enormous.

Scholars of the Global Financial Crisis and the Great Recession of 2008–2009 might argue that the hardships at that time constituted an even larger debt crisis since millions of people purchased homes with little or no chances of repayment. Yet, while the amount of debt was higher, and the emotional toll to the nearly 10 million people who lost their homes in foreclosure[viii] was significant, that debt crisis was different. Prior to the Great Recession, adults borrowed against assets (houses) that had value. Today's student borrowers are generally younger and are borrowing exclusively against their future. These student debtors have fewer rights in the event of financial hardship and bankruptcy, and many people's futures are permanently impaired as a result. As we saw in Chapter 3, many people's degrees do not confer the earning power to repay student loans, and as we will see in Chapter 6, the damage caused by student debt is incalculable. So how did we get here and how big is this problem really? Let's discuss.

HOW DID WE GET HERE?

Like most complex situations, there is no *one* defining moment, piece of legislation, or action that led to a historic outcome. Rather, the explanation for how we, as a country, indebted so many people is nuanced and detailed. But, if it had to be summarized succinctly, it would be this: we can largely (but not entirely) attribute today's student debt crisis to two factors: well-intended but poorly crafted legislation, and mal-intended and well-crafted legislation. So, what is this legislation I speak of? There are several laws to which we can point, and I'll cover the most relevant of each, here.

Early Government Intervention

On October 4, 1957, the Soviet Union launched Earth's first artificial satellite: Sputnik 1. A polished sphere about two feet in diameter with four external radio antennas, Sputnik 1 orbited the earth for three months and transmitted on two frequencies for three weeks. The now-famous Sputnik 1 "beep beep" sounds could be heard around the globe by anybody possessing a short-wave receiver. One month later, the Soviets launched Sputnik 2, which was larger than Sputnik 1, contained more equipment, and even held a dog named Laika. The Soviets timed the launch of Sputnik 2 to coincide with the 40th anniversary of the start of the Bolshevik Revolution and Russian Civil War. Initially, the response by U.S. President Eisenhower was muted and not reassuring to the public. "After all, the Russians have only put one small ball in the air," President Eisenhower told reporters after the launch of Sputnik 1. Future president and then Senate majority leader Lyndon B. Johnson disagreed. In response to the President, Senator Johnson asserted, "It is not very reassuring to be told that next year we'll put an even better satellite in orbit, maybe with chrome trim and automatic windshield wipers. I guess for the first time, I've started to realize that this country of mine might not be ahead in everything."[ix] Two months after the successful launch of Sputnik 1, the Americans attempted to place a satellite into space for the first time. Two seconds after ignition, the rocket lost thrust and the Vanguard TV-3 satellite fell back to earth and exploded. After two months of nonstop media discussion of Soviet advancements in space, Americans were disheartened and frustrated. To add insult to injury, a Soviet delegate to the United Nations publicly offered the U.S. representative aid "under the Soviet program of technical assistance to backwards nations."[x]

The public consensus at the onset of the space race was that the Americans had fallen behind, and that America needed more scientists, mathematicians, and engineers—and America needed them *now*. Clearly universities were a major part of the solution since they were fertile grounds to train young Americans to fill the technical roles that were now considered to be of national importance. But, the question of how to pay for it remained. The two solutions that were chosen were scholarships and loans. The former proposal lacked significant sponsorship because of budgetary constraints and concerns that tuition money would not go to the neediest of students; but Congress rallied around a proposal that would provide loans to students via the universities themselves. Thus, the National Defense Student Loan program was conceived, and on September 2, 1958, President Eisenhower signed the National Defense Education Act into law.[xi]

While modest in scale by today's standards, this act marked a significant milestone in American higher education in general, and the student loan industry in particular. The terms of the act were relatively simple: schools would receive funds from the U.S. Treasury. The schools would then determine which students were eligible to receive scholarships. Eligible students would receive up to $1,000 per year but no more than $5,000 in loans. Interest on loans was deferred until one year after leaving the program (or graduating), and students were expected to repay loans in 10 years. In total, nearly 1,600 institutions participated in the program, extending $443 million in loans to approximately 600,000 students over a five-year period. The initial program had a sunset provision—it authorized funds through 1962, and after that only such funds deemed "necessary for students previously receiving . . . loans to continue their education."[xii] So by 1964, the program had been exhausted and needed to be extended, replaced, or allowed to end.

As far as then-President Lyndon Johnson was concerned, not only would the existing student loan program not abruptly end, but government intervention into the student loan market should be expanded. Sworn in as President on November 22, 1963, following the assassination of John F. Kennedy, President Johnson was a former schoolteacher and recipient of student loans himself; he viewed access to higher education as both a moral imperative as well as being critical to a country's national defense and to the success of its democracy. In a letter to all members of Congress in 1965,[xiii] President Johnson argued:

> *"Nothing matters more to the future of our country: not our military preparedness—for armed might is worthless if we lack the brain power to build a world of peace; not our productive economy—for we cannot sustain growth without trained manpower; not our democratic system of government—for freedom is fragile if citizens are ignorant."*

Later that year, President Johnson signed the Higher Education Act (HEA) into law; this law included the Guaranteed Student Loan Program (GSLP)[1] that was intended to further improve student access to student loans.[xiv] By utilizing this program, the states or other non-profit agencies could establish "guarantee agencies" that had pools of capital that would insure student loans. A participating bank would extend a student loan to a person, and the guaranteeing agency would cosign the loan. If the student defaulted, the agency would reimburse the lender for loan principal and accrued interest. In turn, the guarantee agency would be reimbursed by the federal government for 80 percent of principal losses per year.[xv] Finally, interest rates on the student loans were six percent, and the U.S. Treasury would pay the interest on the debt until the student began loan repayment (nine months after graduation).[xvi]

This complicated system attempted to align incentives among several stakeholders. For the government, it would subsidize student loans (pay the interest) while the student was in college, but the government would not originate the loans. As a result, federal outlays would be limited. With respect to principal reimbursement, the U.S. Treasury would reimburse most, but not all, of potential principal losses; as a result, loan originators would keep some *skin in the game* and ensure that loans are thoughtfully originated. With respect to banks, they would have access to significant protection from default; as a result, they would be far more willing to extend loans to students with a lower likelihood of full repayment. Finally, students would benefit from moderate interest rates (6%), interest that does not accrue while they are in school, and greater access to bank lending because the federal government would reimburse most, if not all, of the principal in the event of default. In short, it was a thoughtful attempt to fully align incentives.

In terms of stimulating student loan origination, the program was a hit. Between 1963 and 1970, student debt outstanding increased tenfold to $1.2 billion.[xvii] Despite its success, by 1970, student loan origination began to slow. Inflation rose to 5.9 percent per year in 1970 and 6.2 percent per year in 1973;[xviii] as a result, the interest rate that banks paid to depositors rose while the interest rate that banks could charge student debtors was fixed by the federal government. In addition to this, participating banks already had significant exposure to student borrowers, so there was a reluctance to extend more loans to these borrowers. Meanwhile, at the same time that the banks were less willing to extend student loans, the demand for student loans was increasing as college enrollment swelled—even while colleges raised the price of tuition. The solution to all of these issues came in the form of a new

---

[1] A loan made under the GSLP was later known as a Federal Family Education Loan (FFEL).

government agency: the Student Loan Market Association (Sallie Mae). This entity was created in 1972 during the Nixon administration and following the passage of the 1972 amendments to the HEA.[xix]

The Creation of Sallie Mae

Sallie Mae was envisioned to be a government sponsored enterprise— something of a hybrid between public and private interests. The 21-member board of directors would be comprised of representatives from seven banks, seven educational institutions, and seven presidential appointees. Sallie Mae's goal was to ensure that banks always had sufficient capital available in order to originate student loans—not unlike how Fannie Mae and Ginnie Mae partner with banks to ensure that they can originate home loans. Sallie Mae would enhance the ability for banks to originate student loans in two ways. First, it could buy the student loans directly from banks. As a result, at any time, banks could shed their exposure to student loans and free up capital to originate more loans. Second, Sallie Mae could lend to banks that would pledge student loans as collateral. In this way, banks could continue to hold the risk of the student loan, but the banks could now easily raise cash with which they could—again—extend more student loans. From the perspective of the students, they would continue to borrow from banks, and the U.S. Treasury would continue to guarantee the principal of those loans as per the conditions of the Guaranteed Student Loan program. Sallie Mae would operate as a for-profit entity and would pay income tax to the federal government.

The initial growth of Sallie Mae's balance sheet was modest; it lent $75 million to banks in 1973 and $191.6 million in 1974.[xx] And for all its complexity, the system was thoughtful, well intended, and reasonably well crafted. While the availability of student loans no doubt led to people attending college who should otherwise have entered a trade school, and while this excess demand for college no doubt led to tuition inflation, the mechanisms in place to ensure that capital flowed to needy students were functioning. In fact, there were (albeit imperfect) market forces to discourage bad behavior. Banks had skin in the game because they didn't fully recoup losses when students defaulted. Sallie Mae investors had skin in the game because their portfolio would also incur losses in the event that a student defaulted.

In addition—and I apologize to the people whose eyes cross when they think of finance—Sallie Mae's cost of borrowing was indirectly determined by both the riskiness of student loan debt as well as the ability of banks to extend to creditworthy student borrowers. That is, if student loans became riskier (i.e., defaults increased), the Sallie Mae cost of debt would increase, and in turn, less capital would flow to the banks, which in turn, would originate fewer bad loans. That's a good thing because it functions as an incentive (to profit-maximizing entities) to stop extending loans to students with little or no chances of repaying their student debt. In plain speak, as long as Sallie Mae's cost of funding (and by extension profitability) was tied to the likelihood of student loan repayment, and as long as profitability for the banks was tied to the likelihood of student loan repayment, then the growth of bad student loans would be kept in check. Then within three years, two major legislative pieces severed the market forces that checked the growth of bad student debt, forever changing the trajectory of student debt in America.

> *". . . two major legislative pieces severed the market forces that checked the growth of bad student debt, forever changing the trajectory of student debt in America."*

Misaligned Incentives and Bad Debt: The Growth of Sallie Mae

In 1973, the U.S. Congress created the Federal Financing Bank.[xxi] This bank, which was an extension of the U.S. Treasury Department, had the authority to lend up to $5 billion—a staggering sum at the time—to Sallie Mae. The interest rate of this loan was equal to 0.125 percent above the three-month U.S. Treasury Bills. In short, Sallie Mae now had (essentially) unlimited financing at a rate equivalent to the most creditworthy institutions in the world. This was an enormous windfall to Sallie Mae shareholders. Salle Mae is a for-profit entity that could borrow at (essentially) a risk-free rate. As such, it's net interest margin—the spread between where it borrows and where it lends—was wider than it should have been. Furthermore, the cost to borrow each additional $1 billion (up to $5 billion) was the same; normally, as entities lever (borrow more), their cost of financing rises. But not in this case. The net result? Sallie Mae was given the green light to grow far larger than would have been warranted by market conditions.

The other major piece of legislation was the 1976 revision and extension of the HEA. Buried in 161 pages of edits was a line that stated that federally insured student loans would now be insured at 100 percent of their principal in the event of default (up from 80%).[xxii] As a result, the holders of defaulted student debt, whether that is the originating bank or Sallie Mae, would no longer incur a loss in the event of a default. Now, lending to students became a risk-free endeavor on the part of the banks and Sallie Mae. Only taxpayers would lose in the event that a student defaulted on his or her loan. As a result, students who may have otherwise been deterred by a banker from investing time and capital into earning a *worthless* degree, were given the green light to *invest* in their education—and *invest* they did. Between 1975 and 1980, the number of full-time enrolled students increased by four percent from 8.5 million to 8.8 million. Meanwhile, the amount of student debt increased 157 percent from $7.5 billion to $19.3 billion.[xxiii] Some of that growth came from students who chose to borrow $2,500 a year, place that cash in a bank account, and then repay the debt in four years after having earned interest on the cash.[2] The remainder came from students who would otherwise have been dissuaded from borrowing to take courses, whether at a non-profit or for-profit educational institution.

Also found in the 1976 HEA reauthorization was seemingly innocuous language allowing the payment for a "special allowance" to servicers and lenders. This allowance was intended to induce greater bank participation in the program.[xxiv] In short, when the interest paid by student borrowers fell below a threshold, then the government would pay a special allowance to loan servicers (such as Sallie Mae).[xxv] Doing so would ensure that banks would continue to originate student loans, even when the rate on student loans was less than the borrowing rates for banks. How much was this allowance? This rate has changed over the years, but it was around 3.5 percent of outstanding student loan balances.[xxvi] Perhaps unbeknownst to the legislators (but certainly known to the bank executives) was that the formula to calculate the special interest payment also had the three-month T-bill rate as an input.[3] In addition, since 1973, Sallie Mae has been able to borrow at the three-month T-bill rate plus 0.125 percent. Thus, by putting the two legislative pieces together, Sallie Mae was now guaranteed a profit margin equal to 3.375 percent (3.50% − 0.125%). In finance speak, Congress provided Sallie Mae an exceptionally generous net interest margin.

Now, banks regularly charge borrowers a higher rate than what the banks pay to depositors. That's part of their business, and banks get paid this margin both for the services they provide (linking borrowers and depositors) and for

---

[2] This was a popular *arbitrage* opportunity for wealthy families. Even if a family could pay the full cost of tuition, they could borrow $2,500 per year, which would not be charged interest while the student was enrolled. The borrowed cash could then be placed in a bank account and accrue interest (earning 10% or more), while the student was in college. Once the student graduated, she could repay the student debt in full and pocket the accrued interest.

[3] The calculation on the special allowance is [(average interest rate of 3-month Treasury Bills and Commercial Paper) − the interest rate of the applicable loan + a spread (around 3.5 percent)] × loan balance outstanding. The interest rate of the loans is set by the government (which was generally at or slightly above the borrowing cost for the federal government), while the borrowing cost for Sallie Mae was set at 3-month Treasury Bills + 0.125%.

assuming the risk that a borrower may default. So, why is it so appalling that Sallie Mae could now lock in a 3.375 percent net interest margin? First, Sallie Mae did not perform the services of a typical bank—Sallie Mae didn't originate loans, it merely purchased loans that were already originated. Second, there was absolutely no default risk! Since 1976, if a student borrower defaulted on a loan, the U.S. Treasury would make the holder of that loan whole.

". . . between 1973 and 1980, Sallie Mae went from an obscure program that was intended to encourage banks to originate student loans, to a literal money-making machine."

So, with the passage of three bills between 1973 and 1980, Sallie Mae went from an obscure program that was intended to encourage banks to originate student loans, to a literal money-making machine. The only thing that limited its profits was the size of its loan book. And to increase that, Sallie Mae was motivated to ensure that more students had loans and that those loans were larger. It didn't matter to Sallie Mae, or to the other banks that were originating the loans, whether or not the student loans were likely to be repaid.

Banks, Student Loans, and the Government: 1980 to 1992

Between 1980 and 1985, Sallie Mae's after-tax annual earnings grew from $9.4 million to $99.3 million. In addition to this rapid earnings growth, its return on equity (a financial measurement of overall profitability) varied between 20.2 and 44.8 percent. Readers who are not also financial experts will be forgiven for not knowing that these percentages are astronomical and roughly four times as high as the typical profitable bank during the same period.[xxvii] Meanwhile, Sallie Mae's total book of student loans reached $10 billion by 1984; by then, Sallie Mae had already reached its financing peak of $5 billion in subsidized debt (courtesy of the Federal Financing Bank) and had turned to private lenders for an additional $5 billion in financing.[xxviii] This private financing, while slightly more expensive than the $5 billion offered by the U.S. Treasury, was nevertheless extremely attractive since Sallie Mae was viewed as having an *implicit guarantee* by the U.S. Treasury. This means that investors assume that if Sallie Mae became vulnerable to default that the U.S. government would infuse capital, ensuring that operations continue and debt holders are made whole. As a result, Sallie Mae had the ability to continue to borrow from private lenders at a rate that was commensurate with the most creditworthy institutions around the world.

While Sallie Mae executives and equity holders found themselves making money hand over fist, another group was losing even more—the taxpayers.

"While Sallie Mae executives and equity holders found themselves making money hand over fist, another group was losing even more—the taxpayers."

By fiscal year 1980, Congress had made over $1.4 billion in payments to holders of student loans (banks and Sallie Mae) under the GSLP program. (Reminder: the GSLP is the program where the government will cover any principal lost in the event of a student default.) Default rates were in excess of 12 percent and payments exceeded $200 million per year. Meanwhile, payments by the U.S. Treasury to banks that were under the special allowance program had ballooned from $106 million in 1977 to $1.5 billion in 1981! (Reminder: the *special allowance* is a subsidy paid to banks to offer student loans at lower rates than would otherwise be available given banks' cost of borrowing.)[xxix]

Despite the egregious cost of the federal subsidization of student loans, these programs were viewed as a success. If measured by the quantity of student debt growth following the passage of the 1976 HEA, it is apparent that the legislation had its desired effect. Student debt grew from about $8 billion in 1975 to $22 billion in 1980 (in 2020 dollars). As shown in Figure 5.1, student debt outstanding would march steadily higher every year.

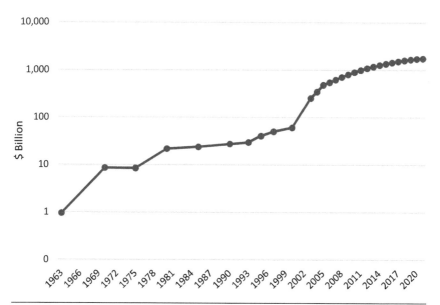

Figure 5.1   Student Debt ($Bn) 2020 Dollars. Log Scale. *Sources:* Urban Institute,[xxx] College Board,[xxxi] U.S. Federal Reserve,[xxxii] and author's calculations.

With an entirely profit-driven motivation,[4,xxxiii,xxxiv] Sallie Mae would continue to lobby Congress to enact legislation that would further enhance the availability of student loans under the GSLP program. In 1980, the U.S. Congress created the PLUS Program (later called Parent PLUS) that allows the parents of dependent undergraduate students the ability to borrow on behalf of their children.[xxxv] A year later, the U.S. Congress extended the program to include the parents of graduate and professional students (later called the Supplemental Loans to Students (SLS) Program).[xxxvi] Meanwhile, the U.S. Congress also increased the limits on loans in the GSLP program in 1986 and again in 1992. Sallie Mae continued to ride the wave of privatizing government subsidies while passing losses from bad student loans to taxpayers. By 1990, Sallie Mae had grown to 2,500 employees with $37 billion in assets and was 39th on *Fortune* magazine's list of the largest U.S. corporations. It held 30 percent of the country's outstanding student loans.[xxxvii] In 1990, the Sallie Mae president and CEO retired from the firm and became the dean of Dartmouth University's business school. He reportedly left with Sallie Mae stock worth $7 million;[xxxviii] at its peak, that stock would be worth $300 million.[xxxix]

Of concern during this period was the rising default rate of borrowers. By 1987, 17.6 percent of borrowers defaulted on their student loans within two years of entering repayment. In an attempt to address this, in the 1986 reauthorization of the HEA, the U.S. Congress implemented a series of policies designed to reduce the overall default rate. These policies included a provision preventing a student who was in default from taking out another subsidized loan. In addition, loan originators were prevented from falsely advertising to prospective students or giving incentives to institutions to direct borrowers to them.[xl] These new rules had a modest impact and by 1990 the two-year default rate had risen to 22.4 percent. In response, in 1990 the U.S. Congress enacted the Omnibus Budget Reconciliation Act,[5] which eliminated students from accessing government student loan programs if they were enrolled at schools with high default rates.[xli] Restricting loans from high-default institutions was effective, and two-year default rates fell from 22.4 percent in 1990 to 10.7 percent in 1994, and would fall to a low of 4.5 percent in 2003.[xlii]

---

[4] Edward Fox, Sallie Mae's first president and CEO stated to the *Washington Post* in 1983, "Since day one we have run this corporation as a business." When speaking to the Subcommittee on Education, Arts and Humanities, Committee on Labor and Human Resources, he stated in 1982, "Our duty is to shareholders and bondholders—not to subsidize education credit."

[5] Also included in this act was a provision requiring government agencies that extended loans to account for an estimated *subsidy* cost to account for future costs to the government. Previously, losses and subsidies were recognized only in the years they were paid out, distorting the true cost of the program.

Also contained in the 1990 Budget Reconciliation Act was a provision colloquially known as *PAYGO*. The intention of this rule was to force fiscal restraint, and the mechanism to do this was that any new proposal must be "budget neutral," meaning new spending would be offset by either new taxes, or there must be expense reductions elsewhere. This provision had its desired effect as members of Congress began searching for areas of waste; the GSLP—by now known as the FFEL program—became a prime target. As such, included in the 1993 Omnibus Budget Reconciliation Act was a mandate to create a Federal Direct Loan Program, which would directly compete with other student loan originators (and by extension, compete with Sallie Mae).[xliii] Sallie Mae, and the banks who originated student loans, were the beneficiaries of billions of dollars in annual subsidies. So, replacing them as middlemen seemed like a sensible and fiscally prudent policy decision. In the initial mandate, the U.S. Department of Education (DOE) would launch a pilot program with 300 participating institutions. These institutions would provide students access to a Free Application for Federal Student Aid (FAFSA) form; students would complete the form and if students qualified for the loan, the loan would come directly from the DOE.[xliv] And with the passage of this legislation, the U.S. government would become fully entrenched in student debt, for better or worse.

The Student Loan Explosion: 1992 to the Present

In 1992, Congress approved the sixth reauthorization of the HEA. The most relevant provision in this act was the creation of an unsubsidized *Stafford* loan program. The loan was considered *unsubsidized* because interest would begin accruing once the loan was originated, as opposed to subsidized loans where interest did not accrue until after a student completed or left the educational program. In addition, unsubsidized loans would be available to students of all income levels, whereas previously, they were only available to students that were judged by colleges to be unable to pay full tuition. Finally, the 1992 legislation increased annual loan limits to $2,625 for first-year students, $3,500 for second-year students, and $5,500 for all other undergraduates.[xlv] To Sallie Mae's delight, the legislation had the desired effect—student loan originations exploded. As shown in Figure 5.2, annual loan originations would roughly double between 1993 and 1995, reaching $22.4 billion in 1995 and peaking at $107 billion in 2012, only 20 years after the passage of this fateful act.

Meanwhile, the entrance of the DOE as a direct lender in 1993 constituted an existential crisis for Sallie Mae. But its executives weren't going to simply watch their money printing machine wither away. Sallie Mae would reinvent itself. In 1996, Sallie Mae shed its Government Sponsored Entity status,

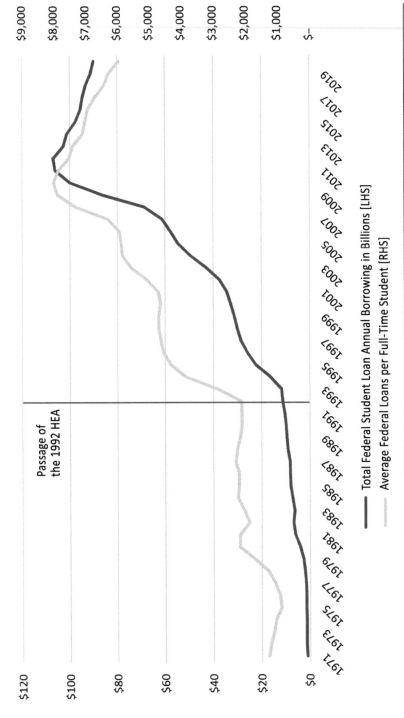

Figure 5.2   Annual Aggregate Student Loan Borrowing Versus Size of Each Loan. *Sources:* College Board: Trends in Student Aid 2021, Tables 2 and 3.

allowing it to operate as a private company and extend loans directly under the GSLP.[xlvi] Sallie Mae quickly began regaining market share and diversifying its product opportunities by offering both federal and private loans, loan origination and servicing (collecting money from borrowers), enhanced support for universities, and online resources for borrowers. Sallie Mae's fortunes would peak in 2007 when an investor group announced it would take Sallie Mae private and purchase the business for $25 billion.[xlvii] That deal fell through following the passage of the 2007 College Cost Reduction and Access Act, which reduced Sallie Mae's reimbursement for defaulted loans from 99 to 95 percent.[xlviii] Sallie Mae's fortunes further deteriorated during the 2008–2009 recession. With exploding toxic debt and a freezing of the financial markets, Sallie Mae turned to the U.S. federal government for a bailout.[6] In February 2009, Sallie Mae's stock was down 94 percent from its 2007 peak.[7] Sallie Mae's status as a driving force in the student loan market came to an end in March 2010 when President Obama signed the

> *"With exploding toxic debt and a freezing of the financial markets, Sallie Mae turned to the U.S. federal government for a bailout."*

Student Aid and Fiscal Responsibility Act into law. This legislation ended subsidies for private student loans (like the ones Sallie Mae originated and owned). Filling the void would be an expansion of Federal Direct Student Loans, meaning that now, a vast majority of all new student loans would be originated and owned directly by the U.S. government.[xlix]

While Sallie Mae and the DOE tussled for control over the student debt market in the 1990s and 2000s, the stage had been set for an explosion of student debt. Ease and accessibility of student loans, both directly from the DOE as well as originated by banks participating in the FFEL program, meant obtaining financing to earn a degree was easier than receiving a credit card.

---

[6] The Ensuring Continued Access to Student Loans Act (ECASLA-Pub. L. No. 110-350) allowed the U. S. Treasury to buy student loans from eligible lenders (like Sallie Mae). This both allowed lenders to transfer bad debt to the federal government while also ensuring that lenders had sufficient cash to operate normally.

[7] Sallie Mae exists today; although, both its influence on Capitol Hill, as well as its earnings power, have been diminished. In 2010, the U.S. Congress passed the Health Care and Education Reconciliation Act; this eliminated the federally guaranteed loan program known as the FFEL, which had been a major source of guaranteed income for Sallie Mae. After the passage of this act, all subsidized federal loans would be originated by the DOE. Separately, in 2013 Sallie Mae separated into two companies. One company called Navient continues to own student loans and service them (collect interest and principal). The other company, which retained the name Sallie Mae, offers private education loans.

Meanwhile, as detailed in Chapter 2, universities continued to raise tuition at rates far in excess of both inflation and household income; this means that a college degree continued to become significantly more expensive (i.e., less affordable). Remember, college debt is used as something of a *plug*—students (and their parents) would take out debt once all other sources had been exhausted. This includes savings, current income, grants, and other scholarships. So, is there a *moment* to which we can point when college expenses rose to an amount that necessitated ever-growing amounts of student debt? The answer, surprisingly, is yes. Data suggests that the maximum amount a household can spend on a member toward earning a college degree is about 30 percent of that household's annual income. After that, households (both student and parent) generally need to borrow to cover the gap in willingness and ability to pay for college.

That's pretty specific (and prescriptive); so, how do I arrive at that? I arrive at this figure (30% of household income) by examining both the cost of tuition as a percentage of household income as well as the total student debt by household. By looking at both tuition and debt in this manner, we can see if there's a point after which debt begins to rapidly rise; this would suggest households can no longer afford a postsecondary education and are turning to debt to finance each incremental dollar in tuition increases. What Figure 5.3 shows is that prior to the year 2000, the average cost of tuition was less than 30 percent of the median household's income; so, if the average household made $50,000 per year, average annual college expenses were less than $15,000. In addition, prior to the year 2000, college debt per household remained relatively low and stable. However, after 2000, tuition continued its upward march, peaking above 45 percent in 2014. This means if the average household still earned $50,000 per year, average annual college expenses would have grown from $15,000 to $22,500. As a result, in the year 2000, student debt began to expand at an exceptional pace, rising from $580 per household in 2000 to over $13,000 in 2021.

The takeaway—once the cost of college exceeded 30 percent of household income, households turned to borrowing in order to plug the gap between their means and their ability to pay for college. The aforementioned hypothetical household would not have borrowed money when college expenses were $15,000, but would have borrowed (again, on average) $7,500 once college expenses had risen to $22,500. To be fair, there are a couple of problems with this analysis. First, it shows averages but ignores the distribution around the mean. So, some families would have borrowed once college exceeded 25 percent of household income, while others would have only

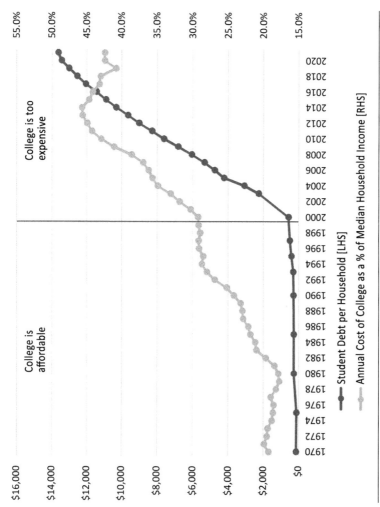

Figure 5.3   Student Debt per Household vs College Cost.[8] *Sources:* Urban Institute, College Board, U.S. Federal Reserve, U.S. DOE, National Center for Education Statistics, United States Census Bureau, and author's calculations.

[8] Beginning in 2003, the U.S. Federal Reserve began reporting aggregate student debt data. Prior to this, the most reliable source of data on aggregate student debt is the College Board. Due to the mixing of data sets, it's possible that the jump in student debt from 2000 to 2003 was exaggerated, as data prior to 2003 was likely incomplete.

borrowed once the cost exceeded 35 percent of household income. Household incomes also vary dramatically as well. Therefore, my type of analysis is what economists call a *univariate analysis*, meaning we're trying to explain one phenomenon (student debt outstanding) with one other variable (cost as a percentage of household income). While this is a good approach, it does ignore other confounding variables. This includes changes in household wealth, availability of financing, and availability of grants or other means of payment for college. For example, after consistent growth in household wealth through 1999, household wealth flatlined (and even briefly fell) in 2000 following the dot-com stock market bust. This modest decline in wealth likely contributed to a modest increase in student borrowing since households had fewer assets (like stocks) that they could sell to pay for college. With that said, I believe that these impacts are relatively minor and the most important input to determine college debt per household is the cost of college versus household income. Also, because the cost of college varies by household income (wealthy parents pay more), focusing on the 50th percentile of household income seems reasonable.

WHERE ARE WE NOW?

As of 4Q 2021, total student debt outstanding exceeded $1.7 trillion and total student debtors in the United States exceeded 45.7 million. So, how does that break down by type of loan, by borrower, and by repayment status? Figure 5.4 attempts to answer the first part of that question—loans by type. There are currently six different types of public or federal loans, five of which are ongoing. The largest portion of this public loan market (by balance) are direct unsubsidized loans, with $563.5 billion in debt outstanding, extended to some 30 million borrowers. These loans are less desirable than subsidized loans because interest begins accruing immediately, whereas subsidized loans do not accrue interest while the student is in college. The second largest portion of the public student loan market are consolidated student loans with $555.1 billion outstanding. This is where borrowers with multiple direct loans consolidate into one loan. This seems like a good idea as this reduces the number of loans a borrower needs to remember to repay; but I'll show later in this chapter that consolidation may put borrowers at a disadvantage. Direct subsidized loans outstanding aggregate to $291.5 billion and are also extended to roughly 30 million borrowers. Meanwhile, private loans make up a comparatively small portion of this market. With only $136.3 billion in debt outstanding, private lenders generally lend to borrowers who have exhausted all direct (federal) loan options and still need more money. Private loans generally carry higher interest rates because they are considered more risky.

Who Has Student Loans?

The bulk of student debt is currently owed by 29.3 million adults aged 25 to 49—basically, adults in their prime earning years. Figure 5.5 shows the distribution of loan balances by age, as of 4Q 2021. Interestingly, this shows that while the size of the population of borrowers with outstanding debt tends to fall as people move from the 25–34 cohort to older cohorts, the total balance per borrower initially increases! In other words, the data suggest that a large portion of debtors are *not* able to pay down their debt while between the ages of 25 and 34. Instead, most borrowers' balances remain unchanged or grow in the initial years after graduation. This is what the U.S. Federal Reserve found in a 2018 study of student debt. They

> "... *the data suggest that a large portion of debtors are* not *able to pay down their debt while between the ages of 25 and 34.*"

showed that between 2003 and 2017, on average, only 38 percent of borrowers with outstanding debt saw their debt balances fall year over year. Meanwhile, between 50 and 58 percent of borrowers saw their balances remain unchanged or grow year over year. Finally, between five and 11 percent of borrowers defaulted in any given year.[1]

While student debt impacts all age groups, the racial group most negatively impacted by student debt is overwhelmingly Black. Unfortunately, our understanding of the racial disparities among student borrowers is incomplete because the FAFSA form does not ask for racial information. But that inconvenient fact did not stop Columbia University professor and former Brookings Institution Nonresident Senior Fellow Judith Scott-Clayton from assembling a more complete picture of the racial breakdown of student debt. In 2016, Professor Scott-Clayton, along with coauthor Jing Li, drew upon data from the DOE's Baccalaureate and Beyond (B&B:08/12) survey[9] as well as data from both the DOE and the Census Bureau. Figure 5.6 shows a brief snapshot of the results of their findings. In short, Black borrowers have significantly more student debt than White, Hispanic, or Asian borrowers. In addition, nearly half of Black borrowers have more debt outstanding than

---

[9] This survey follows graduates from the 2008 cohort through 2012.

As of 4Q 2021*

Loans	Dollars Outstanding (Billions)[1,2]	Loan Recipients (Millions)[1,3]	Status	Credit Considered	Need Considered	Cosigner Required	Alternative Repayment Options[c]	Interest Accrual Start	Repayment Start	Max Loan Size per School Year
Public Loans, aka Federal Direct Student Loans (FDLP loans)										
Direct Subsidized Loans (aka Subsidized Direct Stafford Loans)	$291.5	30.0	Ongoing	No	Yes	No	Yes	6 months after graduation	6 months after graduation	Between $3,500 and $5,500[b]
Direct Unsubsidized Loans (aka Unsubsidized Direct Stafford Loans)	$563.5	30.0	Ongoing	No	No	No	Yes	Immediately	6 months after graduation	Between $2,000 and $7,000[b]
Direct PLUS Loans (aka Grad PLUS Loans)	$90.7	1.6	Ongoing	Yes	Yes	No	Yes	Immediately	6 months after graduation	Cost of attendance minus other financial aid
Federal Parental Loans (aka Parent PLUS)	$105.4	3.7	Ongoing	Yes	Yes	Yes, if credit is poor	Yes	Immediately	6 months after graduation with deferment	Cost of attendance minus other financial aid
Consolidated Federal Loans	$555.1	11.3	Ongoing	No	No	No	Yes	Immediately	6 months after graduation	N/A
Perkins Loans	$4.4	1.5	Ended in 2018	No	Yes	No	No	9 months after graduation	9 months after graduation	Undergraduate: $5,500/yr Graduate: $8,000/yr

Figure 5.4   Current Student Debt Programs in the United States.

Loans	Dollars Outstanding (Billions)[1,2]	Loan Recipients (Millions)[1,3]	Status	Credit Considered	Need Considered	Cosigner Required	Alternative Repayment Options[c]	Interest Accrual Start	Repayment Start	Max Loan Size per School Year
Private Loans										
School-Channel Loans & Direct-to-Consumer Private Loans	$136.3[a]	2.4+[a]	Ongoing	Yes	No	Varies	Varies	Immediately	Varies	Varies; may have no maximum
Total Public	$1,611.7	45.7								
Total Private	$136.3[a]	2.4+[a]								
Total	$1,748.0[a]	45.7+[a]								

* Private loan data as of 1Q 2021

Sources:

[1] Public loan outstanding and recipient data: U.S. DOE. Federal Student Aid Office. Webite: https://studentaid.gov/data-center/student/portfolio.

[2] Private loan oustanding data: MeasureOne. The MeasureOne Private Student Loan Report, June 15, 2021.

[3] Private loan recipient data: Melanie Hanson. "How Many People Have Student Loans?" EducationData.org, August 11, 2021.

General loan details: U.S. DOE. Websites include: https://studentaid.gov/understand-aid/types/loans/subsidized-unsubsidized, https://studentaid.gov/understand-aid/types/loans/plus/grad, and https://studentaid.gov/manage-loans/repayment/plans.

Notes:

[a] These figures should be considered reasonable indications. This is because there is greater transparency into the public student loan market as the U.S. DOE regularly publishes updated data regarding the publicly owned student loan portfolio.

[b] The maximum size of a loan depends on the length of time a borrower is in school (third- and fourth-year students can borrow $2k more than first-year students) and on the borrower's dependency status.

[c] Alternative repayment options include: Extended Repayment Plan, Revised Pay As You Earn Repayment Plan, Pay As You Earn Repayment Plan, Income-Based Repayment Plan, Income-Contingent Repayment Plan, and Income-Sensitive Repayment Plan.

Figure 5.4 *(continued)*

Age	Borrowers (M)	Balance ($M)	Balance per Borrower
24 and Younger	7.6	$109,700	$14,434
25 to 34	14.9	$500,200	$33,570
35 to 49	14.4	$622,200	$43,208
50 to 61	6.4	$281,800	$44,031
62 and Older	2.4	$97,800	$40,750
Total	45.7	$1,611,700	$35,267

Figure 5.5   Federal Student Loan Borrowers by Age. *Source*: U.S. DOE.[li]

	Average Total Debt ($)	Owes More than Borrowed (%)	Loan Payments >15% Income	Default Rate (%)
White	$28,006	17%	16%	2%
Black	$52,726	48%	23%	8%
Hispanic	$29,949	23%	18%	6%
Asian	$26,253	12%	17%	1%

Figure 5.6   Student Loan Borrowers by Race as of 2016. *Source: Brookings Institution*[liii]

originally borrowed, and for these reasons a larger portion of Black borrowers have debt exceeding 15 percent of their income. Finally, the Black default rate is higher than other racial groups, which is expected, given the comparatively higher average balance owed by Black students at graduation.[lii]

Who Defaults?

Students with all backgrounds may find repayment difficult, but there are clear disparities among various racial, socioeconomic, and educational cohorts that correlate to higher default rates. That's a bit academic, but the bottom line is that if I had to summarize the profile of the *typical* defaulter of a student loan, it would be this: a Black person who has dependents, was considered poor prior to entering college, attended a for-profit college, and did not finish earning his or her degree. It's tragic and it's true.

As mentioned, there are clear disparities among racial groups with respect to their default rates. In a 2017 report, the Center for American Progress (CAP)[10] noted that of students who entered college in 2003 and took

---

[10] The CAP is a D.C.-based public policy think tank.

out federal loans, 49 percent of Black borrowers had defaulted as opposed to 21 percent of White borrowers.[liv] In addition to racial disparities among defaulters, there are significant differences among the institutions to which defaulters have attended. In another 2017 paper, researchers from the National Center for Education Statistics showed that among students who had entered college in 2003, the average cumulative default rate for public or private four-year programs was 9 and 8.5 percent, respectively. Meanwhile, students entering a two-year or for-profit program had default rates of 15.7 and 34.8 percent, respectively.[lv]

For-profit administrators were quick to counter this result by arguing that the typical profile of a student entering a for-profit program is very different than the profile of someone entering a public or private four-year program. Basically, it's not the program that's causing the higher relative default rate, it's all of the other extenuating circumstances. And to be fair, they have a good point. In a separate Brookings publication, economists from the U.S. Department of Treasury and the NYU Stern School of Business utilized advanced statistical techniques that corroborated the for-profit administrators' argument. Specifically, when adjusting for all other factors, including age, marital status, whether or not they have children, family income, whether or not they attended graduate school, and future income, people who enter for-profit colleges have a *lower* default rate than those who enter a two-year program, a *somewhat selective* four-year program, or a *nonselective* program! Factors that lead to higher default rates (irrespective of the institution) include low family income and when the borrower has children. Factors that lead to lower default rates include marriage (married people are less likely to default), attending graduate school, and earning more after graduation. Interestingly, women are less likely to default than men.[lvi]

Whether or not a student earns a degree or drops out is also a significant predictor of whether or not they will default. Returning to the 2017 CAP report, the authors found that the default rate 12 years after entering a program among people who earned a bachelor's or associate degree is nine and 22 percent, respectively. Meanwhile, people who earned a *certificate* or dropped out of a program altogether had a 46 percent default rate.[lvii] Finally, another interesting variable is somewhat counterintuitive—people with lower balances default at higher rates. In a 2015 study, economists at the U.S. Federal Reserve found that the default rate among the 2009 cohort of students was highest among people with balances from $1,000 to $5,000 (34%) and lowest among people with balances of $100,000 or more (18%).[lviii] That default rate is a single snapshot in time for a single cohort; so, it might not be fully indicative of the default rate

". . . people with lower balances default at higher rates."

among the full life of loans. But it is telling that people struggle to repay even comparatively modest amounts.

LAWS, CONSUMER PROTECTIONS, AND BANKRUPTCY

Think student debt is like any other debt? Think again. Unlike mortgage debt, federal student loans cannot be refinanced if interest rates fall; instead, if you want to benefit from lower rates, you need to use a private lender. What happens if you default on a federal loan? Unlike other mortgage, credit card, or auto debt where a creditor must first file a lawsuit and receive a judgment, the federal government can immediately begin garnishing your wages, and it can do so indefinitely. How about discharging student loans in bankruptcy? Well, it's not impossible, but it's not easy either. A 2012 study estimated that only about one in 1,000 people who declare bankruptcy even try to jettison their student debt. And how successful are the people who try? About 25 percent of people who try are able to fully discharge their debt. Those odds get better if the person is unemployed (40%) or has a medical hardship (35%).[lix] So, why is student debt treated differently from all other debts—and should it be? The typical rationale is that student debt is treated differently because the proceeds from incurring the debt are spent differently. Unlike a mortgage or a car loan that has an asset to which the debt is pledged, a student loan has no collateral that the lender can seize. Therefore, the creditor needs additional protections in the event that the debtor attempts to refinance loans or declares bankruptcy. As an economist by trade, I can tell you that logic is dubious at best, and I'll explain why later in this chapter. In the meantime, let's better understand the current state of laws surrounding student debt and how we got here.

Refinancing and Consolidating Loans

Imagine that a student enters college in 2008, and she realizes that she and her parents can't quite make ends meet. So, the student takes out a $5,000 Federal Stafford loan. The interest rate at the time is 6.8 percent, and the student feels good about the decision because the interest on Stafford loans do not accrue while she's a full-time student. She continues taking out $5,000 student loans each year while she is attending college. The subsequent three loan interest rates are 6.0, 5.6, and 4.5 percent respectively.[lx] Finally, in 2012, she graduates with $20,000 in debt and intends to start repaying her loans within six months of graduation. With four separate Stafford loans, the weighted average interest rate of her debt is 5.725 percent, while newly issued Stafford loan debt is being offered at 3.4 percent. That's great!—right? Unfortunately, because the borrower's loan is federally subsidized, she is *not* eligible to refinance her loans to a lower interest rate. She can consolidate her loans, so that she will have a single federal loan and a single monthly payment (instead of four separate balances and payments). Alternatively, she may repay her loans in full by taking out a loan with a private lender. So, should she do either? Maybe.

With respect to loan consolidation (i.e., turning four Stafford loans into one Stafford loan), the primary benefit is that it is easier to manage one rather than four payments. What do borrowers give up when they do this? Plenty. First, the new interest rate on the loan is the blended average (5.725%) of the earlier loans, and that is set for the lifetime of the loan. However, if a borrower is able to repay the loan early (likely in parts), he or she will no longer have the option of prioritizing the repayment of the highest interest rate loans. How does this work? Imagine at the end of a recently minted college graduate's first year of working full-time, she receives a $5,000 bonus and wants to repay student debt with it. For simplicity, let's assume that the student loan principal balance is still $20,000. If the borrower hadn't consolidated that debt, she could pay off the loan with the highest rate (6.8%) in full. As a result, the average interest rate on the three remaining loans would fall to 5.37 percent. However, because she consolidated the debt, the interest rate on the remaining $15,000 loan is still 5.75 percent.

What about the option of consolidating and repaying all four loans by borrowing from a private lender (a bank and not a government agency)? That option has the advantage of potentially reducing a borrower's interest rate on one or more of a borrower's existing student loans. But there are significant trade-offs. First, private loans generally do not have income-driven repayment (IDR) plans. With many federal loans, if a borrower qualifies for an IDR, the monthly payment may fall because the payment will be calculated as a percentage of the borrower's discretionary income.[11] An added benefit to an IDR plan is that the remaining loan balances may be forgiven after 20 or 25 years; however, this is conditional on Congress not unilaterally changing a borrower's existing terms prior to this period. A second reason not to refinance with a private lender is that the borrower will likely lose access to loan forgiveness programs such as the Public Service Loan Forgiveness (PSLF) or

---

[11] This website is a good resource to estimate loan payments using an IDR: https://studentaid.gov/loan-simulator.

Teacher Loan Forgiveness (TLF) programs. Under the PSLF program, if a borrower works for 10 years for an eligible government entity or non-profit organization, is enrolled in an IDR plan, and makes 10 years of on-time payments, all remaining debt is forgiven at the end of this period. Similarly, the TLF program may allow eligible borrowers to enjoy up to $17,500 in debt forgiveness after five years if the borrower works at a school that is servicing low-income students. The final reason not to refinance with a private lender is that a borrower is no longer eligible for federal deferment or forbearance. Federal loans offer generous deferment or forbearance[12] options in case a borrower returns to school, experiences a financial hardship, develops a serious medical condition, or meets another qualifying criterion.[lxi] More recently, the Coronavirus Aid, Relief and Economic Security (CARES) Act, passed in March 2020, granted eligible borrowers automatic loan forbearance during which time interest rates fell to zero percent, borrowers were not required to make payments, and all fees would stop accruing.[lxii]

General Consumer Protections

Fortunately, a myriad of federal (and state) laws protect student borrowers from unscrupulous lenders and collectors. These laws include the Equal Credit Opportunity Act, the Fair Credit Reporting Act, the Truth in Lending Act, the Federal Trade Commission Act, the Consumer Financial Protection Act, and the Fair Debt Collection Practices Act. Broadly speaking, borrowers are protected from three actors: schools, lenders, and collectors. With respect to schools, if they provide students with a preferred lenders list, the school must make its selection criteria for preferred lenders available to students. Schools must not financially benefit if a student receives a loan from one of its preferred lenders, schools must also include at least three options on their preferred lenders list, and schools must make it clear that students don't have to use a preferred lender.[lxiii] Lenders, meanwhile, have a host of requirements as well. For example, lenders may not discriminate against borrowers on the basis of race, color, religion, national origin, sex, marital status, age, or any other protected class.[lxiv] In addition, lenders must "plain speak" critical terms of the loan to borrowers; such terms include the size of the loan, the cost (in terms of an interest rate), and other relevant fees.[lxv] Finally, collectors may not use abusive or deceptive practices to collect student loans. For example,

---

[12] With both deferment and forbearance, the borrower does not make loan payments. With deferment, interest does not accrue during this period (i.e., the loan balance is frozen). With forbearance, interest continues to accrue and the loan's principal balance will increase.

debt collectors may not communicate with anybody other than the borrower, and they must do it during normal business hours. When they do speak with a borrower, the collector may not use intimidating, obscene, or threatening language. They must also not make false or misleading statements—like suggesting they have the power to garnish wages, may have the borrower arrested, or place children into foster care. Finally, debt collectors must provide borrowers with information about the debt, giving the borrower an opportunity to dispute the debt.[lxvi]

Discharging Loans

So, when did student debt begin to receive unique treatment during bankruptcy, and why? The answer is that unique treatment of student debt was the recommendation of a congressional commission that was established in 1970. In that year, the U.S. Congress established the Bankruptcy Act Commission to review the Bankruptcy Act of 1898 and make recommendations for updating the Act. In 1970, while the use of student debt was minimal by today's standards, it had recently crossed $1.0 billion and was up from around $100 million just seven years prior.[lxvii] In addition, following the creation of the Guaranteed Student Loan program in 1965, the U.S. Treasury (and by extension, taxpayers) were perceived as in need of protection from unscrupulous borrowers. While at the time there were few instances of improper use of bankruptcy law to discharge student debt, members of the commission nevertheless identified the potential moral hazard that was associated with the current bankruptcy law. One member of the commission, Representative Allen Ertel, noted that existing bankruptcy law "encouraged fraud." When describing the need to update the Bankruptcy Act, Rep. Ertel compares two students, both of whom have debt at graduation. He noted that the student who immediately declares bankruptcy after graduation (and discharges student loans) has a superior financial outlook than the student who repays his or her debt.[lxviii] Thus, irrespective of actual fraud, the commission recommended that the law should be updated to address the potential for fraud. So, in 1976, Congress amended the HEA to specify that federally guaranteed student loans could only be discharged in two circumstances: if more than five years have passed since entering repayment of the loan, or in less than five years if repayment would cause undue hardship.[lxix]

Two years later, Congress codified the unique treatment of student debt (as specified in the HEA) into the Bankruptcy Reform Act of 1978.[lxx] Between 1979 and 2005, Congress further revised the legal treatment of student debt at least five times.[13,14,15,16,17] In each instance, the result of the revised bankruptcy laws was twofold: Congress expanded the breadth of debt that fell under the student-debt umbrella (and thus had a unique treatment during bankruptcy), and Congress increased the hurdle for achieving a full discharge of those loans. The cumulative impact of these amendments is that all student debt (regardless of use and originator) is now treated separately from other debt. In addition, this debt can only be discharged if the repayment of this debt would cause undue hardship, regardless of how long ago the debt was originated.

The Brunner Test

So, what is *undue hardship*, and under what circumstances might a person successfully discharge their student debt? Unfortunately, the U.S. Congress never defined that critical term, and so it was left to the courts to define. One court did just that in 1985 in a landmark case—*Marie Brunner v. New York State Higher Education Services Corp.* In 1982, Marie Brunner earned a master's degree in social work, but she had difficulty finding work commensurate with

---

[13] 1979 Act. This Act specified that student loans that are treated differently would now include loans originated by programs funded by the government or by a higher-education non-profit entity. In addition, the new law specified that the five-year period after which student loans could be discharged might be *reset* if there were any deferments or forbearances. Source: PUBLIC LAW 96–56—AUG. 14, 1979.

[14] Federal Judiciary Act of 1984. This Act removed the phrase "of higher education" when specifying a loan originated by a non-profit institution, meaning it would be more difficult to discharge. As a result, a student loan originated by any non-profit institution would now be treated differently during bankruptcy. Source: PUBLIC LAW 98–353—JULY 10, 1984.

[15] Crime Control Act of 1990. This Act specified that conditional grants for education (such as an ROTC scholarship) would now be treated like other student debt. In addition, this Act increased the waiting period to discharge debt from five to seven years. Source: PUBLIC LAW 101–647—NOV. 29, 1990.

[16] Higher Education Amendments of 1998. These amendments eliminated the seven-year period after which student debt would no longer be treated differently from any other debt. As a result, student debt would permanently be a unique form of debt during bankruptcy, and only *undue hardship* would allow a debtor to discharge this debt. Source: PUBLIC LAW No: 105–244 (10/07/1998).

[17] Bankruptcy Abuse Prevention and Consumer Protection Act (BAPCPA) of 2005. This law specifies that any "qualified education loan," irrespective of the originator, may only be discharged if it causes "undue hardship." Previously, only student loans associated with a non-profit institution (or the government) would be treated differently under bankruptcy code. Source: PUBLIC LAW No: 109–256 (Jan. 4, 2005).

her level of education and at a salary that would allow her to repay her debt. So, seven months after graduating, she declared bankruptcy, and her $9,000 student debt was successfully discharged.[lxxi] The New York State Higher Education Services Corp., which held the loans, challenged that decision. Ms. Brunner represented herself and lost two subsequent cases, which meant she had to repay her debt.[lxxii] In the 1985 case, the judge clarified what constitutes *undue hardship*, and this has since become known as the *Brunner Test*. This test, which is cited in nearly every bankruptcy proceeding that involves student debt, states that the repayment of student debt would constitute *undue hardship* if the holder of the debt passes all three criteria:

1. *That the debtor cannot maintain, based on current income and expenses, a minimal standard of living for herself and her dependents if forced to repay the loans*
2. *That additional circumstances exist indicating that this state of affairs is likely to persist for a significant portion of the repayment period of the student loans*
3. *That the debtor has made good faith efforts to repay the loans*

In justifying the decision, the judge admitted that this three-part test is "draconian," but rationalized the decision in two ways. First, the governmental entities that were extending loans at the time did so without regard to the credit worthiness of the borrower. Therefore, lenders were entitled to some protection. Second, the *undue hardship* standard only applied for the first five years after the borrower graduates.[lxxiii] Perhaps if the judge knew that in 1998 Congress would jettison the window requiring repayment, meaning only the *undue hardship* definition would apply for the life of the loan, he would have defined *undue hardship* more generously.

As mentioned previously, passing the *Brunner Test* is extremely challenging; therefore, only a tiny percentage of people declaring bankruptcy even try. So, what makes passing the test more or less likely? With respect to the first criteria (maintaining a minimal standard of living) there are several factors that judges consider. For example, income-driven plans are more difficult to discharge because the monthly payments fall with income. Loans with lower balances or with lower rates of interest are also more difficult to discharge. Conversely, people with higher incomes or people with spouses (who also earn an income) are less successful at shedding their student debt. Similarly, people with other assets, such as retirement accounts or home equity, are also less likely to be successful. With respect to the second criteria—additional circumstances—debtors who have major medical expenses or disabilities, have suffered a loss of employment, have one or more dependents, or who have a dependent with a disability are more successful at discharging their loans. With respect to the final criteria—good faith efforts—a debtor who has made payments for several years and/or utilized deferments or forbearances is more likely to successfully shed their student debt during bankruptcy. With all that said, the decision of whether or not a person who is attempting to discharge their debt meets the *undue hardship* criteria is at the discretion of the judge presiding over the case. So, if you find yourself attempting to discharge your student debt during bankruptcy, the most important factor is not your personal circumstances, but your judge.

". . . if you find yourself attempting to discharge your student debt during bankruptcy, the most important factor is not your personal circumstances, but your judge."

Default and Wage Garnishment

Regardless of the issuer of a student loan, the loan will be considered delinquent the first day after a missed payment. Generally, after 90 days of delinquency, the status of the loan will be reported to credit agencies, after which the borrower's credit score will fall. If the borrower does not enter forbearance or deferment, the loan is generally considered in default after 120 days for private loans and 270 days for federal loans. What happens next depends most heavily on whether the student debt is private or federal. Starting with private loans, the borrower will (should) have been contacted several times by the lender; the lender must have made a good faith effort to learn why the borrower hasn't made repayments as well as discussed loan repayment options. For example, a lender may offer the borrower forbearance, whereby interest continues to accrue (and is added to the principal balance), but late fees and other charges cease. Lenders may also offer some sort of repayment agreement whereby a borrower makes payments for a time before the loan is brought out of default. Lenders may also offer some other negotiated settlement. On the other hand, private lenders are not *required* to do any of these things, and they will generally act in their own best interest. Generally, after 120 days (but up to 270 days) of delinquency, the lenders will *charge off* the loan, whereby the lender will take a write-down on the loan and the defaulted loan will be transferred to another party, usually a collections agency. Once this happens, borrowers will continue to receive notices from collectors; however, the tools that the collectors may choose to utilize have grown.

Specifically, because the *owner* of the defaulted loan is now a collections agency, they likely will be unable or unwilling to offer loan forbearance or other temporary repayment agreements to bring the loan current. Instead, the collections agency may choose to sue the debtor in order to garnish their wages or have a lien placed on their house or other assets. The collection agency's willingness to do this will be a function of several considerations: the expected legal expense to sue, the loan balance currently outstanding (if the anticipated legal expense exceeds the balance outstanding, agencies are less likely to sue), and the statute of limitations during which the agency can sue (if the statute has passed, the collection agency can't sue). Interestingly, the statute of limitations for a lawsuit varies by state and is anywhere from three to 20 years in length.[lxxiv] After this period, a private student lender cannot sue a defaulted borrower in hopes of garnishing their wages. So, when does this clock start? That varies by state, but in general, it starts when the borrower becomes delinquent. So, if a defaulted borrower is near the statute of limitations, a single payment may *reset the clock*. Don't expect a collection agency to explain that to a defaulted borrower. Finally, only if a private lender files a lawsuit (within the statute of limitations) against a defaulted borrower and wins a judgment, may the private lender begin garnishing the wages of a borrower. The amount of the garnishment is generally the lesser of 25 percent of disposable income or an amount exceeding 30 times the minimum wage in the debtor's state (whichever is lower). If the collection agency chooses not to file a lawsuit or fails to win in court, the defaulted loan will remain on the borrower's credit report for seven years, after which it will no longer appear on their credit report. After this period, the borrower is still technically required to repay the loan; however, if the statute of limitations has passed and no judgment has been granted, the collection agency's ability to collect on the debt has been blunted.

So, that's what happens if a borrower defaults on a private student loan. But what about federal student loans? There's good and bad news. I'll start with the good news. Federal student loan borrowers who are in default have the option of getting out of default through *loan rehabilitation*. To rehabilitate a loan, the borrower must make nine consecutive, full, on-time payments. After this, the defaulted loan is removed from a debtor's credit report and collection fees are reduced or eliminated. But what if that fails and the borrower eventually finds their wages garnished? The other good news is that the federal government will likely garnish no more than 15 percent of disposable income, as opposed to 25 percent for private loans.

And now the bad news. First, a defaulted federal loan borrower loses accesses to deferment, forbearance, repayment plans, forgiveness programs, and additional federal student aid. Next, if a loan owned by the DOE is sent to a collection agency, a 17.92 percent fee will immediately be applied to the outstanding principal balance.[lxxv] So, a loan with a $10,000 balance will immediately jump to $11,792. Next, unlike the default on a private student loan, there is no statute of limitations for the federal government to sue a debtor, nor is there a need to file a lawsuit to get a judgment in order to garnish wages. Rather, the DOE has that power without judicial oversight. As a result, the DOE will seize a debtor's tax refunds, garnish paychecks, and garnish up to 15 percent of his or her federal benefits (such as social security). Therefore, the federal government can place a lien on homes, seize assets in the future (such as if the borrower receives an inheritance), or sue the borrower at any time. Finally, in some states, teachers, dentists, nurses, and other professionals are unable to renew their professional licenses if they are in default on their student loans.[lxxvi] Scared yet?

CONCLUSION

If you've made it this far in the chapter, you're probably angry. Angry that our government has enabled excessive borrowing. Angry that our universities have raised tuition despite a decline in their students' ability to repay. Angry that university endowments don't support the neediest of schools. Angry that banks and executives made fortunes over our misfortunes. Angry that our current system exacerbates racial disparities. And if you read the next chapter, you're likely to get even more angry because I detail all the ways in which student debt impairs our economic, social, and mental health.

Fortunately, we can trace every suboptimal outcome (high tuition, high debt, high default, high inequality) to one or more misaligned incentives. For example, for decades banks were incentivized to lend freely because it was profitable. The government was incentivized to support the student loan program because it was popular. The government was incentivized to reduce bankruptcy protections for student debtors in order to protect against hypothetical bad actors. Universities were incentivized to raise tuition because their students' ability to borrow was essentially limitless (Chapter 2), students were incentivized to attend college because of significant societal pressure and the expectation that attending college was a path to financial success (Chapter 3), and endowments were incentivized to maximize their tax advantages by growing their portfolios while shrinking the number of students supported by the endowment (Chapter 4). So, what's the solution? Simple. We craft legislation to align incentives (Chapter 8). But before we go there, let's spend some time fully analyzing the different ways student loans have impacted debtors (Chapter 6) and how the postsecondary system has disproportionately harmed racial minorities (Chapter 7).

6

How Student Loans Have Impaired a Generation

On net, student debt is a burden to some households, but the increase in student debt does not appear to have substantially altered the macroeconomic conditions . . . Most individuals, and the economy as a whole, will benefit from the education made possible by student loans. Nonetheless, the rise in defaults and high debt among low earners show that student loans can have negative effects on some individuals and merit a policy response.[i]

—July 2016 Report by the Council of Economic
Advisors to President Obama

The 78-page report to President Obama, titled *Investing in Higher Education: Benefits, Challenges, and the State of Student Debt,* covers many of the same items in this book, including the growing stock of student debt and many of the adverse consequences of that stock of debt. This report even concludes (albeit meekly) that the current state warrants a policy response. Sadly, no material or effective policy responses have been implemented since this report's composition. Perhaps this is because the report was submitted in the waning days of the Obama presidency. Maybe the authors failed to appreciate either the magnitude or trajectory of the debt; in fact, the authors concluded current policies were "building on a record of success." Or perhaps the lack of a policy response can be attributed to the fact that tuition inflation and student debt are chronic issues and not acute issues. Specifically, the stock of debt is a burden that is cumulative and spread among a large population that has largely accepted its existence. By contrast, recessions, wars, commodity price shocks, and pandemics are acute and generally receive the appropriate legislative focus warranted by

". . . like a chronic health condition, the growth in student debt needs to be addressed before it becomes fatal."

time-sensitive and critical situations. However, like a chronic health condition, the growth in student debt needs to be addressed before it becomes fatal. And like any appropriate medical treatment, the treatment must address the disease (incentive misalignment leading to tuition inflation) and not the symptom (too much debt).

As a country, we are in a student debt crisis. It's a chronic crisis that is felt by tens of millions of people, and it is felt in ways that do not always translate into GDP or casualty figures. Rather, this crisis has caused delayed household formation, lower birthrates, and higher depression. We can guestimate how this crisis has impacted the economic outlook of our country, but this analysis often misses the point: we know that tens of millions of individuals would be far better off if they had not assumed student debt. We know this because debtors report it when surveyed and because savvy researchers are utilizing statistical techniques that prove it. So how is student debt damaging people and society? In short—student debt harms the individual in the form of delaying and preventing many of life's milestones while inflicting psychological harm, and student debt also harms the taxpayers (society) since they ultimately assume the cost of defaulted loans. To be fair, student loan availability has the potential to unlock educational options for those who may not otherwise have access to a college education—and that's a great thing. So, let's take a closer look at the benefits and harms of student debt availability in order to determine whether we think current legislators have a record of success, or not.

THE BENEFITS OF STUDENT LOAN AVAILABILITY

While the bulk of this chapter will focus on the harm done to individuals and society by excessive student debt, a complete analysis of the current situation should also include a discussion of the benefits of the availability of student loans. As discussed in Chapter 3, education benefits both individuals and society. For example, recipients of a bachelor's degree have a higher earnings potential, which yields higher tax revenue and lower government expenditures on transfer programs. In addition, higher educational obtainment also correlates to higher civic engagement[ii] and lower criminal activity.[iii] Because student loans facilitate the advancement of peoples' education, we shouldn't necessarily avoid loans if we hope to address the ills of student debt. So, in what ways do individuals and society benefit from the availability of student loans, in general, and federally subsidized loans, in particular? The three benefits of student loan availability are: (1) greater access to higher education, (2) the realization of greater educational *externalities*, and (3) a correction for *market failures*.

Greater Access to Higher Education

Holding all things equal,[1] the ability to use financing to pay for an education should increase peoples' ability to afford college and therefore, should increase the number of both students and recipients of advanced degrees. So the most relevant policy question is: What percentage of the prospective pool of students are able to attend college (that otherwise wouldn't) because student loans are available? Unfortunately, there is limited data in the United States that can allow us to directly observe the impact of student loan availability—rather, we need to look to South Africa and Chile to gain this kind of insight. In order to tease out whether credit availability (e.g., a loan) impacts enrollment, in 2010, researchers created a database that combined South African student enrollment with student credit scores and whether or not they were approved for a loan. To be approved for an *Eduloan* in South Africa, students must have a minimum credit score; unfortunately, the algorithm for calculating the score and the credit score minimum to be approved for the loan are not publicly available. So, when prospective students apply for a loan, they generally don't know if they will be approved. In addition, only students who have already been accepted to a university may apply for a loan. By comparing the cohort of students with a credit score just below the limit (and denied a loan) to the cohort of students with scores just above the credit limit (and approved for a loan), researchers determined how the credit score and loan availability impacted enrollment rates. The results? Students just below the credit threshold (and denied loans) have a 50 percent chance of enrolling the next semester, while students who are just above the credit threshold (and approved loans) have a 73 percent chance of enrolling the next semester. Therefore, researchers reckoned there is a nearly 50 percent

---

[1] This is a nontrivial assumption. As discussed in Chapter 2, the availability of student loans has contributed to tuition inflation. As a result, the availability of student loans has simultaneously led to both decreased affordability and increased accessibility of a postsecondary education. This increased cost of the education and, by extension, decreased demand for education, should partially offset the increase in demand for education that is facilitated by the availability of student loans.

[(0.73 / 0.50) − 1] increase in postsecondary enrollment when student loans are made available to students.[iv]

These results closely align with a study completed by a Swedish researcher in 2011 that focused on loan availability to Chilean postsecondary students. Like in South Africa, there is a discrete point at which students can or cannot qualify for a loan; unlike in South Africa, the metric isn't a credit score but a score on a standardized university entrance exam. Students who have been admitted into one of 44 accredited universities are eligible for a state-sponsored loan if they score at least 475 (mean 500, standard deviation 100) on a standard assessment test and if their family is not in the top 20 percent of income earners. The researcher discovered the average enrollment rate of students who had been admitted into a university but scored just below the cutoff was 18.5 percent, whereas the average enrollment of students who scored just above the cutoff was 34.7 percent. So, in this case the availability of student loans led to a nearly 88 percent [(0.347 / 0.185) − 1] increase in postsecondary enrollment.[v]

Since there is no discrete point that leads to the availability of student loans (or lack thereof) in the United States, we can't run a similar experiment. Fortunately, Professor Constantine Yannelis at the University of Chicago (then a student at Stanford), along with another colleague at Peking University, came up with a clever way to estimate how student loan availability impacts enrollment among students who may or may not attend college due to financial constraints. Between the late 1970s through the mid-1990s, states deregulated the U.S. banking industry and allowed banks to open branches across state lines. As a result, during that 20-year period, the availability of private student loans varied by state. These researchers then combined this state-by-state data with information found in the National Longitudinal Surveys (NLS), which is a set of surveys sponsored by the Bureau of Labor Statistics (BLS) of the U.S. Department of Labor. This survey includes participants who were born between 1957 and 1964. The participants were first interviewed in 1976 and then reinterviewed either each year or every other year, thereafter. By combining the state-by-state loan availability data with the educational obtainment data found in the NLS document, and while simultaneously controlling for all other relevant factors (age, race, income, wealth, parents' education, etc.), researchers could then determine how loan availability impacted educational attainment. The results of their analysis showed that once banks were deregulated (and loans were more available to students), enrollment among recent high school graduates increased from 53.0 percent to 55.6 percent. This means that an increase in private loan availability led to a nearly 4.9 percent [(0.556 / 0.530) − 1] increase in college enrollment.[vi]

Positive Externalities and Market Failure Corrections

There are two arguments that are widely accepted among academics and are utilized to validate the policy of providing subsidized public loans to college students. The first argument goes like this: Students and society both benefit every time a person enrolls in a college course. Individuals benefit from the education they receive along with the likely higher earnings that education will enable. Similarly, society benefits from the higher tax receipts, a larger and more productive economy, higher civic engagement, and reduced criminal activity when people earn degrees. The ways in which society benefits from an individual's education is termed an *externality*, which is a side effect of an activity. Externalities can be positive (like walking to work, thereby reducing traffic congestion for other drivers) or negative (like a factory creating air or water pollution). When individuals decide whether or not they want to receive a college degree, they typically make that decision based on a cost-benefit analysis that applies to only them, such as: by going to college will I earn more than the cost of my degree? However, as a society we all benefit when people earn college degrees. So, we should subsidize college degrees, thereby making people more likely to attend college on the margin. By doing this, we all reap the benefit of positive college degree externalities. Publicly provided and subsidized student loans are that form of subsidy.

The second argument for publicly subsidized student loans is that without government intervention, the private market would be unwilling to supply educational loans in a sufficient quantity to prospective students (curing a market failure). This is because of the unique nature of student loans. Unlike car loans or home mortgages (which are secured by a car or house), there is no collateral for a student loan. So, if a student defaults, the lender cannot seize an asset and be made whole. As a result, private lenders would be unwilling to extend credit to a typical 18-year-old with no assets and no credit history. This also suggests that the most disadvantaged students would be unable to attend college despite their academic credentials.

WAYS IN WHICH TODAY'S YOUNG ADULTS HAVE BEEN IMPAIRED

No doubt there are benefits to the availability of student loans because it enables some students to earn a college degree when a lack of wealth or liquidity would otherwise prevent them from doing so. The questions we should ask now are: What are the harms caused by student debt, and do the harms outweigh the benefits? On an individual level, the harms caused by excessive student debt include (but are not limited to): regret attending college, delayed household formation, delayed home purchases, delayed marriages, delayed first child, lower fertility, lower entrepreneurship, fewer job opportunities, higher economic inequality, fewer career choices, lower job satisfaction, damaged physical and mental health, and higher instances of depression. That's a lot—so let's cover each harm in turn.

Regret Attending College

Despite the benefits of earning a college degree—including higher earning potential—an increasingly large portion of former students report that they wish they had made different life choices. Morning Consult, a private data and market research firm, conducted an online survey in September 2020 and found that a whopping 45 percent of millennials (born between 1981 and 1996) believe taking out student debt was either "definitely" or "probably not worth attending college."[vii] This figure was up three percent since March 2019.[viii] By contrast, in September 2020, 24 percent of baby boomers answered that taking out student debt was either "definitely" or "probably not worth attending college." The most recent uptick in disillusionment with a college degree (and its associated debt) can be partially attributed to the 2020 recession and COVID-19 pandemic. In September 2020, 16 percent of all surveyed adults reported that they lost income due to the economic recession, while 24 percent of millennials reported lost income—meaning millennials were disproportionately financially hurt by the pandemic and recession.

The results of this Morning Consult survey closely align with a separate 2019 online survey conducted by PayScale, a data company that assists companies by providing job market and compensation information. In their survey, taken by 248,000 respondents, people who had at least a bachelor's degree were asked if they had any regrets regarding their college education. Among millennials, only 28.7 percent indicated they had no regrets. Meanwhile, student loans were their largest regrets (28.8%), followed by not taking advantage of networking opportunities (13.2%), and their area of study (13.1%). By contrast, 51.3 percent of baby boomers indicated having no regrets and only 13.4 percent indicated that student loans were their largest regrets. Not surprisingly, the students' choice of major correlated with whether or not they

> *"Not surprisingly, the students' choice of major correlated with whether or not they had regrets."*

had regrets. Students who earned engineering degrees had the lowest post-college regrets, with 42.2 percent indicating that they had no regrets and only 18.7 percent indicated that their college debts were their largest regrets. Meanwhile, among health science and art majors, 33.0 and 27.2 percent indicated no regrets, respectively, and 37.7 and 32.1 percent indicated that their largest regrets were college debts. A similar percentage of college graduates from public and private colleges indicated no regrets at 31.7 percent and 31.1 percent, respectively. However, should they have college regrets, graduates from private colleges were significantly more likely to indicate that their debts were their primary regrets.[ix]

Delayed Household Formation

Perhaps one of the reasons that college graduates regret taking on student debt is that their debt burden forces many of them to move back home! In fact, upon graduation young adults are increasingly less likely to form their own household and become fully independent. According to the Pew Research Center, for the first time in more than 130 years, in 2014 adults between the ages of 18 to 34 were more likely to be living in their parents' home than they were to be living with a spouse or a partner in their own household. Since 1960, the percentage of adults from 18 to 34 years old who were still living with their parents has roughly doubled for both college-educated and non-college-educated adults; as of 2014, the figures reached 19 and 36 percent, respectively.[x] Looking into this development, researchers at the U.S. Federal Reserve examined the causal relationship between debt and parental co-residence among young adults. These researchers obtained data from a large reporting bureau, which included data on young adults' credit history as well as their address, which could be matched against their parents' address to determine their living arrangements. Their results were not surprising—young adults with debt are increasingly likely to move in with their parents as the amount of debt increases; in addition, young adults who have been forced to defer student loan payments have notably longer durations of parental co-residence.[xi] The recent trend of moving back in with parents has become so common (29 percent among those aged 25 to 34 by 2012) that people researching and reporting on these phenomena have coined the phrase the *Boomerang Generation*.[xii]

". . . young adults with debt are increasingly likely to move in with their parents as the amount of debt increases . . ."

In 2019, The Harris Poll, a market research and consulting firm, conducted a survey on behalf of TD Ameritrade, a brokerage firm. The objective of the survey was to ascertain how student debt had impacted planning for the future among both children and their parents. TD Ameritrade presented the results of this survey in a report aptly titled *Boomerang Generation, Returning to the Nest*. Survey respondents that fell into the *young millennial* cohort (ages 22–28) reported that they anticipate, or have already experienced, significant delays in major life milestones. Respondents indicated delays in the following categories: moving out of their parents' home (31%), buying a home (47%), getting married (21%), having children (21%), and saving for retirement (41%). In addition, 50 percent of young millennials reported planning on moving back in with their parents after college, while 59 percent of students actually did return to the nest. The duration of their move was fairly long, indicating there was a significant financial incentive to co-reside with their parents. Specifically, 25 percent lived with their parents for one to two years, while 31 percent co-resided with parents for greater than two years. Fortunately for the former students, 82 percent of parents indicated they would "welcome their children moving back home after college," although, 34 percent of parents intend to (or did) charge their kids rent.[xiii]

Delayed Home Purchases

Purchasing a home, in the eyes of many, is an essential part of the American dream. Homeownership can be a source of pride, geographic and financial stability, a mechanism for long-term wealth generation, and an important step prior to having children. Unfortunately, homeownership has been on the decline since 2005 and its decline has been particularly acute among young adults. While the U.S. average homeownership rate has fallen by 3.7 percent to 65.3 percent from 4Q 2005 to 1Q 2020, during the same period, the homeownership rate among the under-35 cohort has declined by 5.8 percent to 37.3 percent and the homeownership rate among the 35 to 44 cohort has declined by 8.2 percent to 61.5 percent.[xiv,2] An increase in the stock of student debt among the same cohort of potential homebuyers is a frequently cited contributor to this decline in homeownership. The causal link between higher student debt and lower homeownership is self-evident. To qualify for a home mortgage, a borrower generally needs a 10–20 percent down payment (the minimum Federal Housing Administration down payment is 3.5%), may not exceed a maximum debt-to-income ratio, and must generally have a sufficiently high credit score. Student loans act as a natural impediment to saving for a down payment and maintaining a low debt-to-income ratio. In

---

[2] Interestingly, in 2Q and 3Q 2020 there was a significant jump in homeownership in the United States. Likely related to the Coronavirus-related lockdowns, many prospective homebuyers purchased their first homes. As a result, homeownership rates rose 2.9 percent in the under 35 cohort and 2.4 percent in the 35 to 44 cohort. Despite this one-time jump in homeownership, overall homeownership among these two age cohorts is still well below its 2005 peak.

addition, should a student ever become delinquent on their loans (even if it is temporarily), this blemish may impact a borrower's credit score for years. As a result, we might expect young adults with student debt to have a lower homeownership rate—or at least experience delays in home purchases.

Despite the obvious link between increasing student debt and declining homeownership, estimating the direct impact on student debt and homeownership is a tricky proposition because many variables contribute to the stock of student debt as well as the decision to buy a home. For example, pre-med students who successfully complete medical school generally graduate with significant student debt; but they also tend to repay their debt and become homeowners later in life. Therefore, controlling for all variables simultaneously is critical to identifying exactly how student debt impacts people's homeownership later in life. In 2016, economists at the Federal Reserve did just that and published their findings in a paper titled *Student Loans and Homeownership*. In it, the researchers constructed a database of former college students and included variables such as level of educational attainment, the type of school they attended, their home state and economic conditions in that state, and their college major (among several others). By including all variables that might impact homeownership, they could isolate the impact of debt on homeownership. Their findings? For each $1,000 increase in student loan debt, the former student homeownership rate is reduced by about 1.5 percentage points. This also translates into delaying home purchases by about 2.5 months per $1,000 in debt.[xv] In other words,

> *"For each $1,000 increase in student loan debt, the former student homeownership rate is reduced by about 1.5 percentage points."*

imagine you had two groups of identical 26-year-old former college students. Group A graduated college with an average of $10,000 in student loans apiece, while Group B graduated college with an average of $30,000 in student loans apiece. Four years after graduating college, on average, Group B would have a homeownership rate 30 percent lower than Group A, and those in Group B who purchase homes, do so an average of 50 months (over four years) later than those in Group A.

Delayed Marriages

A large purchase, such as a house, is not the only thing that is delayed following the accumulation of student debt. Former students with student debt tend to delay marriage as well. Like purchasing a home, the decision to marry cannot be distilled to a single variable (quantity of student debt). So, to simplify the problem of estimating how student debt impacts future marriage decisions, Associate Professor Dora Gicheva at the University of North Carolina at Greensboro focused solely on former business school graduate students. By doing this, she examined a largely homogeneous population since business school students tend to be roughly the same age, have identical educational attainment, and hold similar jobs. Dr. Gicheva used registrant surveys that were sent to people who had taken the Graduate Management Admission Test, an entrance exam that is used by business schools. These surveys included the data she needed—a question about marriage status and a question about student debt. The result? The data indicates a roughly three to four percent decline in the rate of marriage per $10,000 in student debt. This result was the same for both men and women.[xvi]

That's insightful for business school students; but, what about undergraduates who earn a bachelor's degree? How does debt impact their marriage plans? This is what Robert Bozick at the Rand Corporation and Angela Estacion at Quill Research Associates answered in their 2014 paper titled *Do Student Loans Delay Marriage*? These researchers analyzed a data set of 1993 bachelor's degree recipients; this data set also had complete loan disbursement and repayment histories, as well as dates of first marriage. The authors noted that marriage rates vary considerably by sociodemographic characteristics, so the researchers included controls for age, race/ethnicity, and parental education in their analysis. In short, the researchers wanted to determine if, after controlling for all relevant factors, the existence and size of student debt could explain marriage rates for the first 48 months after receiving a bachelor's degree. The results? The authors determined that each $1,000 in debt reduces the likelihood of marriage by one percent at any given period. Interestingly, this effect is only present with women. This means each $1,000 in student debt reduces the likelihood that the woman will be married within the first four years after college graduation by two percent but has no impact on the likelihood of whether or not a man would be married.[xvii]

Both of these studies are consistent with a more recent 2019 paper published in the *Journal of Family and Economic Issues*. In this study, researchers used data collected from the NLS, and compared data from two cohorts: one cohort born between 1965 and 1974 and the other cohort born between 1980 and 1984. Survey data included student debt and marriage status, as well as a host of other relevant data points including race, age, highest educational attainment, employment, homeownership, and much more. After utilizing a multi-variate statistical analysis, researchers found that the younger cohort of women were significantly more likely to cohabitate prior to marriage and delay marriage, and that these decisions were directly related to the size of their debt.[xviii] Specifically, women were about two percent less likely to marry in a given year for a one percent change in student loan debt.[xix] Furthermore, the authors believe these living arrangements have contributed to higher nonmarital births and a lower overall marriage rate. Interestingly, this study also showed that student debt does not seem to be an impediment for men to marry; although, men are also more likely to cohabitate if they have student debt.[xx]

Delayed First Child

Student debt has become a major impediment for young adults who would like to start a family. While people don't *need* to be financially secure to have children, most college-educated people view this as an important prerequisite. In 2012, NORC at the University of Chicago (an independent research institution) conducted their General Social Survey and asked young adults about the importance they place on various milestones. One question was, "People differ in their ideas about what it takes for a young person to become an adult these days. How important is it for them to be . . . ?" Ninety-five percent of respondents indicated it was extremely or somewhat important to complete formal schooling while 90 percent of respondents indicated it was extremely or somewhat important to be financially independent. In addition, respondents, on average, indicated they feel the ideal age to have a child was four years *after* becoming financially independent.[xxi] The repayment of student debt is a major component of becoming financially independent; so, intuition suggests that the more debt a student assumes, the longer it will take to repay the debt, and the later in life a person will marry and/or have their first child. The results of this NORC survey and our intuition correlate with the TD Ameritrade survey that was highlighted earlier in this chapter; specifically, 21 percent of current and former college students (ages 22–28) reported student debt forced delays in having children.[xxii]

So, while surveyed people indicate they anticipate or have experienced delays in having children because of a desire to reduce or eliminate student debt, do they in reality? Three professors at the Department of Sociology at Ohio State University wanted to know. So in 2014, they constructed a data set from the U.S. Bureau of Labor Statistics and identified a representative cohort of women born between 1980 and 1984. Their analysis included the year women first became mothers (if at all), and how much debt they had at the time. In addition, the researchers disaggregated the debt into student debt, credit card debt, and home mortgage debt. The researchers did this because they suspected that people treated student loans separately from other forms of debt. They needed to ascertain whether people considered student debt to be an impediment toward having a child while mortgage or credit card debt was not. Not surprisingly, the data confirmed the surveys: student loans are a major hurdle to starting families. Specifically, each $1,000 increase in student debt reduced the annual likelihood of transitioning to motherhood by 1.2 percent. Interestingly, the existence of home mortgage debt showed an increase in the likelihood of transitioning to motherhood; this can be explained by the idea that household formation (buying a house) is a typical precursor to motherhood. Thus, a home mortgage may *not* be viewed as an impediment to having a child, but rather an enabler.[xxiii]

Lower Fertility

Much research had been completed in the 2010s describing how attending college impacts women's careers and their family planning. However, not until 2011 did researchers at the Department of Sociology at the University of California, Los Angeles (UCLA) ask the question as to whether the impacts of college attendance were uniform across all student backgrounds. Specifically, the authors wanted to know: If an affluent young White woman from Brentwood and a young Black woman of modest means from Compton both attend UCLA, could we expect their choice to attend college to have similar impacts on the timing and number of children they have later in their lives. Asked in the vernacular of their research paper: Is the treatment effect (decision to attend college) heterogenous or homogenous among various populations?

To answer this question, researchers first assembled data found in the NLS from the BLS. Researchers then narrowed their database to women who enrolled in college by age 19 and completed college by age 23. The authors then divided women into six *stratum*, which were general categories measuring a women's precollege affluence and propensity to attend college. Women whose parents are high school dropouts, who have four or more siblings, who were not enrolled in a college-preparatory track, and who would generally be considered to be disadvantaged fell into Stratum 1. By contrast, women with college educated parents, who have two siblings, who were enrolled in a college-preparatory track, and who were generally considered to be advantaged fell into Stratum 6. At this point, the researchers observed how many children the women in each stratum had by age 41. The results? Women in Stratum 1 (considered disadvantaged) have 66 percent fewer children, whereas women in Stratum 6 (considered advantaged) have 35 percent more children. The researches postulated that women falling into the lower stratums were more economically motivated than women in higher stratums, and this explains their lower fertility.[xxiv] However, I suspect the financial situations among women once they graduate college is even more relevant. Specifically, we could expect women in the lower stratums to have more student debt, whereas women in the higher stratums would likely have less student debt. Thus, if college-educated women believe that financial independence is a critical prerequisite to having children, then disadvantaged women who are saddled with student debt are disproportionately harmed if they should aspire to have children later in life.

So, is the fact that student debt causes so many delays relevant to an eventual outcome? Or, in other words, if a person buys a house, gets married, and starts a family five or 10 years later, does it really matter as long as they still hit those milestones? For many women (and some men), the answer is: yes! The most compelling way in which delaying life milestones directly impacts people's lives has to do with fertility. Women are generally most fertile in their 20s, after which fertility declines, particularly after age 35. A healthy 30-year-old woman has a 20 percent likelihood of becoming pregnant each cycle, whereas the likelihood drops to five percent by age 40. In addition, while menopause begins (on average) at age 51, many women become infertile prior to menopause. Men also experience declining fertility as they age; although, the effect of declining sperm quality generally is not an impediment to pregnancy until men are in their 60s.

Many people believe that fertility treatments will help women overcome failures to conceive naturally; however, this is often not the case. In women over age 40, the success rate of superovulation with timed intrauterine insemination is generally less than five percent per cycle. This compares to success rates around 10 percent for women ages 35 to 40. Similarly, in vitro fertilization has a success rate of around 20 percent for women age 40 and older.[xxv] Why is this all relevant? The answer is that women who choose or are forced to delay family formation because of their student debt are significantly more likely to experience fertility issues later in life. As a result, women with student debt in their 20s are more likely to experience the heart-wrenching situation of being unable to conceive, experience repeat miscarriages, spend significant resources on fertility treatments, and have fewer children (if any).

> *". . . women who choose or are forced to delay family formation because of their student debt are significantly more likely to experience fertility issues later in life."*

Lower Entrepreneurship, Fewer Job Opportunities, and Higher Economic Inequality

In 2017, the Economic Innovation Group (EIG)—a public policy organization based in Washington, D.C.—published an ominous report on the state of entrepreneurism and innovation in America. Their study, titled *Dynamism in*

Retreat: Consequences for Regions, Markets, and Workers, identified a number of ways in which the U.S. economy has become less dynamic and equitable. For example, in 1977, when the federal government first started recording the data, over 16 percent of all firms in the United States were less than one year old; by 2014, that figure had declined to eight percent. Similarly, the number of individuals employed in a new company peaked in 1987 at 3.6 million and has since declined to 2.5 million by 2014. This decline in new business formation coincided with a change in the corporate landscape in America. The share of firms age 16 years and older rose from 23 percent to 36 percent between 1992 and 2014; meanwhile, the share of total jobs attributable to firms age 16 years and older rose from 60 percent to 74 percent over the same period. Corporate profits also became an increasingly large percentage of U.S. GDP, rising from around 5.5 percent in the early 1990s to around 10 percent by the 2010s.

Why are these trends so alarming? The authors of the report contend that this reduction in economic dynamism (i.e., fewer entrepreneurs and startups) has significant negative effects for U.S. workers. Specifically, a less dynamic economy employs fewer people, has slower wage growth, and generates more inequality among workers. The first way a less dynamic economy impacts workers is that new firms are generally the source of new jobs; each new company creates an average of six new jobs in its first year, whereas established companies tend to shed more jobs than they create in any given year. The authors note that the U.S. economy launched 154,000 fewer companies in 2014 than in 2006; if the United States had launched the same number of startups, the labor force would have expanded by an additional 924,000 jobs in 2014 alone. Extrapolating this finding, the authors estimate the U.S. economy didn't create a net 3.4 million jobs between 2006 and 2014 because of the decline in entrepreneurism. The authors further point to the 3.3 percent decline in the labor force participation rate among people 25 to 54 years old as evidence that they have correctly identified the causal link. A decline in new companies may also contribute to declining wage growth since fewer companies are bidding for the labor. Finally, declining economic dynamism may generate economic inequality because a minority of people are employed by large incumbent firms that reap an increasingly large percentage of economic profits. Thus, declining entrepreneurism can partially explain the increase in income inequality in the United States since the 1970s.[xxvi]

While these trends are concerning, to what degree can we attribute the growth in student debt to the decline in economic dynamism and entrepreneurism in the United States? In 2020, the Ewing Marion Kauffman Foundation, a Kansas City based non-profit that focuses on improving education and encouraging entrepreneurism, published a short white paper arguing that student debt was a major impediment to entrepreneurism and new business formation. Specifically, young adults with student debt have fewer financial resources, thereby inhibiting their ability to save enough capital to launch a venture. Other young adults may believe that starting a business is too risky, lest they fall behind on their payments.[xxvii] These assertions correspond to what recent college alumni have reported when surveyed. In a 2015 Gallup and Purdue University survey of 29,000 U.S. college graduates, 12 percent of respondents who had borrowed up to $25,000 to attend college reported that student loans had caused a delay in starting a business; meanwhile, 25 percent of respondents who had borrowed more than $25,000 indicated that student debt had caused a delay in starting a business.[xxviii] These results corresponded to a 2016 poll that was conducted by the Young Invincibles, a Washington, D.C.-based advocacy group for adults aged 18 to 34. In a poll of young adults, 48 percent of respondents with plans to launch a business (or had already done so) indicated that student debt was an impediment to starting their business.[xxix]

In 2018, an associate professor and a Ph.D. student at Northeastern University decided to quantify the magnitude to which student debt impedes entrepreneurism among young adults. Specifically, how much debt must a former student assume before they decide not to start a business? To answer this question, the researchers collected data from the Survey of Consumer Finances, which is commissioned by the Federal Reserve every three years. In addition to the two figures most relevant to the survey—amount of student debt and whether someone in the household recently started a business—this survey also has other relevant datapoints including age, gender, race, income, education, and several more. The results of their analysis were statistically significant and compelling.

When incorporating all variables relevant to the propensity to start a business, researchers estimated that each $10,000 in student debt reduced the instance of starting a business by roughly 1.4 percent. Because only 19 percent of those in the survey started a business over each period surveyed, this suggests that student debt is a significant deterrent to entrepreneurship.

> "... researchers estimated that each $10,000 in student debt reduced the instance of starting a business by roughly 1.4 percent."

Interestingly, researchers also came across a highly relevant and statistically significant explanation regarding why entrepreneurs fail to launch their venture if they have student debt. Unlike earlier explanations suggesting that people who were making student loan payments didn't have the ability to save enough capital to launch a business, researchers found that the financial impact of a failed venture was likely the greater deterrent. Specifically, the cost to a person who fails to launch a business is significantly higher if the person has student debt. As discussed in Chapter 5, the Higher Education Act of 1998 rendered student loans largely nondischargeable during bankruptcy; all other forms of debt remain dischargeable. So, if two people are considering launching a business, the cost of failure for a person with student debt is significantly higher than the cost of failure for a person with credit card debt.[xxx]

How does this work in practice? Imagine that two people—Amy and Adam—are considering launching separate businesses. Amy has $40,000 in student debt, whereas Adam has $40,000 in credit card debt. Each of them saves enough capital ($20,000) to launch a small carwash business, both are current on their debts, and the interest rate on each of their debts is 10 percent. When they launch their businesses, they each elect to defer payments on their debt in order to reinvest as much capital as possible into their respective carwash businesses. After one year, both Amy's and Adam's debt has grown to just under $45,000, their original capital has been exhausted, and both are struggling to make ends meet with their respective business. Despite their best efforts over the next two years, both find they are unable to operate profitably. Both have seen their respective debts rise to $53,000, and both decide that they must close their small business. Adam, whose debt is exclusively credit card debt, immediately files for personal bankruptcy with the expectation of discharging his debt. Amy, on the other hand, after working for over two years to launch this business, has exhausted her $20,000 in savings and has seen her debt increase by $13,000. Following bankruptcy proceedings, Adam is able to move on to his next business venture, whereas Amy can be expected to see her life's trajectory permanently impaired by this failed business venture. Rewinding the clock back to the original decision of whether or not they should launch a business, we can expect Amy to be far more reluctant than Adam because the cost of failure would be so high for her. Since about half of new businesses fail within five years,[xxxi] Amy knows that if she starts a business, she has a roughly 50 percent chance of falling victim to a student debt trap that can permanently impair her ability to buy a house, start a family, or start a business later in life. Adam doesn't have that concern.

If this is a realistic scenario for young entrepreneurs, researchers at Northeastern University reckoned they could identify this in what statisticians refer to as an *event study*. In a 2019 paper titled *The Cost of Financing Education: Can Student Debt Hinder Entrepreneurship*, researches looked at students who had enrolled in college prior to 1998 (when student debt became nondischargeable)[3] and students who enrolled in college after 1998, in order to see if they would have different rates of business formation. Again, this is exactly what the data indicates. When controlling for all other variables, researchers estimated that the inability to discharge student loans reduced the rate of new business formation by 0.5 percent per year per household.[xxxii] That may not seem like much, but since few households start businesses and since business formulation is cumulative, a 0.5 percent decline in business formation per household per year is quite significant. In fact, this analysis confirms what we can discern and what surveyed entrepreneurs have indicated: student debt is a major impediment to business formation, which has potentially contributed to a reduction in U.S. GDP growth, lower workforce participation, lower wage growth, and an increase in economic inequality among workers.

Fewer Career Choices and Lower Job Satisfaction

If young adults feel compelled to refrain from starting a business because of their student debt, no doubt many feel compelled to take a job, any job, that will help them repay their student debt. This is exactly what recent college graduates regularly report when asked. In 2015, American Student Assistance (a non-profit organization that previously assisted in the expansion of student loans) released a report titled *Life Delayed: The Impact of Student Debt on the Daily Lives of Young Americans.* In this survey, 47 percent of college graduates indicated "the need to pay student loan debt is hampering my ability to further my career."[xxxiii] This figure is up from 11 percent in 1987 and 17 percent in 1997.[xxxiv] This upward trend in college graduates who are reporting that their student debt is negatively impacting their careers corresponds to the larger debt burden that students have upon graduation and the greater percentage of students who are graduating with debt. In addition to choosing to not start a business, the existence of student debt impacts people's career choices in a variety of ways. Some feel trapped by a career path from which they cannot deviate until debt is repaid. Others report they've entered their field of interest but have taken higher paying jobs at less desirable companies in order to more quickly repay debt. Meanwhile, others have chosen to avoid more interesting lower-paying public sector jobs and instead have taken jobs in the private sector. Finally, some people forgo graduate school in order to begin their careers.

---

[3] The Higher Education Amendments of 1998 eliminated the seven-year period after which student debt would no longer be treated differently from any other debt. As a result, for a debtor to discharge student debt he or she would have to pass the Brunner Test by demonstrating *undue hardship*, irrespective of when the debt was assumed.

In 2007, researchers at Princeton University took a crack at quantifying the impact of student loans and the choice of career paths. Specifically, they wanted to determine how large of an impact student debt makes on graduating students' decisions to enter high-paying versus low-paying jobs, public versus private sector positions, and whether or not they were less likely to attend graduate school. To do this, the researchers took data from an *anonymous* highly selective (and well-endowed) university that had recently phased in a "no-loans" policy; this policy offered financial aid recipients no-strings grants instead of loans. Researchers could then compare the post-graduation choices of cohorts of nearly identical groups of students while simultaneously controlling for whether or not members of the student body had student debt at graduation. Their results corresponded to what students regularly report in surveys. Specifically, the presence of student debt caused a significant increase in the number of students gaining employment in high-paying positions including consulting, finance, and banking. In fact, students were about five percent more likely to enter a high-paying field for every $10,000 in student debt. Conversely, students with debt generally avoided lower-paying positions in non-profits, the public sector, and education. The likelihood of entering one of these fields declined by about one-third for every $10,000 in student debt. The analysis didn't provide a clear answer as to whether or not student debt caused students to avoid graduate school (analysis by other economists have since demonstrated that student debt accumulated while earning an undergraduate degree negatively impacts attendance in a graduate school program).[4] Interestingly, researchers also discovered that student debt led to lower academic performance; students with debt had lower GPAs and were less likely to graduate with honors. Finally, the analysis indicated that students with debt were less likely to make a pledge (donation) to the university the first year after graduation.[xxxv] Who could blame them?

> "... students with debt had lower GPAs and were less likely to graduate with honors."

---

[4] See Malcolm, L. and A. Down, "The Impact of Undergraduate Debt on the Graduate School Enrollment of STEM Baccalaureates," The Review of Higher Education, 35:265–305, 2012. Zhang, L., "Effects of College Educational Debt on Graduate School Attendance and Early Career and Lifestyle Choices," Education Economics, 21:154–175, 2013. Fos, Vyacheslav, Andres Liberman, and Constantine Yannelis. "Debt and human capital: Evidence from student loans." Available at SSRN (2017).

Damaged Mental Health

To summarize, young adults who attend college today are more likely to take on debt and graduate with more debt than at any time in the past. As a result, they regret going to college, are more likely to move back in with their parents, and experience delays when it comes to buying a home, getting married, and starting a family. They're also more likely to pick careers that they don't want in order to repay their loans, and these young indebted adults are less likely to start a business. Furthermore, once they're out of debt and start a family, they're more likely to experience fertility issues. Somewhat depressing? Well, it's about to get more depressing; student debt is negatively associated with physical health and mental health, as well as lower psychological functioning.

In 2015, researchers published a paper in the Social Science & Medicine Journal titled *Student Borrowing and the Mental Health of Young Adults in the United States*. Like several other studies mentioned in this chapter, researchers utilized data reported by the NLS from the BLS. Specifically, researchers utilized survey data of people born between 1980 and 1984 who had enrolled in at least one college course by 2010. The survey data includes questions regarding self-rated health (4 = excellent, 1 = fair/poor) and psychological functioning (e.g., in the past month, were you nervous, calm, peaceful, depressed, etc.). Data in the surveys also included relevant inputs including educational attainment, employment situation, marital status, income, wealth, family's wealth, and more. The results should be apparent by this point in the chapter: Adults with student loans reported statistically much lower levels of self-rated health as well as poorer psychological functioning (i.e., more depression, anxiety, and other mental health issues). Interestingly, this study also demonstrated that people without a bachelor's degree also reported lower health and psychological functioning while active military personnel reported significantly better health and better psychological functioning.[xxxvi]

Since the publication of this paper, several other researchers have demonstrated a negative causal link between student debt and mental health. In 2019, three researchers at the University of Sussex in England utilized data from an unnamed British university in order to ascertain whether or not financial concerns predicted a deterioration in mental or physical health; these researchers also attempted to determine whether there was reverse-causality. Specifically, if initial levels of physical or mental health led to subsequent changes in financial concerns. As expected, statistical analysis demonstrated financial concerns, such as those attributable to student debt, led to physical and mental deterioration, while there was no evidence that initial health impacted future financial concerns.[xxxvii] Separately, in 2020, researchers at the University of

South Carolina and the University of Southern California thought to ask the question: If parents take out loans to pay for their children's college education, how does the presence of this debt impact the parents' mental health? By using data from the NLS, and examining responses from people born between 1957 and 1964 who had at least one child in college, these researchers found something interesting. Fathers tend to show a deterioration in mental health if they assume child-related student debt, but mothers don't show any such mental health deterioration.[xxxviii]

THE COST TO THE TAXPAYER

Clearly, the excessively large stock of student debt has caused an incalculable toll on millions of Americans. But, is that where the story ends? Unfortunately, no. As discussed earlier in the chapter, there are positive externalities associated with a highly educated workforce, which includes higher incomes, higher civic engagement, and reduced crime. And if recent college graduates regularly entered the workforce with little or no debt, then there would be few, if any, negative externalities. Unfortunately, that's not the case. In addition to a less dynamic economy with fewer entrepreneurs and less small business formation, publicly owned student debt is extremely costly to taxpayers.

There are two ways we can measure the cost of publicly (government) held student debt. The first is by estimating the amount of principal that will never be repaid when debtors default. The second method involves estimating how much in annual subsidies will be paid to debtors in the form of debt forgiveness, interest subsidies, deferred interest, or other write-offs. Keep in mind that roughly $1.6 trillion of student debt is held by the U.S. Treasury (as of 2022), and while the debt is a liability to the borrower, it is an asset to the entity that anticipates repayment (which is the government, and by extension, the taxpayer). So, how much of that $1.6 trillion debt won't be repaid? Unfortunately, the U.S. Department of Education (DOE) doesn't release that data. But, according to documents reviewed by the *Wall Street Journal* in 2020, the DOE worked with two external consultants and estimated that of the $1.37 trillion worth of debt held at that time, $435 billion (roughly 32%) will not be repaid.[xxxix] Given the increase of publicly held student debt, that $435 billion figure had likely crossed the $500 billion threshold by 2023. Ultimately, by 2023, taxpayers are going to be on the hook for half a trillion dollars in student debt—and that figure is growing by the day!

". . . by 2023, taxpayers are going to be on the hook for half a trillion dollars in student debt . . ."

What about the annual expense of the government loan program? As recently as 2019, the Congressional Budget Office estimated the total expense that is associated with federal student loans over a ten-year period would total $31.5 billion, which comes out to about $3.2 billion per year.[xl] That's not so bad, considering the 2019 federal budget was $4.4 trillion.[xli] But, since that time, the DOE has blown past their budget like a 22-year-old on a Las Vegas bender. According to the 2021 DOE Financial Report, total annual expenses connected to publicly held student debt reached $61.5 billion in 2019, $100.9 billion in 2020, and $93.9 billion in 2021. Of the $195 billion in expenses between 2020 and 2021 alone, $88.1 billion was Covid-related deferrals,[5] $57.9 billion was related to people enrolling in income-driven repayment (IDR) plans,[6] $20.3 billion was changes in *assumptions* for future repayments,[7] and $19.8 billion was reductions in principal due to disability of the borrower.[xlii] The nearly $100 billion in annual expenses are enormous and in line with other significant federal programs including housing assistance ($89.8 billion in 2021) or elementary, secondary, and vocational education ($90.5 billion in 2021).[xliii] In short, these expenses are real and material. So, if we believe college education should be subsidized because it creates positive externalities, the appropriate question is whether the $100 billion annual expense could be spent in a way that generates greater public externalities. Would we be better off as a society if the government spent an extra $100 billion on infrastructure, public parks, health care and medical research, or any number of other programs? It's not my place to answer that question, but rather to point out that the current system is egregiously costly to the taxpayer and should be evaluated alongside other major social programs.

---

[5] In 2020 and 2021, Congress passed several Covid-19 relief bills, which included the suspension of federal loan payments. As of the writing of this book, payments have been suspended through August 2023. The suspension of payments constitutes a loss to taxpayers since people can defer their payments without accruing interest.

[6] IDRs allow a borrower to pay the government a percentage of monthly discretionary income; in addition, after 20 or 25 years, the remaining balance may be forgiven. As of June 2021, nearly 8.3 million direct loan recipients were enrolled in IDR plans. The DOE currently estimates that for the 2021 loan cohort, the government will recover 44 percent less for loans in IDR plans as compared to loans in standard plans.

[7] These assumptions include length of time in school, future repayment plan, likelihood of repayment in full, default, forbearance, disability, or other developments that would impact repayment.

In June 2023, the U.S. Supreme Court blocked President Biden's executive action forgiving between $10,000 and $20,000 of student debt for individuals making less than $125,000 or couples making less than $250,000 per year. The rationale provided by the Supreme Court was that the President did not have the authority to discharge debt under the 2003 HEROS Act; this Act gave the Secretary of Education the ability to modify federal student loan programs during times of war or national emergency. Well before the Supreme Court decision, most legislators and legal scholars agreed that such an action would be an overreach and struck down in court. For example, then-House Speaker Nancy Pelosi stated in a press conference in 2021 that "People think that the President of the United States has the power for debt forgiveness. He does not."[i] Meanwhile, in December 2021, the U.S. Department of Education Office of the General Counsel composed an internal memo stating, "Congress never intended the HEROES Act as authority for mass cancellation, compromise, discharge, or forgiveness of student loan principal balances."[ii] Had student loan forgiveness gone ahead as initially announced, the U.S. Congressional Budget Office (CBO) estimated that the cost of this proposal would have been around $400 billion[iii] or around $2,500 per taxpayer.

So, what's next? Likely anticipating the Supreme Court's decision, in January 2023, the Biden administration proposed new guidelines for federal student loan income-driven repayment plans. The new guidelines would reduce monthly payments by more than half, stop the accrual of principal balances during repayment, and shorten the time until the remaining principal balance is discharged from around 20 years to approximately 10 years.[iv] What'll that cost? The CBO estimates that figure to be about $230 billion[v] or $1,500 per taxpayer.

---

[i] Adam S. Minsky. July 28, 2021. Pelosi: President Biden Does Not Have the Power to Cancel Student Loan Debt—What It Means for Borrowers. https://www.forbes.com/.

[ii] U.S. Department of Education, the Office of the General Counsel. 1/12/2021. *Student Loan Principal Balance Cancellation, Compromise, Discharge, and Forgiveness Authority.* https://static.politico.com/d6/ce/3edf6a3946afa98eb13c210afd7d/ogcmemohealoans.pdf.

[iii] U.S. Congressional Budget Office. 9/26/2022. Letter to Congress. *Costs of Suspending Student Loan Payments and Canceling Debt.* https://www.cbo.gov/publication/58494.

[iv] https://www2.ed.gov/policy/highered/reg/hearulemaking/2021/idrfactsheetfin.pdf.

[v] U.S. Congressional Budget Office. 3/13/2023. Letter to Congress. *Costs of the Proposed Income-Driven Repayment Plan for Student Loans.* https://www.cbo.gov/system/files/2023-03/58983-IDR.pdf.

CONCLUSION

There is no better investment that young adults can make than in their own human capital. An education has the potential to unlock an individual's capacity for excellence—and the more this occurs, the more we all benefit. Similarly (with a few exceptions), there is nothing worse that young adults can do than to assume excessive student debt. This debt has the potential to permanently impair their ability to reach their potential, and it regularly does. For tens of millions of individuals, student debt has caused them to regret college, delay a major life milestone, reduce job satisfaction, reduce entrepreneurship, and increase anxiety and depression. In addition, defaults and deferments have cost tax payers hundreds of billions of dollars that could have been spent on programs that have far greater societal benefits.

There is nothing inherently bad about debt; the availability of loans can ensure that people of modest means will have the ability to earn a degree that would otherwise be unobtainable. But the data is clear—students have taken out too much debt. It's bad for them and it's bad for the taxpayer. Past administrations who thought their policies demonstrated a "record of success" were woefully ignorant at best, and willingly complicit at worst. As we'll see in Chapter 7, while student debt is harmful to all who assume it, it's particularly pernicious among those who are in the most need of help. Specifically, student debt has contributed to an increase in the racial wealth gap. Stick with me and we'll see why that's the case, and then we'll pivot into what we can do to address these issues.

7

Disparate Outcomes: How Postsecondary Institutions Harm Minority Communities

The objectives for this book are to identify the causes of today's explosion of student debt, discuss whether the U.S. postsecondary education system is optimal as it relates to student outcomes in general and student debt in particular, and offer solutions as to how to improve the situation. But, no discussion of a system as large and significant as postsecondary education would be complete without a frank discussion of how various racial groups fare within the current system. While the primary objective of this book is to improve postsecondary educational outcomes, after reviewing this chapter, I hope readers will understand that we need to spend time thinking about how we can improve educational outcomes as it relates to race. Furthermore, before moving forward with any policy solutions, we should also ask ourselves the question of whether any proposed policy solution would exacerbate or alleviate racial disparities.

So, what are the racial disparities within postsecondary education? On average, minority students are more likely to enter for-profit schools, fail to complete the program, and assume more student debt while in college. Unfortunately, they are less likely to experience a material increase in earnings potential even after the program is completed and are more likely to default on their student debt. In short, Black students are overrepresented in every category of adverse postsecondary outcomes. To state the obvious—that's not good. Education should be a means of equalizing disparities and correcting for past errors. But today, it's not. Let's figure out why and what we can do about it.

STARTING CONDITIONS

In 1988, anti-racist and Harvard-educated university professor Peggy McIntosh penned a seminal essay titled *White Privilege and Male Privilege: A Personal*

Account of Coming to See Correspondences Through Work in Women's Studies that reflected on privilege. In it, Professor McIntosh identifies 46 ways in which her skin color offers her privilege, including: "I did not have to educate our children to be aware of systemic racism for their own daily physical protection," and "I can do well in a challenging situation without being called a credit to my race."[i] Following the release of this paper, educators have borrowed from Professor McIntosh's recognition of privilege and created *privilege walks* or *privilege races* whereby students take steps forward or backward depending on attributes over which they had no control. For example, students can take one step forward if one or both parents went to college, if their parents own a home, if they have two parents, or if neither parent has gone to jail. Students then take stock of their starting conditions before completing a race across a field, with the privileged students finishing the race well ahead of their less privileged peers. The objective of this teaching moment is to drive home the point that starting conditions matter, and that observation is certainly true when it comes to college outcomes.

Parental Financial Resources

Because student debt fills the gap between a person's ability to pay for college and the expense of college, the financial resources of parents and students correlate to a student's (and their parents) financial means. In other words, students whose parents earn more and save more generally graduate with less student debt. So, what are the factors that determine whether or not parents save for their kids' education, and if so, how much? These are the questions that Professors Natasha Quadlin (UCLA) and Jordan Conwell (University of Wisconsin-Madison) answered in their 2021 paper *Race, Gender, and Parental College Savings: Assessing Economic and Academic Factors*. These researchers used data from the 2009 High School Longitudinal Study, a survey conducted by the National Center for Education Statistics. In this survey, over 23,000 parents and high school students answer a variety of questions concerning race, college savings, previous academic performance, interests, and others. Follow-up surveys occurred (or will occur) in 2012, 2013, and 2025. With this data, and some savvy statistical analysis, researchers could tease out what the primary factors are that contribute to parental college savings.

So, what were the results? White families were more likely to save for their children's college education, and among those that did have college savings, White families saved more. Specifically, the percentage of parents (who had saved for college) of White boys and girls were 56 and 54 percent respectively, while the percentage of parents (who had saved for college) of Black boys and girls were 34 and 38 percent, respectively. At the time of the survey, among parents who had saved, total savings for White boys and girls were roughly $25,000 and $22,000, respectively, while savings for Black boys and girls were roughly $12,000 and $10,000, respectively. But, to what degree does race play a role in the determination of whether or not to save, and if so, how much? Interestingly, once accounting for all variables including economic (how much you make), family (married or not), and academic (how well do the kids do in school), the racial disparity of whether or not parents had saved for college fell away. That is, Black and White parents are equally likely to save for their children if the parents are in similar economic and family situations, and their kids are equally likely to attend college. However, the total savings among Black parents remained lower (by about $5,000) than the savings among White parents, with all other things equal.[ii]

Primary and Secondary Educational Financial Resources

Another dimension that is relevant to college student outcomes in general, and Black college students in particular, are the academic resources that are available to students prior to enrolling in a college. In 1998, Linda Darling-Hammond, president and CEO of the Learning Policy Institute, published an eye-opening essay on the disparate funding of schools as it relates to race. In her Brookings Institute paper, she asserted that "educational outcomes for minority children are much more a function of their unequal access to key educational resources, including skilled teachers and quality curriculum, than they are a function of race. In fact, the U.S. educational system is one of the most unequal in the industrialized world." She notes that while significant progress has been made since the 1970s, there is still much more to do. At the time of her publication, two-thirds of minority students were attending schools that were located in cities that receive significantly lower funding than neighboring suburban school districts.[iii]

So, what is the source of this disparate funding among school districts? In the United States, funding for public primary and secondary schools is a mixture of state, local, and federal support. The source of local revenue that can be allocated to schools is primarily property tax (72% of local revenue, as of 2016). As of 2019, nearly 45 percent of school funding came from local governments, and because local government revenue is tied to property tax, this means that the more affluent areas with higher property values are able to allocate a comparatively higher amount of financial resources to their communities.[iv] The practice of relying on local governments (and by extension, local property tax receipts) to finance public schools has been challenged in the courts on several occasions. In 1968, John Serrano (a parent and Los Angeles resident) filed a lawsuit against Ivy Baker Priest (the California State

Treasurer), alleging that the use of local funds for local schools (and the disparate educational quality that this entailed) violated the equal protections clause under the 14th amendment. In 1971, the California State Supreme Court agreed with the plaintiff thereby requiring the state government to take steps to equalize funding among students.[v] Other successful lawsuits that challenge the practice of funding schools primarily with local government revenue have been brought in other states, including Abbott v. Burk (New Jersey, 1991)[vi] and Campaign for Fiscal Equity v. the State of New York (1993).[vii]

These lawsuits implicitly required that the states provide additional resources to underfunded school districts in an attempt to bring about funding parity among students. But, how is parity measured? Should states spend an equal amount per pupil? Or, should special consideration be given to special needs students? Or perhaps non-native speakers? What about low-achieving or high-achieving students? The ambiguous guidance can provide *cover* for legislatures and their constituents when allocating resources among various school districts at the state level. So, how well have states done at equalizing funding per pupil? According to a 2019 study by EdBuild, a non-profit that investigates school funding—not good. In fact, they estimate there is a $23 billion annual funding gap between majority White and majority non-White school districts. In their 2019 analysis, EdBuild draws upon data from a variety of sources—including the U.S. Census Bureau's Annual Survey of School System Finances and the U.S. Department of Education's (DOE) National Center for Education Statistics—to calculate the average funding per pupil in majority White and non-White districts, by state. They find that the average student receives $13,118 of support per year; however, majority White districts receive $2,226 more per student than majority non-White districts. Of additional concern is that there is a racial disparity among poor White and non-White districts, which suggests that race rather than economic conditions is impacting state funding. Specifically, Edbuild calculates that poor majority White districts receive $1,487 more per student than poor majority non-White districts.[viii]

College Student Evaluation

Assuming a Black student is able to overcome the obstacles associated with being raised in a less affluent community, during the college admissions process, that student is more likely to face additional barriers than their White counterparts. The first of several barriers to entry into a college relates to the implicit assumption of the student's ability to pay tuition in full. Recall from Chapter 3 that the net price of tuition is well below the posted price, and an admitted student's grants are determined after a student is admitted to a program. While admissions are *need blind*, in reality, that's not always the case. So, how would wealthy students obtain an advantage over less affluent students during the admissions process if colleges don't ask about willingness and ability to pay the full (sticker) price? There are at least three clever tricks that universities use to bias their choice of student admissions toward wealthier students: (1) colleges recruit from wealthy areas, (2) colleges admit a large portion of students via early decision, and (3) colleges favor *legacy* students to *non-legacy* students.

In 2019, researchers at UCLA and the University of Arizona compiled data regarding the off-campus recruiting activities of fifteen prestigious public universities. Researchers utilized median household income (by zip code), the percentage of minority enrollment at high schools, and the size of the high school as predictive indicators as to whether or not a university would try to recruit at any given high school. If these universities' objectives were to build a student body that is representative of the population, then statistical analysis would not show a preference for affluent communities. Not surprisingly, that's not what happens. In their paper, researchers demonstrated that large high schools in high-income communities were significantly more likely to be targeted for recruiting by universities. In addition, many universities' recruiting efforts were negatively correlated (i.e., universities were less likely to recruit) with schools with large minority populations.[ix]

> *". . . large high schools in high-income communities were significantly more likely to be targeted for recruiting by universities."*

Separately, university admissions tilt the odds of finding affluent students by admitting more students via early decision rather than in their regular admission process. In 2001, faculty at Harvard's Kennedy School of Government analyzed five years' worth of admissions records from fourteen selective colleges and more than 500,000 applications. What they found was that the admissions rate for *early-decision* candidates was significantly higher than the general acceptance rate; the most dramatic was Harvard, with a 26 percent early-decision acceptance rate versus a six percent general pool acceptance rate. Researchers further estimated that the decision to apply early was worth the equivalent of around 100 points on the Scholastic Aptitude Test (SAT). Essentially, an early-decision candidate with an SAT score of 1,300 had about the same likelihood of acceptance as a regular-decision candidate with an SAT score of 1,400.[x] So, how does the process of favoring early admissions disadvantage minority candidates? The answer is simple; low-income students are significantly less likely to apply for early decision. According to a 2016 study by the Cooke Foundation, 29 percent of high-achieving students from families making more than $250,000 a year applied for early decision, whereas only 16 percent of high-achieving students from families with incomes less than $50,000 applied early.[xi] And why is that? Many low-income students are simply unaware of the option because their parents likely didn't attend college and therefore can't advise them, or their high schools lack guidance counselors. Some low-income students don't even learn about the early-decision option until it is too late, since in order to apply early, students generally need to earn an SAT score in their junior year of high school (or early in their senior year). Finally (and likely most prohibitively), low-income students generally attend colleges that offer the most substantial financial aid. Therefore, low-income students have to apply in the general pool so they can weigh their options and make an informed decision. In contrast, wealthy students generally are not constrained by the size of their financial aid packages, which enables them to utilize the early-decision process.[xii]

Finally, colleges tilt their student bodies in favor of more affluent students by showing admissions preference to legacy students (or students who had at least one parent attend the university). In 2009, Professor Michael Hurwitz at the Harvard Graduate School of Education assembled over 300,000 applications from thirty selective colleges for entry in fall 2007. Using statistical techniques, Professor Hurwitz calculated the likelihood of two identical candidates being accepted with the only difference being their legacy status. The results of his findings were similar to that of the early-decision findings; the odds of acceptance for applicants with legacy status is 3.1 times that of non-legacy students. So, why would colleges prefer legacy to non-legacy candidates? In general, colleges find that legacy students go on to donate to the schools in higher proportions. However, a 2010 study by the Century Foundation, an independent think tank in New York, suggests that legacy students are not more inclined to donate back to their schools after graduating. By running similar statistical analysis as Professor Hurwitz, the Century Foundation discovered that after adjusting for wealth, legacy and non-legacy students are equally likely to donate to their schools. Realistically, legacy students are more likely to come from wealthy families, and wealthy families are more likely to donate to schools. So, wealthy legacy students and wealthy non-legacy students will go on to make similar donations, while poor legacy students and poor non-legacy students will also make similar donations to their colleges.[xiii] Regardless of the reason, colleges favor legacy candidates, and as a result, minority students are less likely to be admitted to a selective college because they are less likely to have parents who also attended the same college.

Black Students and Enrollment Decisions

Given the disadvantageous starting conditions, it should be no surprise that Black students make different college enrollment decisions than their White or Asian counterparts. For children growing up in working-class neighborhoods, the notion that attending college is the rational next step after high school is not self-evident. So, what happens when Black students graduate high school? Let's find out.[1]

When and Where Black Students Enroll

Since 1972, when the National Center for Education Statistics (NCES) began collecting data on postsecondary enrollment by race, we can observe that Black students are less likely to enroll in postsecondary programs than their White, Asian, or Hispanic counterparts. In 1972, 44.6 percent of Black high school graduates enrolled in a program the following fall versus 49.2 percent of the general population. By 2020, overall enrollment had increased, with 57.5 percent of Black and 62.7 percent of the general population enrolling in a postsecondary program the fall after high school graduation.[xiv] So, while overall Black enrollment in postsecondary programs has improved in the past 50 years, the roughly five percent gap between post-high school Black enrollment and enrollment by the general public has not closed. Separately, the data indicate that the five percent enrollment gap does not close in the years after high school graduation. In other words, Black students don't tend to take *gap years* in disproportionately large numbers. In 2020, 35.8 percent of Black 18- to 24-year-olds were enrolled in a postsecondary program whereas 40 percent of the 18- to 24-year-old general population were enrolled in a postsecondary program.[xv]

Once Black students decide to enroll in a postsecondary program, we find that they make different selections (or have different opportunities) than White, Asian, or Hispanic students. For example, Black men and women are underrepresented at both public and private four-year programs. Of the Black men who enrolled in a postsecondary program as of 2016, 26.8 percent enrolled in a public four-year program versus 32.9 percent of the general male student population, and 13.7 percent of Black men enrolled in a private four-year program versus 14.4 percent of the general male student population. The breakdown is similar for Black women; 27.7 percent enrolled in a public

---

[1] Much of the data cited in this section comes to us from the National Center for Education Statistics (NCES). The NCES is a part of the U.S. DOE and is charged with collecting and aggregating data on public and private schools throughout the United States.

four-year program versus 30 percent of the general female student population, and 12.5 percent of Black women enrolled in a private four-year program versus 15.1 percent of the general female student population. However, Black students are significantly over-represented in for-profit schools. As of 2016, 12.6 and 17.6 percent of Black men and women enrolled in a postsecondary program were enrolled in a for-profit school, respectively, versus 6.5 and 9.2 percent of the overall male and female student populations.[xvi]

The over-representation at for-profit schools (and corresponding under-representation in other programs) is concerning. As described in Chapter 1, for-profit schools have poor historic records of generating graduates with good economic outlooks. On the contrary, there is a long history of these programs targeting the poor and poorly educated students with promises of a brighter future. In addition, for-profit schools generally experience higher attrition rates and poorer economic outcomes than their non-profit counterparts. Essentially, students who enroll in for-profit schools are more likely to drop out, take on more debt, and go on to default on their student loans. So, while I wouldn't advocate an elimination of for-profit schools in order to avoid these outcomes, the over-representation of Black students in these schools suggests that Black adults are more likely to experience poor postsecondary educational outcomes.

Separate from the type of institution (public, private, non-profit, for-profit), Black students are not equally represented among schools when viewed through the lens of selectivity. According to a 2019 report from the American Council on Education, which parsed data from the 2016 U.S. DOE National Postsecondary Student Aid Study, Black students remain significantly under-represented in *very selective* universities and over-represented in *minimally selective* universities.[xvii] But, to what degree is the type of school and the selectivity of a school a function of race or socioeconomic status and not simple geography? Asked another way, are Black people under-represented in highly selective schools simply because highly selective schools are located far away from Black population centers? Alternatively, are Black students over-represented at for-profit schools simply because for-profit schools are located in Black population centers? In 2020, Tomás Monarrez and Kelia Washington, research associates in the Center on Education Data and Policy at the Urban Institute, took a crack at answering just that. In their white paper *Racial and Ethnic Representation in Postsecondary Education*, the authors defined a *college market* as a radius around schools from which they draw students. For example, four-year colleges have a radius between 121 and 139 miles, while two-year colleges have a radius between 15 and 34 miles. Once establishing a radius, researchers could identify the racial breakdown of people within that radius and then compare enrollment to a school's racial *market*. And what were their findings? As of 2017, among for-profit schools, the college market for Black students is 12 percent of the population, but Black students comprise 26.9 percent of the student body, meaning they are over-represented by a factor of 2.2 times (26.9% / 12.0%). Conversely, Black students are significantly under-represented at more selective institutions. Among public colleges, the college market for Black students is 14.1 percent of the population, but Black students comprise only 5.6 percent of the student body; similarly, among private colleges, the college market for Black students is 13.7 percent of the population, but Black students comprise only 5.4 percent of the student body.[xviii]

What Black Students Study

As highlighted in Chapter 3, the economic value proposition of a college degree highly correlates with the area of study. In essence, not all college degrees are of equal value if that value is measured by future earnings. This is true even though students at the same four-year college often pay the same out-of-pocket expense for an engineering degree, a communications degree, or an education degree. So, why is this relevant? Another unfortunate truth that leads to disparate postsecondary educational outcomes among Black students is that they are under-represented in majors that confer high earnings potential and are over-represented in majors that do not confer high earnings potential.

This reality was highlighted in 2016 by the Georgetown University Center on Education and the Workforce. In their report titled *African Americans: College Majors and Earnings*, the authors noted that while African Americans represent 12 percent of the U.S. population, they account for only eight percent of general engineering majors, seven percent of mathematics majors, and only five percent of computer engineering majors. Among Black students who selected health care majors, students were significantly over-represented in the lower-earning medical administrative service studies and under-represented in pharmaceutical studies. Finally, Black students were over-represented in the lowest-earning majors, which include human services and social work, at 20 percent and 19 percent, respectively.[xix] In the years following this study, little has changed in terms of the preferences of study while in college. The U.S. DOE NCES regularly publishes (among other things) bachelor's degrees conferred by race and field of study. As of 2021, Black students remain significantly under-represented in science, technology, engineering, and mathematics (STEM) fields of study. Of total conferred degrees in 2020, 6.3 percent of those degrees were engineering while only 2.7 percent of graduating Black students earned engineering degrees.

Other notable fields with Black under-representation include biological and medical sciences (6.2% all students vs. 5.3% Black students), mathematics (1.3% all students vs. 0.5% Black students), and sciences & technology (1.5% all students vs. 0.8% Black students).[xx]

THE RESULTS FOR BLACK STUDENTS

Given the highly unequal starting conditions, it should be no surprise that Black students are over-represented in adverse postsecondary educational outcomes. In this chapter's introduction, I asserted that Black students are less likely to earn a degree (complete the postsecondary program), more likely to assume student debt while enrolled, less likely to experience a significant increase in earnings potential once the program is completed, and more likely to default on student debt. In the following paragraphs, I'll substantiate those claims.

Lower Completion Rate

Beginning in 1990, colleges and universities were required by law to gather and publish data on the percentage of students who graduate within 150 percent of the *normal* time for completion. In other words, universities had to disclose their program completion rate of students who graduate within six years of starting a four-year program, or within three years of starting a two-year program. Among the cohort of students who entered college in 2013, the percentage of students who completed a four-year program in four years is 45 percent among all students and 26 percent among Black students. Among students who completed a four-year program within six years, the completion rate rises to 63 percent and 44 percent among all students and Black students, respectively.[xxi] That's bad; but the overall completion rate for both Black and non-Black students might not be quite as bad as what is indicated by these statistics. This is because colleges report the four- and six-year completion rate of students who start and complete the program *at their school*, which excludes the students who transfer to other institutions and complete their studies there along with the students who are still enrolled and are making progress toward earning a degree after six years.

To fill the hole in this understanding, the National Student Clearinghouse (NSC) research center published a white paper in 2017 titled *A National View of Student Attainment Rates by Race and Ethnicity—Fall 2010 Cohort*. The NSC was uniquely positioned to fill this gap in knowledge because the primary business of the NSC is to assist colleges and universities with collecting and reporting student data to the DOE. By following students as they either moved to alternate institutions or maintained their enrollment (likely part-time) after six years, the NSC could test the hypothesis that minority students simply take longer to complete their degree or that they are more likely to transfer to other institutions to complete their studies. Unfortunately, that's not the case. Researchers identified the percentage of students who (as of 2010) had begun a four-year program, after six years had not earned a degree, and were not currently enrolled at the time of the study—31 percent of all students and 45 percent of Black students fell into this category.[xxii]

Higher Assumption of Debt

As detailed earlier in this chapter, on average, Black students face comparatively higher financial hurdles when entering and completing their postsecondary education. As a result, Black students are more likely to receive financial aid in the form of grants, loans, or both. According to data compiled and released by the DOE NCES, in 2016 roughly 64 percent of all students received financial aid, whereas 73 percent of Black students received financial aid. Fortunately, low-income students in general, and Black students in particular, seem to do a good job of applying for and receiving grants (which generally don't need to be repaid). Currently, 65 percent of Black students receive a grant while 55 percent of all students receive a grant. However, Black students are also over-represented among students who assumed student loans. Forty-two percent of Black students received a student loan in 2016, whereas 29 percent of the general student body did. Of note, the average grant and loan amounts for both all students and Black students were about $4,500 in grants and $7,500 in loans.[xxiii] The relative size of grants to loans suggests that our most needy students require larger grants, that our colleges need to reduce the cost of tuition, or both.

Given these unequal conditions, it should be no surprise that Black students on average assume more student debt (see Figure 7.1). As highlighted in Chapter 5, in 2016 Professor Judith Scott-Clayton assembled data from several sources and provided meaningful insight into the racial breakdown of student debt. Her findings can be found in the Brookings Institute paper titled *Black-white Disparity in Student Loan Debt More Than Triples After Graduation*. What Professor Scott-Clayton shows is that Black students have significantly more student debt than other ethnic groups, and of equal concern, at the time

	Average Total Debt ($)	Owes More than Borrowed (%)	Loan Payments >15% Income	Default Rate (%)
White	$28,006	17%	16%	2%
Black	$52,726	48%	23%	8%
Hispanic	$29,949	23%	18%	6%
Asian	$26,253	12%	17%	1%

Figure 7.1   Student Loan Borrowers by Race as of 2016. *Source*: Brookings Institution[xxvi]

". . . almost half of borrowers owed more to their lenders than their initial borrowed amount."

that she assembled her data, almost half of borrowers owed more to their lenders than their initial borrowed amount. This suggests that *at least* half of Black borrowers accrued interest while still studying, engaged in student loan forbearance (payments stop but interest still accrues), had missed payments and incurred fees, defaulted, or all of these. In part, due to this higher debt balance, a large percentage of Black borrowers have loan payments that exceed 15 percent of their income. This correlates to higher default rates among Black borrowers.[xxiv] Finally, the burden of student debt is particularly acute among young households. According to an analysis by the *Wall Street Journal*, among households with at least one college-educated adult in his or her 30s, 84 percent of Black and 53 percent of White households have student debt.[xxv]

High Instances of Default

The most complete analysis of student default trends comes to us from the Brookings Institute in a paper ominously titled *The Looming Student Loan Default Crisis Is Worse Than We Thought*. In this paper, Columbia Professor Scott-Clayton (the same person mentioned in the previous section) analyzed DOE data that followed two separate cohorts: first-time postsecondary entrants from either 1995–96 or 2003–04. Using this data, she could compare cumulative default rates by all relevant dimensions including type of institution (four-year, two-year, public, private, for-profit), degree obtainment, and race. Also, because she was able to compare two entirely separate cohorts (one from 1995 and the other from 2003), she was also able to ascertain whether the situation in terms of debt loads and default rates had improved or worsened over time. And what did she find? Well, as the title of the paper indicates, the situation is worse than we thought. Here are some of the highlights (or should I say, low lights?).

The cumulative 12-year[2] student loan default rates among all borrowers who did *not* attend a for-profit school were 8.1 percent in the 1995–96 cohort and 11.4 percent in the 2003–04 cohort. Said another way, if you entered a public or private two- or four-year program in 1995, 12 years later, 8.1 percent of your peers had defaulted on their student debt. In contrast, among Black students, the 12-year cumulative default rates among the 1995–96 and the 2003–04 cohorts were 19.5 percent and 27.9 percent, respectively. What if the school is a for-profit institution? In that case, the cumulative 12-year default rates among all students in the 1995–96 and the 2003–04 cohorts were 23.3 percent and 43.2 percent, respectively. Among Black students who attended for-profit schools, the cumulative 12-year default rates rise to 37.4 percent and 58.2 percent. In her paper, Professor Scott-Clayton also speculated that the path of defaults among the 2003–04 cohort may follow the same trajectory as the 1995–96 cohort. If that's the case, the total 20-year cumulative default rate of student debt among Black students who entered college in 2003 may surpass 70 percent! Professor Scott-Clayton described this finding as a "crisis."[xxvii] I agree.

> *". . . the total 20-year cumulative default rate of student debt among Black students who entered college in 2003 may surpass 70 percent!"*

Fewer Postsecondary Job Opportunities

So, once Black students enroll in a college program and complete their degree, presumably they have the same opportunities as all other college-educated adults? Sadly, the data suggest otherwise. In 2014, researchers at the progressive Washington, D.C.-based think tank, Center for Economic and Policy Research, analyzed data from the National Bureau of Economic Research to better understand postsecondary employment outcomes by race. Their white paper titled *A College Degree Is No Guarantee* highlights a number of concerning findings. First, from 1980 through 2013 (the years in the study), Black college graduates consistently had higher unemployment rates than all college graduates; in 2013, the Black college graduate unemployment

---

[2] The statistic calculates all people who have defaulted within 12 years of originally entering a postsecondary program. So, a five percent figure means that a total of one out of 20 borrowers had defaulted sometime within 12 years after entering a postsecondary program.

rate was 6.2 percent versus 3.9 percent among all U.S. college graduates. Similarly, Black college graduates had higher under-employment (employed at a job that did not require an advanced degree) rates than college graduates. The gap in employment opportunities between all college graduates and Black college graduates was widest at graduation, but fortunately closed by the time the workers reached their mid-30s. As mentioned earlier in this chapter, Black students are generally less likely to choose STEM majors; so, presumably, some of the disparate employment outcomes can be attributed to the student's field of study. However, even when normalizing for field of study, Black students have a more difficult time finding full-time employment in a field that required a bachelor's degree in their area of study. For example, among students who earned an engineering degree, 10 percent of recent Black college graduates and six percent of all recent college graduates were unemployed, respectively. Similarly, 32 percent of recent Black engineering degree recipients and 22 percent of all recent engineering degree recipients, respectively, were employed in an occupation that did not require an engineering degree.[xxviii]

> "... Black students have a more difficult time finding full-time employment in a field that required a bachelor's degree in their area of study."

A 2021 study conducted by the U.S. DOE's Institute of Education Sciences reaffirmed several of these concerning disparate outcomes. Titled *Baccalaureate and Beyond (B&B:08/18): First Look at the 2018 Employment and Educational Experiences of 2007–08 College Graduates*, this DOE report utilized survey data from roughly 14,700 college graduates. These college graduates agreed to participate in a *longitudinal* study, which is another way of saying *a study that tracks the same people over time*, and the data for this study was gathered 10 years after former students had completed their studies. Their findings showed Black bachelor's degree holders were under-represented in "positive" categories including home ownership (46.9% vs. 62.7% of all graduates) and having a retirement account (79.7% vs. 86.5%). Conversely, Black bachelor's degree holders were over-represented in "negative" categories including reporting negative net worth (37.2% vs. 20.1% of all graduates) and not meeting essential expenses in the past 12 months (29.3% vs. 13.6% of all graduates). Black degree holders also reported a higher percentage of utilizing student loans (85.9% vs. 71.7% of all graduates) and borrowing more than other racial groups ($51,395 vs. $32,116 median borrower among all graduates). Finally, Black degree holders reported having spent more time unemployed (9.4% vs. 6.5% of all graduates) over the 10-year period covered by the survey.[xxix]

So, why do Black bachelor's degree holders experience different postsecondary outcomes? The DOE study was silent on this, but the authors of a

2014 Center for Economic and Policy Research study took a crack at explaining these disparate outcomes. Authors of that study point to "a large and growing body of recent research documenting extensive, ongoing discrimination in the labor market."[xxx] The evidence cited includes the highly influential 2003 study by Devah Pager,[3] a former professor of sociology at Harvard University. In her study, two teams of male job applicants (one Black, one White) applied for similar jobs with identical fictitious resumes and criminal backgrounds (50% with and 50% without). Her findings were that White applicants were significantly more likely to receive a callback for the position, and a White person with a criminal record was more likely to receive a callback than a Black person without a criminal record![xxxi] A 2009 follow-up study focusing on entry-level jobs in New York revealed similar results—White men were more likely to receive call backs than Black men.[xxxii] Once on the job, Black employees may experience additional scrutiny in terms of job performance. In 2014, workplace consulting firm Nextions released a white paper suggesting that legal briefs that were prepared by Black associates were more heavily scrutinized by other lawyers.[4,xxxiii] Separately, a 2007 paper by the National Bureau of Economic Research that analyzed Major League Baseball data showed that when umpires and pitchers are of the same race, the umpire is more likely to call a pitch a *strike*. This suggests an unconscious bias on behalf of the umpire to favor same-race pitchers.[xxxiv] More recently, a 2019 study conducted by the Harvard T.H. Chan School of Public Health found that Black adults reported (via survey) higher instances of racial discrimination in areas as diverse as clinical settings, employment, and police encounters. Also of note, having a college degree was associated with higher instances of racial discrimination among the Black population.[xxxv]

> *". . . a White person with a criminal record was more likely to receive a callback than a Black person without a criminal record!"*

> *". . . having a college degree was associated with higher instances of racial discrimination among the Black population."*

---

[3] Devah Pager sadly died in 2018 at the age of 46 after a battle with pancreatic cancer. She was a highly influential researcher, writer, and public policy expert. Her seminal paper, mentioned above, was first presented during her doctoral dissertation in 2003 at the University of Wisconsin-Madison.

[4] The sample size for this study was small (53) meaning we cannot draw any conclusions that are statistically significant.

POLICY SOLUTIONS: BENEFITS AND SHORTCOMINGS

As highlighted in Peggy McIntosh's 1988 essay on privilege, and expanded upon by many others since, some groups are born with greater privilege than others. This uncomfortable truth impacts starting conditions, and those starting conditions impact outcomes. What does this mean in terms of post-secondary educational outcomes? Well, the data is clear: Students with two parents, have parents who attended college, have saved for college, and have attended high-performing high schools are significantly more likely to both attend college and have a positive outcome as a result. Therefore, if the objective is to ensure that college graduates (of all races) have similar outcomes across metrics such as amount of debt, educational obtainment, and career opportunities, then policies cannot focus on college alone and the time frame for reform must be measured in decades, not years. Further, because starting conditions matter, in order to achieve racial educational parity at the collegiate level, there must first be racial educational parity among high school graduates. But high school parity requires middle school parity, and before that elementary school parity, and before that preschool parity, and so on.

And how do we achieve *that*? The answer to how we achieve racial and socioeconomic parity across all relevant dimensions is well outside the scope of this book. In addition, remedies for workforce, legal, medical, and other areas of racial discrimination also will not be found here. That's a punt, but I bring this up to make a point—addressing current shortcomings in our college education system is not a panacea, and truth be told, may not always be ideal toward addressing all racial inequities in the U.S. But, highlighting racial issues in the U.S. can help, and the postsecondary reforms proposed in this book have the potential to be part of a broader policy package that is intended to achieve racial equality. So, while the policy proposals that you will read about in Chapter 8 aren't laser-focused on addressing the gaps that are associated with racial wealth and educational achievement, meaningful postsecondary reform has the potential to improve the educational outcome for all races—and that's a start.

College Reform: Contribution to Parity

As highlighted earlier in this chapter, Black students are over-represented in all adverse educational outcomes. Specifically, they're more likely to fail to earn a degree once entering a program, assume student debt, graduate with significant debt, and default on their student loans later in life. But adverse postsecondary education outcomes are not unique to Black students. All students, irrespective of race, run the risk of a bad outcome once they enroll in college. But if we were to construct a postsecondary system whereby everybody graduated and nobody assumed college debt, then Black students would disproportionately benefit from these reforms. In other words, an idyllic system whereby adverse educational outcomes are eliminated would most positively impact the currently disadvantaged groups.

While we will never construct a postsecondary education system whereby adverse outcomes are entirely eliminated, we can improve postsecondary outcomes with thoughtful policy solutions. The foundation of the reforms proposed in Chapter 8 involve incentive alignment among the government, universities, students, and other postsecondary stakeholders. In order to align incentives, all participants must share in the pain of an adverse outcome and all stakeholders must benefit from a positive outcome. That sounds good, so in practice what does this mean? If all participants have skin in the game, then universities will generally only accept students whom they believe will complete the program. Colleges and universities will also dedicate more resources to students who are at risk of failing to earn a degree, thereby reducing total attrition. Colleges and universities will reduce the number of offerings of majors and degrees that correspond to high post-graduation default rates; that means colleges will graduate fewer Arts & Humanities[5] majors but will graduate more STEM majors. Separately, price controls will end tuition inflation and gradually bring the cost of a college degree back within the means of a majority of American families. This will reduce the overall need to assume student debt. Finally, endowment reform will enable colleges with fewer resources to *catch up* with more heavily endowed schools, while heavily endowed schools will be required to educate more students in order to maintain their preferential tax treatment.

How does this benefit Black students? First, poorly performing colleges in general, and for-profit schools in particular, will reduce their overall enrollment. If institutions are adversely financially impacted when their students fail to achieve their stated objective (earning a degree that unlocks financial security), then poorly performing institutions will either reform or close. That's a good thing, and it would be largely driven by the schools themselves rather than a government bureaucracy. Why is this relevant? Well, even the

---

[5] According to the Education Data Initiative (a team of researchers that parses through large education data sets), the major with the highest default rate is Arts & Humanities at nonselective schools. Statistically, 26.3 percent of such students default on their student loans, as of 2021. See: Hanson, Melanie. "Student Loan Default Rate" EducationData.org, December 19, 2021, https://educationdata.org/student-loan-default-rat.

most efficiently run bureaucracy will have difficulty parsing the data,[l] and even if they could, there's no guarantee that such a bureaucracy would correctly identify and reform poorly performing schools via government mandate. On the contrary, the only way to improve the outcomes for students in general, and Black students in particular, is to ensure that colleges, universities, and lending institutions are all financially incentivized to work together to minimize adverse educational outcomes.

College Reform: Potential Problems

For every solution created by a new government policy, another problem is also created. Postsecondary education reform is no exception, and while my proposed policy solutions (which are revealed in Chapter 8) will improve student outcomes in general, they will not improve all educational outcomes. In fact, they may have the opposite effect in some limited cases. Let's explore that idea a little further.

Once colleges become financially incentivized to only admit students who are likely to complete the program, then they will only admit students who are likely to complete the program. Okay, that sounds obvious—so what's the issue? Unfortunately, this is where starting conditions matter. Black students are significantly more likely to attend high-poverty elementary, middle, and high schools.[xxxvi] In addition, on average, schools that serve high-poverty areas have less college-preparatory coursework available, a lower experience level of teachers, and students with less access to guidance counselors.[xxxvii] As a result, Black students are less likely to meet college readiness standards.[xxxviii] And all of this contributes to the lower completion rate of Black students.[xxxix] This is a very long-winded way of saying that Black students will face new and additional barriers to entry if colleges only admit students with a low probability of attrition. This suggests that a more comprehensive policy package that is aimed at addressing racial disparities should also include a carve-out for additional support for students who are at risk of college noncompletion.

An additional unintended problem of postsecondary educational reform might arise if colleges and universities are capped at the total tuition that they can charge. As highlighted earlier, White adults were more likely to save for their children's future college expenses.[xl] Furthermore, there is a sizable racial disparity among household incomes. According to the U.S. Census Bureau 2020 Current Population Report, the median Black household income is $45,870, whereas the median White and Asian household incomes are $71,231 and $94,903, respectively.[xli] As a result of lower financial resources in 2016, roughly 64 percent of all students received financial aid, whereas 73 percent of Black students received financial aid.[xlii] So, how might tuition caps impact students with lower financial resources in general and Black students in particular? In response to tuition caps, colleges and universities may choose to admit fewer low-income students in order to avoid offering financial aid packages. This adverse impact, however, might be mitigated if colleges and universities limit the *average* price charged to students and not the price charged to every student. I'll explain that in greater detail in Chapter 8.

CONCLUSION

The unfortunate truth is that America's colleges and universities are failing Black and minority communities. I am not assigning blame, simply because there's no need to. To improve the current situation, we should take stock of where we are today and look forward in order to identify how to make things better. Black students face hurdles that other students don't. On average, Black college students come from poorer communities and underperforming high schools, are less prepared to enter college, and have fewer financial resources to attend college. Once in college, Black students are more likely to attend poorly performing (and high-cost) for-profit institutions, fail to complete the program, or fail to earn a degree that will lead to a high-income job. Finally, Black students take on more student debt, and this debt becomes a major financial impediment. In totality, it is unclear if today's postsecondary education system is reducing the interracial wealth gap; in fact, it may be contributing to it.

So, what can (and should) society do? Well, the primary contributor to high college cost, student debt growth, and poor educational outcomes is a fundamental misalignment between students' and schools' incentives and objectives. Colleges and universities need to be financially incentivized in order to ensure that once a student leaves the program, that student has a brighter future than prior to his or her admission. Otherwise, postsecondary institutions—whether intentional or not—will continue to fail our Black communities. In Chapter 8, I will describe exactly which policies have the potential to better serve all students in general, and Black students in particular.

8

Policy Solutions: How We Fix This Mess

The objectives of good policy solutions to our student crisis are to align incentives so that the government, banks, students, and universities are all incentivized to realize the same outcome: creating a well-educated, debt free, highly productive, and equitable society. In this chapter, I'll explain how I think our legislators can do this. Truth be told, while most people I interviewed for this book agree that the current university system has problems, there was no consensus regarding legislative solutions. In 2011, Jeff Sandefer, an entrepreneur, former University of Texas professor, and founder of the Acton Business School, proposed seven "breakthrough solutions" to many of the issues described in this book. Several of his proposals included treating students like customers, de-emphasizing research, ranking faculty and treating them as cost centers, and introducing several other market-based mechanisms to align students and universities.[i] The response was swift and overwhelming—administrators, faculty, and some legislatures locked arms in opposition. Professor Sandefer, and several of his colleagues who had initially supported the proposal, were pressured to resign (and several did). When I asked Mr. Sandefer about the capacity for legislatures to come up with solutions to our current debt crisis, he responded, "I've seen very few good decisions emerge from a legislature, except voting to adjourn." I'm a bit more optimistic.

I've divided this chapter into three sections in which I review the current incentive structure for (1) universities, (2) endowments, and (3) lenders and borrowers; I then analyze both bad and good policy options through the lens of incentive alignment. In general, good policy solutions are prescriptive, tailored to each stakeholder, and ensure that incentives are properly aligned. Basically, with a good policy, every entity must make money when the outcome is a high-earning student and every entity must lose money when a student drops outs, earns a degree with little economic value, or defaults. Furthermore, good policies are not dramatically disruptive; rather, while the incentive realignment is quick, all stakeholders have time to adapt. This means that bringing down the cost of tuition and helping students repay their debt will not occur over a single two- or four-year election cycle; instead, good policies will take decades to fully manifest themselves. In contrast, poor policy solutions are quick wins that fail to address the underlying structure, incentive, or profit motive of the entities. In addition, proposals like *free college* or general debt forgiveness have the potential to further misalign incentives and only exacerbate the situation.

Let's see what our elected officials should (and shouldn't) do to solve these problems.

UNIVERSITIES

As detailed in Chapter 1, colleges and universities have a tacit societal responsibility to offer training that would enable their students to better produce goods and services of monetary value, as well as to offer training that would enable students to elevate society through advancements in the arts, sciences, religion, and public service. But, while university mission statements pay lip service to these noble aims, in general, administrators and faculty are not incentivized to achieve these lofty objectives. Rather, today's institutions of higher education are largely incentivized to do three things: (1) maximize university peer rankings, (2) maximize the school's financial security, and (3) maximize the happiness of all its constituents. In other words, universities and proprietary (for-profit) schools are not (directly) incentivized to produce graduates who have both the ability and means to benefit society, either economically or socially.[1]

Current Incentives and Outcomes

For better or worse, maximizing rankings in the *U.S. News & World Report*'s annual college rankings is top of mind for most, if not all, university administrators. These rankings impact applications, alumni engagement (and by extension, donations), and overall trustee satisfaction with the schools'

---

[1] In 2014, the U.S. Department of Education (DOE) implemented a *gainful employment* rule whereby all postsecondary institutions had to calculate and report the student debt loan payment-to-earnings ratio and student debt-to-discretionary-income ratio. Schools that failed to meet the required threshold were at risk of their students losing access to federal financial aid and of their students being unable to gain access to federal student loans. In 2019, the gainful employment rule was revoked and has not been reinstated.

administrators. As a quick reminder (from Chapter 2), aggregate scores for schools are based on nine dimensions:

- Graduation and retention rates (22%)
- Social mobility (5%), which is the percent of students receiving Pell Grants
- Graduation rate performance (8%), which is actual versus forecast graduation rates
- Undergraduate academic reputation (20%)
- Faculty resources including class size and faculty compensation (20%)
- Student selectivity (7%)
- Financial resources (10%), which is per student spending
- Alumni giving rate (3%)
- Graduate indebtedness (5%)

So, all things being equal, because universities are motivated to improve rankings, they're motivated to improve retention and graduation rates, admit students who will receive Pell grants, improve their reputation, reduce class size, increase selectivity (reject as many students as possible), and raise tuition. Wait—raise tuition? Yes, that's right. The *financial resources* component of rankings (10%) include an estimation of how much a school spends per student to educate them; this includes tuition. Only five percent of the rankings include student indebtedness. Therefore, raising tuition (all other things equal) will improve rankings. In addition, if raising tuition means more resources can be spent to improve academic reputation (by hiring high-profile faculty) or reduce class size (by hiring more faculty), then again, raising tuition to hire new faculty will likely improve rankings.

Next, universities are motivated to maximize financial security. This is not unique to universities; rather, it is foundational to the longevity of any institution. Also, like any business or organization, revenue and expenses will fluctuate over time. Most for-profit businesses have retained earnings (or equity) that ensure an organization can survive short-term periods when expenses exceed revenue. However, universities are not businesses with retained earnings. Rather, university revenue roughly equals expenses each year, and much of a university's expenses are fixed. Therefore, raising tuition is the most natural outlet for revenue shortfalls. The other potential source of revenue is an increase in endowment spending. However, as I'll discuss in more detail later in this chapter, universities are economically motivated to maintain comparatively low endowment payouts; so, current incentives indicate that raising tuition remains the *least bad* option to address revenue declines.

Finally, universities in general, and their administrators in particular, are motivated to maximize the overall happiness of each of their stakeholders.

And like any business, this diverse group of people includes more than just the customers (students). Rather, it also includes trustees, administrators, faculty, nonfaculty employees, and alumni. Each constituent has his or her own objectives with respect to school policy and operations, and only one constituent (the students) is directly impacted by tuition increases. As a result, cost of attendance is but one of several considerations with respect to a student's desire to attend a school. Other considerations include school prestige, accumulation of marketable skills, and overall experience. I point this out because cost (and by extension, tuition) minimization is usually not a material consideration for university policymakers, but it is a consideration for the stakeholders—including students, their parents, and to a far lesser extent, legislators and legislators' constituents. Besides, tuition is but one of several considerations that impact their decision to attend any given school. As a result, cost rationalization falls near the bottom of most university's list of priorities.

With this in mind, we shouldn't be surprised to learn that among all categories of goods and services tracked by the U.S. Bureau of Labor Statistics, college tuition and related fees have increased more than any other category since 1977. Figure 8.1 highlights those increases. The annual price increases of college tuition appears modest—only an average of inflation plus 3.2 percent per year. But, when compounded over more than fifty years, this has led to a roughly fourfold inflation-adjusted increase in the cost of a college degree. To be fair, household income has also increased over this period; but, the cost of a college degree has far outpaced increases in income. I calculate that the cost of college tuition and fees as a percentage of household income (among the 50th percentile or *average* household) has risen from 19 percent in 1969 to 42 percent in 2020. In other words, a college degree is anywhere from 2.5 to 4 times more expensive today than it was 50 years ago (depending on how you want to measure it).

> *". . . a college degree is anywhere from 2.5 to 4 times more expensive today than it was 50 years ago . . ."*

One policy proposal that has been considered, and continues to be, is eliminating tuition and related fees altogether for all but the wealthiest families. The *College for All Act* is a proposal that would eliminate tuition for public colleges, universities, and trade schools. It would also fund Historically Black Colleges and Universities. This act was put forward by former presidential candidate Senator Bernie Sanders in 2015,[ii] 2017,[iii] and 2021.[iv] In the most recent version of the policy proposal, the federal government would cover between 75 and 90 percent of the expense of college tuition and related fees,

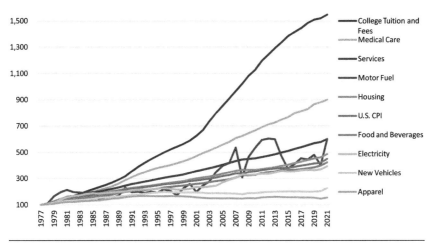

Figure 8.1   Historical Cumulative Category Inflation. *Sources*: U.S. Bureau of Labor Statistics and author's calculations.

with states covering the balance. To pay for this, Senator Sanders and several others also submitted a bill known as the *Tax on Wall Street Speculation Act*. This act would impose taxes on financial transactions, including stocks, bonds, and derivatives. An analysis by three economists at the University of Massachusetts Amherst estimated that this proposal could raise as much as $220 billion per year.[v,2] At the time of this book's publication, there has been no study by the Congressional Budget Office on either of these proposals; so, the total *cost* of these policy options remains unknown.

We've established that incentives among university and college stakeholders are not aligned in such a way that either cost control or educational value maximization are of pinnacle importance. For this reason, tuition has continued to increase at a rate well in excess of inflation and universities have been able to utilize tuition revenue to build increasingly elaborate facilities. Meanwhile, an increasingly large number of students graduate each year with degrees that do not enable significant increases in income earnings potential. So, does the *College for All Act* address the foundational issue, which is poor incentive alignment? Of course not. In fact, it exacerbates the problem.

If colleges could now send tuition bills to the federal government and not their students, then university cost control would be of even lower importance.

---

[2] I believe this paper is extremely (perhaps excessively) optimistic with respect to the calculation of tax revenue from this proposed policy. Little consideration is also given to the adverse impacts of this tax.

Colleges would immediately charge the government the absolute maximum per student allowed by law. Universities, now unfettered from any semblance of financial constraint, would further engage in an arms race of perks to attract top students, which may include more faculty and smaller class sizes; but it would also include nicer facilities, expensive field trips, and superfluous support initiatives. Separately, we could expect college enrollment to rapidly increase and its ranks to be filled primarily with students who should not otherwise be in college. Rather, these young adults would likely benefit from learning a trade or skillset. However, the prospect of free college would elicit a response of drawing in students who would not have otherwise attended college. Most of this incremental enrollment would include students who were unlikely to earn degrees that would confer higher earnings potential. As a result, colleges would likely respond to a surge in applications by capping enrollment, thereby limiting class sizes and potentially excluding students who would have earned a valuable degree without the perverse incentives generated by a *Free College for All* plan.

But, isn't college free in most European countries? And doesn't it work out great there? Well, not exactly. In the United Kingdom, college was (essentially) free from 1962 until 1998. In a 2014 study published in the *Scottish Journal of Political Economy*, the authors noted that despite generous government subsidies, the benefits of a free tertiary education went primarily to the wealthiest families. Specifically, among people earning a degree between 1981 and 1999, the percentage of the poorest students (lowest 20% in family income) rose from six percent to nine percent. Meanwhile, over the same period, the percentage of the richest students earning a degree rose from 20 percent to 47 percent.[vi] Separately, to reduce overcrowding at universities, Germany began charging a tuition in 2006, but was forced to eliminate tuition in 2014 following student backlash.[vii] Perhaps if we want to emulate a European model of tertiary education, Switzerland seems like an appropriate choice. In Switzerland, near the end of primary school (age 11 or 12) students are separated by ability and interest, then they are placed into one of two tracks. One track leads to eventual tertiary (college) attendance and the other track leads to an apprentice program. In Switzerland, roughly 70 percent of students matriculate to an apprenticeship program, while in the U.S., roughly 70 percent of students choose to enter a college program.[viii] Meanwhile in the U.S., over 30 percent of students who enter a public four-year program drop out;[ix] this suggests that 21 percent (70% × 30%) of young Americans would have benefited from a Swiss-like apprenticeship program rather than entering college.

Another potential policy solution falls at the other spectrum of the *Free College for All* proposal: eliminate all government intervention for student loans and public support for tertiary education. While this proposal is generally relegated to angry posts in various periodicals, it does have some merit. Specifically, this proposal recognizes that government intervention is at the source of misaligned incentives. As a result, eliminating government intervention will facilitate the eventual realignment of incentives; specifically, only people who are likely to earn a college degree that will confer higher earnings potential will make the investment in time and resources. Meanwhile, banks will only extend loans to students with a high likelihood of repayment. Finally, colleges that experience high dropout rates or produce graduate students who are unable to reap the financial benefit of their degrees will eventually close. Problem solved, right? Unfortunately, while this proposal will lead to a significant reduction in college education-related waste, it will also lead to a major reduction in the positive benefits from a highly educated workforce.

Economists use the term *externalities* to describe the side effect of an activity. Negative externalities involve things like a factory that generates air or water pollution. The factory owners benefit from producing and selling widgets; but everybody is harmed by the pollution (the negative externality). By contrast, positive externalities are positive side effects of an activity. For example, if a city replaces a freeway by placing it underground, and the city uses the existing space as a park, this project creates positive externalities. Specifically, nearby residents benefit from lower road noise along with the beauty and fresh air created by a park. Pivoting back to the topic, education is a prime example of a policy that has positive externalities, such as lower crime, higher civic engagement, more stable families, and higher tax revenue. These positive externalities would all be reduced if the U.S. workforce became less educated—as would be the case if all university-related government programs were ended. So, eliminating all government support for college students is also not a policy panacea. Fortunately, there is a middle ground.

Good Policy Solutions and Likely Outcomes

To briefly review, a good policy solution is prescriptive and ensures that incentives are aligned. We also know (from Chapter 5) that by the late 1990s, college became *too expensive* and was beyond the reach of most middle-income families. As a result, students turned to borrowing, which has led to the current student debt situation shown in Figure 8.2. We also know that universities are not incentivized to minimize costs and maximize the economic value of their degrees. Finally, we know that there are positive externalities to a highly educated workforce; therefore, to ensure that society receives those externalities, government intervention is appropriate.

So, what are we to do? Simple: cap the total cost that a college or university can charge its students. No doubt, some economists and most university

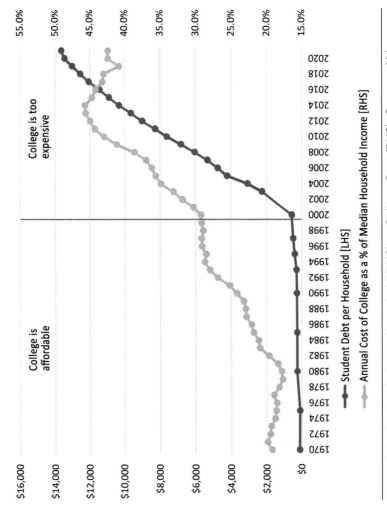

Figure 8.2 Student Debt per Household (LHS) vs College Cost (RHS). *Sources:* Urban Institute, College Board, U.S. Federal Reserve, U.S. DOE, National Center for Education Statistics, U.S. Census Bureau, and author's calculations.

administrators will find this suggestion appalling. But, a thoughtfully constructive price cap has the potential to both align university incentives while also ensuring that students have access to a high-quality education. Allow me to explain how I think it should work.

The maximum amount that a college or university can charge (all expenses including tuition, room, board, and other items) per student, per year, should be no greater than:

- Private schools—annual household income of the prior year × 40 percent
- Public schools—annual household income of the prior year × 20 percent

Here are the caveats:

- Consideration may be given to schools that operate in high-cost areas, such as New York or Los Angeles. In this case, the maximum expense may be no greater than 45 and 25 percent for private and public four-year programs, respectively.
- If a school currently charges more than the maximum allowable amount, current tuition, room, and board fees would be frozen (i.e., they cannot increase) until such time as household income has sufficiently risen and the cost to attend the school has regained compliance.
- Schools may continue to have higher "sticker prices" than the current allowable figure; this allows colleges and universities to charge some students a higher amount while charging others a lower amount. But, the *average* expense of college attendance must be in line with the aforementioned maximum price.
- Schools that are not in compliance with price controls would incur large fines.

Is this feasible? Well, the U.S. Census Bureau already calculates annual household income, while the DOE already monitors and regulates public, private, and for-profit universities. To pass the legislation, Congress need only include the price control criteria in the next passage of the Higher Education Act (HEA). As a reminder, the HEA was first passed in 1965 and has been reauthorized (read: amended) eight times since then.

So, how would the price to attend college change if this policy were adopted? From the perspective of students and parents, the dollar price of a college education would remain unchanged for about 20 years. After 20 years, the price

". . . the dollar price of a college education would remain unchanged for about 20 years."

of a college degree would begin to increase at a rate commensurate with the growth of household income. Meanwhile, for the next 20 years, the real price of a college education, as measured by the total cost to a household, would gradually decline. As shown in Figure 8.3,[3] in the 1990s college became *too expensive* and students began borrowing in order to fill the gap between willingness and ability to afford college. This problem continued to worsen for the next 20 to 30 years. In short, this proposal would take about the same amount of time to undo the problem as it took to get into this mess.

So, would this policy proposal mean that all colleges and universities would charge all students (essentially) the same price for attendance? No! In fact, we can look to a completely different industry to see how this policy has been successfully implemented elsewhere. The Department of Transportation National Highway Traffic Safety Administration was charged with setting an average fuel efficiency for cars sold in the U.S. Known as the Corporate Average Fuel Economy (CAFE) standard, this is the required fuel efficiency for cars sold in the U.S. Begun in 1978, the objective of this standard was to financially incentivize car manufacturers to produce and sell more fuel-efficient cars. However, rather than simply taxing less fuel-efficient cars, manufacturers had the option of producing a *fleet* of cars, some of which would be more or less fuel efficient. So, if the CAFE minimum was 20 mpg, a manufacturer would have three options: (1) 100 percent of their cars get 20 mpg, (2) 50 percent of their cars get 10 mpg and 50 percent of their cars get 30 mpg, or (3) some other mix. Car manufacturers that failed the test had to pay a hefty fine. So how effective has this been? In 1978, the CAFE standard for U.S. passenger cars was 18 mpg and the average fuel efficiency was 19.9 mpg.[x] As of 2021, the CAFE standard is 39.9 mpg[xi] for domestically manufactured passenger cars, meaning the average fuel efficiency has more than doubled since 1978, or alternatively, the average amount of gasoline that a driver consumes has been cut in half. Again, this doesn't mean that we all drive smaller cars; my wife's Toyota Sequoia gets 13 mpg city/17 mpg highway, while my neighbor's Prius gets 48 mpg city/53 mpg highway. Meanwhile, Toyota can average the mpg of both cars when calculating compliance.

This talk of CAFE standards seems random, so why bring it up? Well, universities and colleges (like car manufacturers) will respond to average price caps by continuing to charge wealthier students higher prices and less affluent students' lower prices. This won't change, and in fact, it may become even

---

[3] This graph should be considered an indicator of the future cost of tuition. The most material assumption (which is prone to error) is the future growth of household income. I assume that rate is +2.6 percent per year because this was the rate of annual household income growth for the 20-year period that ended in 2019.

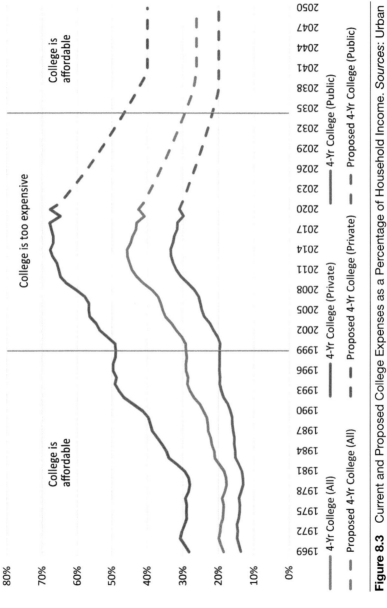

Figure 8.3   Current and Proposed College Expenses as a Percentage of Household Income. *Sources:* Urban Institute, College Board, U.S. Federal Reserve, U.S. DOE, National Center for Education Statistics, U.S. Census Bureau, and author's calculations.

more pronounced. I highlight the success of CAFE standards to demonstrate how thoughtful regulation can drive innovation and positive change over a multi-decade horizon. Establishing a CAFE standard equivalent for colleges will dramatically reduce cost (over time) while minimizing near-term disruption.

Criticisms of Price Controls—and a Brief Rebuttal

Measuring the cost of tuition (as it relates to household income) and proposing price controls are not new ideas. In 1998, the DOE established the National Commission on the Cost of Higher Education. In its seminal report, the Commission stated that it is "statistical gibberish to compare mean gross tuition with median income of all families." Oh, really? It is true that gross tuition expenses don't incorporate grants or scholarships; thus, net tuition is more appropriate (which is what I show in this book). However, using median family income is the *only* relevant metric when attempting to determine how much families can afford to spend on their children's college. The authors fail to suggest any alternative yardstick with which to measure college affordability.

The authors also claim that "price controls invariably stimulate demand and retard supply, creating 'shortages' until the controls collapse."[xii] This argument is so wrong it hurts my head. First, it is true that price controls can stimulate demand. However, haven't we already established that it is optimal to do just that? We know that a highly educated population produces positive externalities; so, we want to stimulate demand. In addition, by enabling students to assume overwhelming debts at age 18–22, the government is already stimulating demand for college education because students who otherwise would balk at the cost of tuition are still able to enroll. Next, the authors argue that price controls retard supply. This is only true in unique situations; if the controlled price of a product is set below the marginal cost to produce that product, then supply is retarded. For example, if the maximum price of a loaf of bread is set at $0.50, but it costs $0.60 to produce additional loaves, producers will stop producing bread. However, if the maximum price of a loaf of bread is $2.00, and it costs $0.60 to produce bread, the price control will not retard supply. For a real-world example, we can look to regulated utility companies in the United States that manage to profitably operate (with limited exceptions) by producing electricity or water at a slightly higher rate than their cost of production.

The authors also claim that "quality [would] deteriorate rapidly," if price controls were implemented. Perhaps. But the quality of what? If we measure quality by the number of A-list bands that perform on campus, the additional square footage of new student apartments, and the upgrading of lavish gyms, then yes, quality may deteriorate from the current country-club status of university perks. Conversely, if we measure "quality" as the percentage of students graduating with the ability to earn a salary that is commensurate with the economic cost of a degree, then quality is unlikely to decline. When conducting research for this book, I spoke with John Katzman, founder of the *Princeton Review* and two other educational technology companies. During our discussion Mr. Katzman argued that universities could reduce net tuition by around 25 percent without reducing engagement between students and faculty. The three areas of operational improvement he identified were: (1) increase in capacity (e.g., online learning and better use of the campus in the summer), (2) streamlining of administrative support, and (3) collaboration at scale. With respect to the final area, Mr. Katzman noted that thousands of schools wove together a variety of licensed and homegrown tech into their own "learning platforms," which were often expensive to maintain and of poor quality. By working together, universities have the potential to improve quality and reduce expense. Separately (and for full disclosure), Mr. Katzman wasn't fully on board with my suggestion that Congress cap the maximum net price of college tuition. He noted a "one-size-fits-all" solution rarely works, and passing a law with this type of mandate would take years to fully implement. Fair points.

ENDOWMENTS

As described in Chapter 2, endowments are permanent pools of capital (money) that generate income; this income is generally tax exempt as long as the income that is generated by the endowment's portfolio is used to support endowment or school operations. The notion that educational institutions should have permanent pools of capital that enjoy a tax-exempt status can be traced back to the 1800s. No doubt, the individuals who crafted the legislation as well as donated their wealth to institutions of higher education were well intended. In addition, it is likely that these endowments have, over time, contributed to the growth and maturation of many elite educational institutions in America. Societal and individual good has certainly come of both donations to endowments as well as the favorable tax treatment. However, now that we have run the experiment for nearly 150 years of enabling universities to grow tax exempt and distribute their earnings, we can determine if the current system is *optimal*.

What is optimal? I define optimal policies as policies that financially incentivize endowments (and the universities which they support) to contribute to the creation of a well-educated, debt-free, highly productive, equitable society. So, are endowments incentivized to do this? Asked another way, are endowments penalized when universities fail to produce well-educated, highly productive graduates? Conversely, are endowments rewarded when universities produce debt-free students or contribute to the reduction of intergenerational poverty? Sadly, no.

Current Incentives and Outcomes

Both endowments and the universities they support have perpetual horizons. As a result, the primary objectives for endowments are to grow to perpetuity while also generating revenue that can be used during current school years. For these reasons, endowment payouts are set to ensure that their capital base may continue to grow while the income they throw off is of relevance to the school. According to surveys, endowment payments are generally around four percent of assets, while target return rates are around 7 to 7.5 percent,[xiii] per year. The difference between their return and their payout is the rate at which the endowment can grow, even if there are no other contributions by alumni or other donors.

Of relevance to our discussion of (mis)aligned incentives is the fact that endowments benefit from preferential tax treatment. Specifically, income and capital gains that are generated by endowments, with a few exceptions,[4] are not taxed. In addition, there is essentially no upper limit on preferential tax treatment, which means that in the distant future, all publicly traded companies, all commercial buildings, and all farmland may be (theoretically) owned exclusively by university endowments. Furthermore, the nature of preferential tax treatment for endowments creates a perverse incentive well outside the intent of legislators' intent. Specifically, current tax code encourages endowments to grow (because the implicit tax subsidy grows), while the universities are encouraged to shrink (or at most, grow slowly). That seems absurd—but, it's clearly the case, as shown in Figure 8.4. In the 1986–87 school year, the fall student body enrollment among all Ivy League schools was roughly 60,000 students. Meanwhile, the aggregate endowment of all of those same schools was $11.3 billion the same year. By 2020, the Ivy League undergraduate student body had grown to roughly 63,000 (a 5% increase), while the aggregate

---

[4] The 2017 Tax Cuts and Jobs Act imposed a 1.4 percent tax on endowment investment income. This tax applies to institutions with greater than 500 students and an endowment equal to at least $500,000 per student. This 1.4 percent tax is still well below the federal capital gains tax for high earners (20 percent) or the tax bracket for ordinary income (which includes interest income) for high earners (37 percent).

	Undergraduate Students		Endowment ($Million)		Change (%)	
	1986–1987	2020–2021	1986–1987	2020–2021	Students	Endowment
Brown University	5,747	6,792	$357	$4,377	18%	1127%
Columbia University	5,790	8,148	$1,387	$11,257	41%	712%
Cornell University	12,622	14,743	$540	$6,883	17%	1174%
Dartmouth College	3,583	4,170	$535	$5,975	16%	1017%
Harvard University	10,394	8,527	$3,850	$41,894	–18%	988%
Princeton University	4,667	4,774	$1,892	$25,944	2%	1271%
University of Pennsylvania	11,722	11,155	$649	$14,877	–5%	2194%
Yale University	5,291	4,703	$2,111	$31,202	–11%	1378%
All Ivy League Colleges	59,816	63,012	$11,321	$142,410	5%	1158%

Figure 8.4 Ivy League Undergraduate Student Body, Endowment Size, and 33-Year Change. *Sources:* National Center for Education Statistics, Integrated Postsecondary Education Data System, Digest of Education Statistics, univstats.com, https://irp.dpb.cornell.edu/, and author's calculations.

> *"If the number of undergraduate students who were educated at Ivy League schools grew at the same rate as their endowments . . . Ivy League undergraduate population would be roughly 690,000 students (rather than 63,000 students)."*

endowment of the same schools had grown to $139 billion (a 1,158% increase). If the number of undergraduate students who were educated at Ivy League schools grew at the same rate as their endowments for the 33-year period that ended in 2020, the fall Ivy League undergraduate population would be roughly 690,000 students (rather than 63,000 students).

So, what does current tax policy mean in terms of the endowment per student, and even more important, the tax subsidy per student? Figure 8.5 shows that in 1986 the average endowment per student attending an Ivy League college was $189,000, ranging from a low of $43,000 (Cornell) to a high of $405,000 (Princeton). Meanwhile, in 2020 the average Ivy League endowment was over $2 million per student. At Princeton and Yale, the average endowment per undergraduate student was $5.4 million and $6.6 million, respectively. We can also combine the endowment per student estimate, with reasonable assumptions of endowment return, to estimate the per student tax subsidy.[5] In 1986, I estimate that the average tax subsidy (in forgone taxes) to Ivy League schools per undergraduate student was $3,761. Thirty-three years later, the average tax subsidy to Ivy League schools per undergraduate student had grown to $40,890. Even more disheartening was the average annual subsidy to Princeton and Yale for their undergraduates: $94k and $101k, respectively. In short, because there is no cap on tax subsidies per student, the most heavily endowed schools are receiving extremely generous tax subsidies. So, the schools that need the subsidies the least, get the most.

> *". . . the schools that need the subsidies the least, get the most."*

The final outcome that results from current tax policy is that endowment wealth has and will continue to become increasingly concentrated in a small handful of institutions. As shown in Figure 8.6, the wealthiest four institutions

---

[5] I assume that annual endowment portfolio return was eight percent and the tax rate that would have been applied was 25 percent. I chose eight percent because the average endowment return for the 10-year period ended June 30, 2020, was 7.9 percent among large endowments (*Source:* 2020 NACUBO-TIAA Study of Endowments). I chose a tax rate of 25 percent as a reasonable blend of the long-term capital gains tax rate (20 percent) and the top marginal federal income tax rate (37 percent) among top earners.

	Endowment ($K) per Student		Tax Subsidy per Student	
	1986–1987	2020–2021	1986–1987	2020–2021
Brown University	$62	$645	$1,241	$12,890
Columbia University	$240	$1,382	$4,791	$27,631
Cornell University	$43	$467	$856	$9,337
Dartmouth College	$149	$1,433	$2,986	$28,658
Harvard University	$370	$4,913	$7,408	$98,263
Princeton University	$405	$5,434	$8,108	$108,690
University of Pennsylvania	$55	$1,334	$1,107	$26,674
Yale University	$399	$6,634	$7,980	$132,688
All Ivy League Colleges	$189	$2,260	$3,785	$45,201

Figure 8.5   Ivy League Endowment and Tax Subsidy per Student Over a 33-Year Period. *Sources*: National Center for Education Statistics, Integrated Postsecondary Education Data System, Digest of Education Statistics, and author's calculations.

Institutions (#)	Endowment ($Bn)	Institutions (%)	Endowment (%)
4	$128.0	0.1%	21.4%
20	$291.6	0.5%	48.7%
40	$399.1	1.0%	66.7%
120	$442.6	3.0%	74.0%
Bottom 3,862	$155.7	97.0%	26.0%
All Institutions	$598.3	100.0%	100.0%

Figure 8.6   Endowment Concentration as of 2020. *Sources*: National Center for Education Statistics and author's calculations.

(Harvard, Yale, Stanford, and Princeton), are 0.1 percent of degree-granting postsecondary institutions, yet they control 21.4 percent of endowment wealth. Similarly, the top 40 institutions (1% of institutions) control 66.7 percent of endowment wealth. Meanwhile, the bottom 97 percent of institutions (3,862 institutions) control only 26.0 percent of endowment wealth. How has this happened? Well, there is a *virtuous cycle* described by former Yale Endowment Chief Investment Officer David Swenson that involves endowments generating income—which make universities more desirable and attracts students who, later in their careers, donate to their schools (and endowments).[xiv] But, for every school that benefits from this virtuous cycle, there are dozens (if not hundreds) that are harmed by having their top faculty or prospective students lured to other schools. As a result of this brain drain, the wealthiest schools are able to maintain their elite status to the detriment of endowment-poor schools. The current tax system perpetuates this inequity because there is no limit to the tax benefits that wealthy schools receive.

Bad Policy Solutions and Likely Outcome

How do we prevent endowments from becoming increasingly concentrated in a small group of elite institutions? One policy option first considered in 1977 and reconsidered in 2008 by the chairman to the Senate Finance Committee, Chuck Grassley, is requiring endowments to pay out a minimum amount every year.[xv] A commonly cited payout proposal is five percent, which is similar to foundations' average payouts. This policy is intended to prevent an "unreasonable accumulation of taxpayer-subsidized funds" among the country's wealthiest endowments.[xvi] In addition, should endowments be forced to pay out higher proportions, these unlocked yearly payouts could be utilized to reduce student tuition.

Unfortunately, this policy proposal has several limitations. First, enforcing a mandatory distribution rate is unlikely to generate significant additional revenue that can be used to support less well-endowed universities (i.e., the lower 97 percent). Second, because this policy proposal would apply to all university endowments, irrespective of their endowment size in aggregate or endowment size per full-time student, this policy is unlikely to lead to redistribution of endowment wealth from larger endowments to smaller endowments. Third, universities generally distribute, on average, 4.5 percent[xvii] of their endowment each year. So, the increase in distributions of 0.5 percent will likely not move the needle. Finally, universities generally engage in policies they perceive to be in their best interest. Overlaying a mandatory distribution rate therefore may not lead to lowering tuition rates; rather, universities may opt to build more lavish buildings, hire more administrators, and increase salaries for their staff.

Another creative policy proposal to address both endowment and tuition growth is to apply a special *endowment tax* should a university raise tuition at a rate faster than inflation.[xviii] This proposal has some advantages; it is simple and better aligns university incentives with those of their students. However, this proposal also comes with a whole host of other problems. First, this proposal doesn't differentiate between heavily endowed and lightly endowed schools. Therefore, this proposal will not, over time, address the inequity associated with some schools that currently benefit from the lion's share of university endowment assets. Second, the proposed tax shows no consideration to the size of endowments per full-time student. As a result, this proposal will not motivate heavily endowed schools to increase their enrollment. Third, the proposal is a disadvantage to schools that currently have low tuition rates versus their peers; a school with a tuition rate far below the average rate will experience taxes as it raises tuition to its peer average, while schools with tuition rates far above its peer average rate will experience no such taxes unless its tuition growth rate exceeds that of inflation.

A variate of the endowment tax was put forward in 2015 by Jorge Klor de Alva, President of the Nexus Research and Policy Center and former president of the University of Phoenix. In a policy paper titled *Rich Schools, Poor Students: Tapping Large University Endowments to Improve Student Outcomes*, the authors propose an annual excise tax that begins at 0.5 percent per year for endowments $500 million or larger, and increasing to up to 2 percent for endowments that are larger than $3 billion.[xix] This proposal does solve some issues—it favors smaller endowments, providing them the opportunity to catch up over time. In addition, the taxes raised would likely have (as the authors point out) "vastly more bang for our buck" if utilized to provide grants to needy students. However, this tax does not vary by the size of the school's student body. In other words, a $1 billion endowment to a school with 1,000 students is a lot; but if the school has 50,000 students, a $1 billion endowment isn't all that much. As a result, the unintended consequence is that this excise tax would encourage heavily endowed schools to shrink their student body, allowing them to become even more elite.

One final policy proposal is to simply do nothing. Beginning in 2017, the federal government imposed a 1.4 percent tax on endowments' investment income. This tax applies to institutions with greater than 500 students and an endowment greater than $500,000 per student. As a result, the problem of endowment wealth concentration has been addressed and it will simply take time for wealth to be redistributed owing to this new and progressive tax rate. However, this law has deficiencies both in its wording and its design. First, the law states that the tax does not apply to income from assets that "are used directly in carrying out the institutions' exempt purpose." This language is confusing and needs clarification. Furthermore, this exemption seems to enable universities to classify significant portions of income as being used for an exempt purpose, thereby nullifying the tax. Second, as highlighted by Sandy Baum and Victoria Lee at the Urban Institute, the tax has significant "cliff effects." Specifically, the tax is applied to institutions that have endowments in excess of $500,000 per full-time enrolled student; therefore, a university with an endowment equal to $500,001 per student will pay a (potentially large) tax whereas an endowment with $499,999 per student will remain tax exempt.

Furthermore, this tax applies to universities with 500 or more students; so, schools with 499 are exempt regardless of the size of their endowments.[xx] Finally, a 1.4 percent tax is far too low to motivate universities to materially alter their behaviors. It's a *token tax* and if we hope to redistribute wealth among the most elite universities, generate tax revenue, and fully align university incentives with those of the students and taxpayers, the 1.4 percent tax isn't enough. Rather, the loss of a tax-exempt status (above or below a certain threshold) has the potential to be a major part of a basket of solutions to our current student-debt crisis.

Good Policy Solutions and Likely Outcomes

So how do we align tax incentives such that: (1) wealth doesn't become excessively concentrated in a small handful of schools and (2) well-endowed schools utilize their endowment income by expanding their student body? Simple: cap the total portion of a university endowment that is tax exempt. Like capping the total college tuition and expenses, some schools will find this suggestion appalling. But, let's be real; if a small state school can educate a young adult for $10k/yr, does Harvard really need a $100k/yr per student tax subsidy to continue to operate? Here's how the endowment cap would work:

- The maximum size of a university endowment that is tax-exempt is equal to $500,000 per full-time student, which includes both undergraduate and graduate students.
- The tax-exempt cap (starting at $500,000) is reset higher each year by an amount equal to the Core CPI (inflation index).
- The percentage of the endowment that exceeds the cap loses its tax-exempt status and becomes taxable.
- The portfolio return generated by the taxable percentage of the endowment is subject to normal capital gains (20% rate) and income tax rate (37%).

That's a lot to wrap your head around; so, I'll include a couple of examples. Imagine a hypothetical well-endowed college with an endowment of $1.5 billion and only 2,000 full-time enrolled students. The total size of the endowment is $750k per student ($1.5bn/2k). Imagine further that the portfolio returns eight percent in a year. What happens? Well, because the school's endowment is above its maximum size per full-time student, it will pay roughly $10 million in capital gains and income taxes. The faculty, keen to avoid these taxes, may look to increase their student body. As shown in Figure 8.7, had the student body been 3,000 students, the endowment would have been $500k

Full-Time Enrolled Students	Endowment ($Bn)	Max Endowment ($Bn)	Endowment Subject to Taxes ($Bn)	Endowment/ Student ($k)	Tax[1]
2,000	$1.5	$1.0	$0.5	$750	$10,000,000
2,500	$1.5	$1.3	$0.3	$600	$5,000,000
3,000	$1.5	$1.5	$—	$500	$—
4,774	$25.9	$2.4	$23.5	$5,425	$470,260,000
51,800	$25.9	$25.9	$—	$500	$—

Figure 8.7 Hypothetical University Size, Endowment, and Taxable Income. *Figure note 1*: Assumes the portfolio returns eight percent in a year. The taxable portion of the endowment is then subjected to blended capital gains and an ordinary income tax rate of 25 percent.

per student, and so the university endowment would have avoided the $10 million in taxes. What about the elite of the elite—what would their tax bill look like? In 2020–21, Princeton had 4,774 full-time undergraduate and graduate students, while its endowment was $25.9 billion. At roughly $5.4 million per student, its endowment is well above the tax-exempt limit. As a result, if its endowment had also generated an eight percent annual return (which is appreciation of its endowment by $2.07 billion), Princeton would have been hit with a $470 million tax bill. In order to avoid similar tax bills in the future, Princeton would need to either shed 85 percent of its endowment, or grow its student body to around 52,000 students (about the size of my alma mater, the University of Southern California).

Is this feasible? Yes, but any change to this tax policy would also require changes to IRS regulations, which would require congressional approval. The IRS, in collaboration with the DOE, would be charged with ensuring compliance and calculating penalties. No doubt, the initial reaction of the most heavily endowed universities would be to protest and claim that this proposal is an existential threat to their ability to offer a superior educational experience. But, should those protests fall on deaf ears, the next response by the most heavily endowed universities would likely be to increase the size of their full-time enrolled student population. This would be a good thing. As discussed earlier, elite universities currently have a perverse incentive to minimize their acceptance rate, thereby improving rankings as well as the tax subsidy per student. If heavily endowed universities are now financially incentivized to increase their student body (or suffer a tax), eventually, several will. From the perspective of less heavily endowed universities, this new tax policy would enable them to close the monetary gap

"Current tax policy heavily favors well-endowed universities; this new approach would level the playing field over time."

between their programs and the most elite programs. Current tax policy heavily favors well-endowed universities; this new approach would level the playing field over time.

Criticisms of Endowment Reform—and a Brief Rebuttal

As mentioned, there is no doubt that Harvard, Yale, Princeton, and others would oppose capping the tax-exempt portion of their endowments. How dare we suggest that the richest institutions in the world pay their *fair share*! In the previous example of the impact to Princeton, it's more than $2bn year-over-year appreciation in its endowment would fall to *only* $1.6bn—that's highway robbery! I think you catch my drift.

Another potentially more palatable argument against endowment reform is that this would neither lead to lower tuition prices nor lower student debt levels. This is because there's no clear link between the endowment tax status at Yale and a person at a state college assuming $40,000 in debt prior to graduation. This may be somewhat true when this proposed policy is viewed in isolation. But, arguing that an elite college's tax status doesn't impact the broader university system ignores both the interconnectedness of the American university system as well as the impact that this policy will have over time. So, in what way are they interconnected? Ivy League colleges currently educate around 63,000 undergraduate students (in aggregate) per year, while in 2020, there were roughly 16.7 million full-time enrolled undergraduate students in the United States. Motivated to avoid large endowment taxes, should (however unlikely) the Ivy League expand enrollment from 68,000 to 680,000 students, the percentage of U.S. students educated by the Ivy League would increase from 0.4 percent to over 4 percent.

This sizable shift in the U.S. student body is a good thing because more students would receive their education at schools with more resources. Meanwhile, over time, other universities' endowments per student will continue to grow tax-exempt, and more schools will reach the $500,000 (plus inflation adjustment) per student limit. These heavily endowed schools will also feel pressure to expand their student body to avoid endowment taxes once they reach the per-student tax-exempt maximum size. Finally, the less heavily endowed schools will have an opportunity to catch up to the more heavily endowed universities—both in terms of the size of their endowments as well as in terms of annual donations from alumni. In the earlier hypothetical example where the Princeton endowment earned an eight percent pre-tax return and a six percent post-tax return, a vast majority of all university endowments would still earn an eight percent return. This two percent incremental return for less-endowed universities might seem insignificant for a single year. However, due to the power of compounding, this marginal difference in return will be extremely significant when measured over a period of several generations.

LENDERS (BANKS AND THE GOVERNMENT) AND BORROWERS (STUDENTS AND THEIR PARENTS)

In most instances lenders and borrowers regularly agree to mutually beneficial terms. Borrowers, such as homebuyers or small business owners, borrow cash, while banks lend that cash. The price of borrowing is the interest rate of the loan, and borrowers often pledge collateral (a house, a car, or other asset) in order to assure that the bank will not incur a major loss should the borrower default. This process of borrowers and lenders transacting is at the foundation of our modern economy. However, when the borrower lacks a credit history, has no collateral to pledge, and their ability to repay is uncertain, lending stops. We can assume it has always been with the best intentions that the government intervened in order to lessen the risk to banks and unlock the borrowing ability of students. However, good intentions may still lead to misaligned incentives and bad outcomes. Fortunately, there are solutions to these problems, which I'll detail here.

Current Incentives and Outcome

The primary lender in the student loan market is now the U.S. Treasury. As detailed in Chapter 5, the 2010 Student Aid and Fiscal Responsibility Act ended subsidies for private student loans as well as expanded the Federal Direct Student Loans program. When signing the act into law, President Obama correctly pointed out that: "For almost two decades, we've been trying to fix a sweetheart deal in federal law that essentially gave billions of dollars to banks . . . padding student lenders' pockets."[xxi] With the government now being the primary lender, what is its incentive? The optimistic assessment is that because the U.S. government is a representative democracy, the government is beholden to the people. Therefore, its incentive is to ensure that the laws and regulations it passes maximize its constituents' well-being. The pessimistic assessment is that the U.S. government is beholden to special interest groups, who fund the reelection campaigns of its representatives. So, it is incentivized to pass laws and regulations that benefit a select few.

Regardless of where you fall on this spectrum, we can agree that the U.S. government's primary motivation is not to maximize the present value of its student loan portfolio (like a typical bank). Rather, whether encouraged by universities or borrowers (students), the U.S. government is primarily incentivized to ensure that student loans are freely available because doing so is a popular policy. Ensuring its loan losses are limited is also a consideration; but, by lending to only students whose propensity to repay is high, the government would restrict lending, which runs counter to its primary objective.

Meanwhile, students and their parents are incentivized to attend college and to borrow whatever is needed to attend. Societal pressure to attend college is extreme and likely counterproductive. Roughly two-thirds of graduating high school students go on to attend college.[xxii] Of those, 60 percent of students earn a four-year Bachelor's degree where they initially enrolled and over 20 percent drop out entirely![xxiii] But don't expect universities to advertise the fact that nearly a quarter of the people entering college would be better off if they hadn't attended college. Prospective students are sadly undereducated when it comes to the value proposition of college. Undoubtedly, administrators, teachers, parents, counselors, and even former first ladies mean well by encouraging everybody to attend college. But the net result is a highly motivated but poorly educated consumer (student) who is willing to purchase a product (college degree) on the expectation that the degree is a positive net present value proposition (i.e., the benefit is greater than the cost).

> *"Prospective students are sadly undereducated when it comes to the value proposition of college."*

Combine the ability of students to borrow and the willingness of the government to lend with the increasing price of tuition, and we come to two unfortunate outcomes. The first outcome is a material decline in the value of a college education net of all risks and expenses. Returning to a study highlighted in Chapter 3, the 2021 analysis by the Foundation for Research on Equal Opportunity estimated that the median return on investment (ROI) for earning a college degree is $306,000 for students who graduate on time. So, if you graduate in four years, you're still probably better off attending college. But, adjust for the risk that someone drops out or takes longer than four years, the median ROI drops to only $129,000. Even worse, when accounting for all direct and indirect expenses and the risk of noncompletion, 37 percent of degrees have a negative ROI. Said another way, 37 percent of college students would have been financially better off by not

". . . 37 percent of college students would have been financially better off by not attending college."

attending college.[xxiv] The second outcome to address is the high indebtedness of adults who have attended college. As shown in Figure 8.8, there are over 22 million borrowers who are age 34 and younger with student loans, and over 45 million people with student debt. These balances are the natural outcome of the intense societal pressure to attend college, of a university system that does not prioritize cost (and price) minimization, and of a willingness to extend loans to students even when the likelihood of repayment is low. It's a big problem—and we can, and should, address it.

Age	Borrowers (M)	Balance ($M)	Balance per Borrower
24 and Younger	7.6	$109,700	$14,434
25 to 34	14.9	$500,200	$33,570
35 to 49	14.4	$622,200	$43,208
50 to 61	6.4	$281,800	$44,031
62 and Older	2.4	$97,800	$40,750
Total	45.7	$1,611,700	$35,267

Figure 8.8   Federal Student Loan Borrowers by Age. *Source*: U.S. DOE[xxv]

Bad Policy Solutions and Likely Outcomes

A highly popular (among some constituents) policy proposal is for the federal government to cancel student debt. These proposals vary with the primary difference coming in the form of how much to cancel. At one end of this spectrum is President Biden, who has called for eliminating $10,000 of debt per borrower[xxvi] at a cost of almost $400 billion to taxpayers. Meanwhile, Senators Elizabeth Warren and Chuck Schumer have proposed eliminating up to $50,000 per debtor[xxvii] costing taxpayers roughly $1 trillion, while Senator Bernie Sanders has proposed eliminating all $1.6 trillion in federally held student debt.[xxviii] Arguments in favor of this proposal are that this elimination of student debt would help close the racial wealth gap in the United States, provide relief to struggling Americans, and stimulate economic activity. So, will debt forgiveness, which would also be the single largest wealth transfer in U.S. history, achieve these objectives? Let's look at them one at a time.

The argument that student debt forgiveness will close the racial gap has some merit. As we saw in Chapter 5, Figure 5.5, Black student loan borrowers have notably higher debt and higher default rates than White, Hispanic, or Asian borrowers. So, a policy that eliminates all student debt should disproportionately help Black student borrowers, thereby reducing the racial wealth gap. If viewed in isolation this seems like a reasonable policy proposal. However, if the primary objective of student debt forgiveness is to reduce the racial wealth gap, it is appropriate to evaluate student debt forgiveness against other programs that also reduce this wealth gap. These programs include transfer payments such as food stamps, supplementary security income, welfare, Medicaid, free school lunches, and several others. According to a Brookings Institute study, recipients of these programs generally have household incomes around $30,000 per year and roughly 25 percent of the recipients are Black. In contrast, income for households that are making student debt payments is roughly $87,000 and only 18 percent of those households are Black.[xxix] Why does this all matter? Well, if we compare student debt forgiveness against these other social welfare programs, we can see the other programs are significantly more effective at transferring wealth (closing the racial wealth gap) to poor Black households.

What about the claim that student debt forgiveness will assist struggling Americans and offer a boost to the U.S. economy? Again, there is some merit to this argument. We saw in Chapter 6 that student debt creates a whole host of problems including (but not limited to) delayed household formation, delayed marriages, lower entrepreneurship, lower job satisfaction, and damaged mental health. So, a sudden elimination of this will no doubt benefit millions of Americans. But, like evaluating the claim that debt forgiveness would reduce the racial wealth gap, we must consider this policy against other policies with the same objective. With respect to assisting struggling Americans, policies targeting those who are struggling should assist those who are struggling the *most*. Generally, 30 to 50 percent of recipients of the aforementioned welfare programs (including food stamps, supplementary security income, etc.) are below the poverty line in the United States. In contrast, only four percent of people making student loan payments are below the poverty line.[xxx] So again, student loan forgiveness ranks poorly as a policy when evaluated against other, more targeted government programs.

What about the final claim that canceling student debt will stimulate economic activity? Sure—it will. But again, we should evaluate the degree to which canceling student debt will stimulate economic activity and then compare that with other potential government plans. The typical metric used to compare a program's economic impact is the *fiscal multiplier*. Specifically, how much economic activity is created for every $1.00 spent on the program.

In general, programs that should be implemented or expanded have a fiscal multiplier greater than $1.00, while programs that should be reduced or eliminated (based on economics alone) are ones that have a fiscal multiplier that is less than $1.00. So, what is the fiscal multiplier of student debt elimination? The Committee for a Responsible Federal Budget (a Washington, D.C.-based, nonpartisan public policy organization) estimates that the fiscal multiplier for student debt forgiveness is between $0.08 to $0.23 per $1.00 spent. Authors cite the poorly targeted nature of the program as well as the state of the U.S. economy (as of 2021) as reasons for the poor multiplier.[xxxi] The implication? Student debt forgiveness is a very poor policy option if the objective is economic stimulation.

In summary, student debt forgiveness will reduce the racial wealth gap and help struggling Americans, but not by nearly as much as other programs, and it will stimulate the economy, but the increase in economic activity will be insufficient to offset the cost to taxpayers. So, what about the reasons *not* to forgive all student debt? In short, the large stock of student debt is a symptom, whereas the disease(s) can be found within the U.S. postsecondary education system. Specifically, a college education costs too much, too many people fail to graduate, too many who graduate fail to earn a sufficient income to repay the debt, and minority students have disproportionately bad outcomes. These problems are the result of decades of incentive misalignment on the part of the government, university administrators, endowments, lenders, and students (including their parents). Debt forgiveness does absolutely nothing to address any of the misaligned incentives that we have painstakingly reviewed. In fact, student debt forgiveness will further exacerbate incentive misalignment, making every problem exponentially worse!

To understand why this is the case, imagine that student loans are forgiven. What happens next? All college stakeholders (college administrators, prospective students, etc.) now consider a future when student debt is forgiven, *again*. Administrators raise prices for college, the government lends more, and more students attend college who would have otherwise entered the workforce (while many of those students fail to complete the degree). College campuses, with this windfall of higher tuition and additional students, will further compete for prospective students by building even more elaborate facilities that do little to improve educational outcomes, but certainly look nice. All the while, students happily borrow thinking they too will benefit from forgiveness in the future, and the $1.7 trillion in debt replenishes itself at an alarming speed. These problems are in addition to the inequity created by transferring wealth to households in the top 50th percentile and the frustration among people who sacrificed (e.g., Ramen noodle dinners) to repay their student debt. And, because this policy proposal has a low fiscal multiplier, student debt forgiveness will add to government debt, which will need to be repaid by future generations.

Good Policy Solutions—Consumer Protections

In these final sections, I will propose solutions that are intended to achieve two objectives: improve the current and future consumer protections for student debtors and better align university incentives to ensure that more students graduate with little debt and/or the ability to repay that debt. With respect to improving consumer protections, we need the U.S. Congress to roll back many of the laws that have been passed since 1976 that relate to student debt. As a quick refresher from Chapter 5, in 1976 Congress passed a law stating that federally guaranteed student loans could only be discharged in two circumstances: (1) if greater than five years have passed since the borrower was required to begin making loan repayments or (2) in less than five years if repayment would cause undue hardship.[xxxii] Between 1979 and 2005, Congress revised the legal treatment of student debt at least five additional times, dramatically reducing the ability of debtors to discharge student loans in the event of bankruptcy. This needs to be addressed.

The first critical change to bankruptcy law that will alleviate the current debt crisis is for legislatures to define *undue hardship* so that this threshold is much less onerous than the current court definition. The second, and perhaps even more meaningful change, is for Congress to limit the length of time in which student debt has unique treatment during bankruptcy. Prior to 1998, if a person declared bankruptcy, that individual would only have to demonstrate undue hardship to discharge student loans if that person had begun making student debt payments within the previous seven years. After 1998, a person would need to demonstrate undue hardship irrespective of when their student debt was assumed, meaning that student debt would be forever treated as a unique class of debt. As a result, there currently are people who declared bankruptcy in the past and are now having social security checks garnished to offset unpaid student debt.[6] That isn't right. Restoring the original five-year window (during which a person needs to demonstrate undue hardship) should alleviate concerns that recently graduated students will immediately declare bankruptcy to discharge student debt, while treating student debt like

---

[6] According to a 2016 United States Government Accountability Office report titled *Social Security Offsets*, between 2002 and 2015 the number of people who had their social security benefits garnished due to defaulted student loans rose from 36,000 to 173,000.

any other debt (five years after leaving a college) will allow people to discharge debt as intended by U.S. bankruptcy law.

What other changes can we make to alleviate the suffering of people who have or will default on student debt? Plenty. Here are a few ideas. Someone who has defaulted on a private loan may have up to 25 percent of their disposable income garnished. That's too high. This figure should be brought down to 15 percent, which is in line with the maximum wage garnishment for defaulted federal student loans. Another consideration is capping the time period during which wages can be garnished. Currently, the only ways to stop wage garnishment for defaulted federal loans are to repay the loan in full, rehabilitation (meeting repayment objectives), or consolidating (repaying multiple loans by taking out another loan). But what about people who fail to do any of these? Well, they'll have income garnished for the rest of their lives. That's too long. A reasonable period of wage garnishment seems to be in order, such as four years for every $10,000 (with an inflation adjustment) in defaulted loans. Therefore, a person who defaults on $5,000 in loans may see their wages garnished for up to two years, while someone who defaults on $40,000 in loans may have their wages garnished for up to 16 years.

Other consumer-friendly changes include reducing the fee associated with default on a federal loan. Currently, if a borrower defaults on a loan, a 17 percent premium is immediately applied to the debt. So, if someone defaults on a $10,000 debt, they now have to repay at least $11,700 in principal. The 17 percent fee is usury and regressive in nature since it is a tax that is being applied to people at the exact time when they are in the most financial distress. Next, the government should allow people to reenter loan forgiveness plans once a loan has been rehabilitated. Rehabilitation (and eventual repayment) should always be the objective of a lender; therefore, removing a borrower's ability to enter forgiveness plans is illogical. Finally, there are some states that will not allow an individual to renew a professional license (nurses, teachers, hair stylists, etc.) if a person defaults on a student loan. Again, removing an individual's ability to work, just when their financial outlook has deteriorated, is punitive and regressive. The U.S. Congress should pass a simple law ensuring that states or municipalities cannot prevent an individual from renewing a professional license if they have defaulted on debt.

Good Policy Solutions—University Incentive Alignment

Capping the price of tuition, revising tax laws relevant to endowments, and returning consumer protections will all help to alleviate the student debt crisis over time through incentive realignment. But there is one final incentive

> *". . . universities currently face no financial repercussion when students have adverse outcomes."*

mismatch that has not yet been addressed—universities currently face no financial repercussion when students have adverse outcomes. These adverse outcomes include: students failing to complete the program, students failing to earn a higher salary after they graduate, or students failing to repay debt quickly and in full. From 2014 to 2020, the DOE did require for-profit colleges to meet a *gainful employment* test in order to have access to government student aid programs. For-profit colleges were targeted due to their high default rates. Students at for-profit colleges represented 11 percent of the total higher education population, but 44 percent of all federal student loan defaults. For these colleges to meet the *gainful employment* test, annual student loan payments of graduates could not exceed 20 percent of discretionary income or eight percent of earnings. The application of this standard was effective and enrollment in for-profit colleges fell by roughly 50 percent in the next five years. Unfortunately, the policy was repealed in 2019.

This experience demonstrates that if schools have skin in the game, then outcomes will be better; a better outcome may mean higher graduation rates, higher income (better skills) among students at graduation, or the closure of schools that primarily produce future student loan defaulters. So, what is the most efficient way to ensure that universities' and students' collective incentives are fully aligned? I am so thrilled you asked. Public, private, and for-profit colleges should be mandated by law to purchase the debt of their students; otherwise, they will lose access to federal student aid programs. Here's how it should work:

> *"Public, private, and for-profit colleges should be mandated by law to purchase the debt of their students . . ."*

- All postsecondary institutions, irrespective of size, must purchase 25 percent of all federally guaranteed student loans that originated at their school, each year.
- The loans must be a representative sample of originated loans. In other words, schools can't cherry-pick loans to their STEM students and avoid loans to their humanities students.
- Because not every school has an endowment sufficiently large to purchase these loans, the U.S. Treasury may lend money to schools (so that the schools may, in turn, purchase the student loans):
  - ▫ The interest rate that the U.S. Treasury will charge postsecondary institutions will be equal to the average interest rate on their portfolio of student loans, plus one percent.

        ◻ The tenor on the loan will equal the tenor of the recently acquired student loans; this loan cannot be extended or rolled at maturity.

That may seem a little convoluted, so here's a working example. Imagine that in one year, a university's students collectively borrow $100 million at an average interest rate of five percent with a duration of 15 years. The university would then be required to purchase $25 million worth of their students' debt. To finance this, it would borrow $25 million from the U.S. Treasury at an average interest rate of six percent for 15 years. In the first year, the university would collect $1,250,000 in interest from its portfolio of student loans ($25 million × 5%) but it would pay $1,500,000 in interest to the U.S. Treasury. The net impact is a $250,000 per year tax on its $100 million in loans originated. From the university's perspective, to minimize the tax it will pay, the university should work to reduce tuition, which, in turn, would lower the amount of borrowing by its students.

    Next, if during the following year, 10 percent of student borrowers default, then the portfolio of loans held by a hypothetical university drops from $25 million to $23.2 million (the lenders can expect to recover around $0.73[7] for every $1.00 after a borrower defaults), then the university must recognize a $1.8 million loss because its students are failing to repay their loans. To minimize future credit losses, the university will want to graduate students with less debt as well as more marketable skills (i.e., their students make more at graduation). This may include revising the programs it offers (more STEM degrees and fewer humanities degrees), admitting students with a higher likelihood of completing the program, better career placement services, or allocating more resources to ensure that students graduate with a good financial footing. Finally, the university will continue to incur losses every year until all loans are repaid (from that year's cohort) or default. Thus, it is in the university's best interest to ensure that students are able to repay loans in full and on time. This may lead to universities working with students to ensure that they have the necessary resources following graduation or that they have received sufficient financial aid earlier in their college careers.

    From the taxpayers' perspective, colleges and universities that fail to adapt to this new environment will eventually falter and close. That's a good thing.

---

[7] According to the White House Office of Management and Budget Supplemental Materials, the recovery rate on student loans is 105%. But this figure is misleading because it suggests that all principal is recovered from student borrowers; that's not the case. Here's how: over the course of the lifetime of a $10,000 15-year student loan at 5%, a borrower will pay $14,234. If the government collects $10,500 (105% of principal) on a particular loan, then the total recovery rate based on what was expected is really $10,500/$14,234, or 73%.

We want to tax out of existence universities that fail to fulfill their obligation to students and society, which is to produce a competent and highly productive citizenry. Doing so will ensure that future generations of students find themselves at colleges that offer academic programs that ensure students will graduate with little or no debt, complete the program, and have marketable skills at graduation. These goals can be accomplished if Congress adds these requirements in the next passage of the HEA.

CONCLUSION

Albert Einstein is credited with saying, "a problem without a solution is a poorly stated problem." In other words, all problems when they are clearly and appropriately defined have solutions. Student debt is no different. Throughout this book, I've tried to convey that student debt isn't the problem—it's the symptom of the problem. The problem is incentive misalignment among constituents. Specifically, governments, banks, students, and universities all work with their own best interest in mind; however, only students are burdened when they do not complete a program, graduate with debt, graduate without marketable skills, or are unable to repay their debt. So, if we are to solve this problem, we must first agree that all actors in postsecondary education must benefit when students graduate on time, with skills, and with little or no debt. Conversely, all actors must feel pain when students fail to achieve these milestones. Fortunately, it is within our government's power to pass legislation that will enable this incentive realignment. It has taken decades for the stock of debt to rise to today's level due to poorly crafted past legislation; so, it will take several more decades before the nation's youth view student debt as a strange relic of the past. But, reducing the cost of colleges, enhancing the economic value of the education, and eliminating student debt is achievable within our lifetimes. The optimal policy solutions aren't fancy, revolutionary, or quick. Rather, they're oriented to ensure future generations are better positioned than the current generation. In other words, these policy solutions are in line with the foundational objectives of the university system: Produce alumni that better create goods and services of monetary value as well as have the tools to elevate society in a manner that can neither be measured nor taxed. Our legislators can do this. Let's make sure they do.

9

What Every Parent, Student, and Prospective Student Should Know

As the parent of three (likely) college-bound children, I wrote this chapter to help me (and them) figure out what is best for my children (and themselves). Hopefully it will help you as well. My analysis is not prescriptive; rather, I hoped to take stock of the pros and cons of earning a four-year degree and then build a framework to determine what is best for each of my children. Earlier in this book, I posed this question:

> *You have a 66.5 percent[1] chance to receive $253,351,[2] and a 33.5 percent chance to be assigned $13,930[3] in debt, lose $41,194[4] in savings, lose $81,952[5] in current income, and possibly incur other damages that may impair your ability to get married, buy a house, start a family, or start a business.[6] What do you do?*

---

[1] 66.5 percent is the average completion rate for students who entered a public four-year bachelor's degree program in 2011. Source: NCES, Beginning Postsecondary Students 2012/2017.

[2] $253,351.00 is the estimated present value net increase in lifetime earnings following the earning of a bachelor's degree. Source: Kim, et al., 2015. Table 4.

[3] $13,929.65 is the average student loan debt at the time of a student's dropout, according to a survey conducted by LendEDU. Source: College Dropouts and Student Debt. February 17, 2021. Mike Brown. Accessed 12/12/2021. https://lendedu.com/blog/college-dropouts-student-loan-debt/.

[4] $20,598.00 is the estimated average annual undergraduate tuition, fees. room and board rates charged for full-time students in degree-granting postsecondary institutions during the 2018–2019 academic year. I am assuming that this student drops out after two full years of a four-year program. Source: NCES. Table 330.10.

[5] The median weekly income for a high-school graduate is $788, according to the U.S. Bureau of weekly statistics. Here, I assume the student forgoes 104 weeks (2 years) of income while attending college. Source: BLS. Usual Weekly Earnings of Wage and Salary Workers News Release. Table 5. Accessed 12/12/2021.

[6] See Chapter 6 for a detailed discussion about the ways that student debt may negatively impact a person's economic and psychological health.

This question is intended to reflect the current value proposition of going to college. The point I am trying to make is that the *right* answer is unclear. Each individual is different. He or she may be *more* or *less* likely to: complete a degree, assume debt while doing so, or use that degree to increase potential earnings. So, what's the right choice for you or your child? In Former First Lady Michelle Obama and Jay Pharoah's "Go to College" music video, they rap, "If you want to stare at grass, don't go to college." While the spirit of the message is well-intentioned, that's unfair, and frankly, awful advice. The truth of the matter is that the choice to continue with postsecondary education is person-specific, nuanced, and complicated. We can predict with greater certainty which students are more likely to complete a degree, assume little or no debt, and earn significantly more following graduation. Do you, or your children, fall into that category? What if they do? What if they don't?

In order to help guide the conversation, I've presented this chapter in the form of a decision tree, and I offer a framework to answering the question at every node. So, as you try to figure out what the *best* decision is with respect to a postsecondary path, this section will provide you with a framework as well as inform you about the options and resources that are available to you so that you can make the most informed decision. Let's take this final journey together.

QUESTION 1: SHOULD SOMEONE CONTINUE WITH POSTSECONDARY EDUCATION?

This is the only question I'm going to answer for my readers—the answer to this question is: *yes*. But that is not to say that all people should go to college, nor am I suggesting that all people continue with a formal education immediately after graduating high school. On the contrary, postsecondary education can take many forms, and it can become a part of people's lives at different times and for different reasons.

So why am I so convinced that postsecondary education should be universal? There are a lot of reasons why we should value education for all people, both young and old. For example, scientists have noted that the more years of education a person has received, the higher the cognitive function as an adult and the lower the likelihood of developing dementia late in life.[7,i] Years

---

[7] The cited study suggests that the lower rate of dementia among highly educated adults may be attributed to factors other than the number of years of formal education; specifically, people with certain cognitive abilities are more likely to attend college and not develop dementia. So, years of education negatively correlates with dementia, but there may not be a causal relationship.

of education also positively correlates with better physical health, such as less smoking[ii] and more exercising.[iii] Separately, years of education are positively correlated with higher civic engagement (such as hours volunteered) and being an involved parent.[iv] Highly educated people also tend to have higher incomes[v] and lower unemployment rates.[vi] Finally, education is the optimal means by which the country can close its skills gap, which is another way of saying that employers are unable to find qualified workers. According to a 2018 survey conducted by the Society for Human Resource Management (a human resources professional association), 75 percent of surveyed human resource representatives who had difficulty recruiting cited a shortage of skilled applicants.[vii]

> *". . . education is the optimal means by which the country can close its skills gap . . ."*

So the more relevant question really is: What form will postsecondary education take? Allow me to elaborate on three specific options.

Option 1: Apprenticeship and Certificates

An apprenticeship is a formal program that is reviewed and approved by the U.S. Department of Labor (DOL). There are two types of apprenticeship programs: the Registered Apprenticeship Program (RAP) and the Industry-Recognized Apprenticeship Program (IRAP). In both instances, apprentices are paid and learn a skill while on the job. A RAP program also includes a minimum of 2,000 hours of on-the-job learning, a minimum of 144 hours of classroom instruction, and a 1:1 ratio of experienced workers to apprentices to ensure proper mentorship. Once completing a RAP, the apprentice will receive a Certificate of Completion from either the DOL or another state apprenticeship agency. In contrast, an IRAP program does not have a minimum requirement for on-the-job learning or mandatory classroom instruction, nor a ratio of mentors to apprentices. At the completion of the program, the apprentice will receive an industry-recognized credential.[viii]

So, why do this? First, it has been shown internationally to be highly successful. In Germany, for example, slightly over half of the students who graduate from general education (the German equivalent of high school) enter an apprentice program that lasts between 2 and 3.5 years.[ix] Second, apprenticeship programs are large and growing in the United States. According to the DOL, in 2020, over 220,000 individuals entered the apprenticeship system in one of over 26,000 apprenticeship programs. Programs exist in a variety of fields including: healthcare, hospitality, cybersecurity, energy, manufacturing, engineering, transportation, construction, and financial services. Finally, people who complete these programs make good money. Among those who complete an apprentice program, 94 percent retain employment and have an annual salary of $70,000.[x] That's nearly three times the average income of a fully employed high school graduate (with no college)! Their average 2021 annual salary was $24,860.[xi]

What if there's a certain occupation that is of interest to a person, but there's no apprenticeship program available? Then a community college certificate program is an excellent option. Most community colleges offer certificate programs that indicate proficiency in areas including: accounting, business administration, computer science, construction, healthcare, mechanics, welding, and many more. This option is becoming increasingly popular; in 2019–2020, community colleges conferred nearly 700,000 certificates, up from 428,000 just 10 years prior.[xii] Certification programs include both *long* certificates (programs that last longer than one year), and *short* certificates (programs that last less than one year). How valuable are these certificates in terms of future earnings, both at graduation and over time? To answer that, researchers Veronica Minaya and Judith Scott-Clayton from Columbia University reviewed data from the Ohio Education Research Center. Their study followed nearly 96,000 young adults over an 11-year period, some of whom earned associate degrees or certificates (long and short) and others who failed to earn a certificate or degree. What they found was that there was a notable increase in quarterly earnings (around $1,800 for women and $1,200 for men) for those who earned a long certificate; however, there was not a statistically significant increase in earnings for people who earned a short certificate. Of note, however, is that it generally takes longer than advertised to complete the certificate programs; researchers found it took an average of 3.8 years to complete a long program and three years to complete a short program.[xiii]

Option 2: The Military

Each year, the branches of the U.S. armed services enlist around 150,000 new recruits.[xiv] Plus, there are roughly 1.3 million active-duty personnel in the U.S., in addition to the roughly one million reserve personnel.[xv] Taken together, the U.S. military is the largest or second largest employer in the United States; Walmart (roughly 2.3 million employees)[xvi] and Amazon (roughly 1.6 million employees)[xvii] are the other two largest employers in the U.S. So, why might joining the military be an attractive option for a recent high school graduate? Common benefits cited in military recruiting materials include increased discipline, worldwide travel, free room and board, free medical care, a stable career, and job skills. With respect to job skills, there are hundreds of roles within the armed forces, many of which translate into civilian skills. In addition to learning skills, each branch offers tuition assistance (TA) for eligible personnel; in fact, the military may pay for up to 100 percent of tuition and required fees while on active duty, and in most cases, TA is available to veterans up to 15 years following an individual's separation from active services. Finally, all branches of the U.S. military (except the Coast Guard) offer Reserve Officers' Training Corps (ROTC) programs hosted at colleges. ROTC is offered at more than 1,700 colleges and universities across the U.S. In exchange for having their college tuition paid in full and graduating as an officer, ROTC officers agree to an eight-year commitment following the completion of their college courses, of which at least four years must be active-duty service. These conditions change over time, so I'd recommend speaking with a recruiter before taking this benefit for granted.

With all that said, there are some drawbacks to enlisting in the military. In general, enlisting comes with an eight-year commitment during which four years are active duty.[xviii] However, this varies by branch and may include up to a six-year active-duty commitment.[xix] The remaining time of the eight-year commitment may be completed as a reserve, which means that the soldier may be recalled to active duty during that time. In addition, while on active duty, the government has control over where the person is deployed. Life during this time may be highly regimented, and soldiers may become lonely or miss family life events. In the long run, once a person completes his or her service, the data suggest that the financial benefits of military service are lifelong. In 2019, Florida-based law firm Hill & Ponton analyzed data from the University of Minnesota's Integrated Public Use Microdata Series in order to compare veterans' incomes versus their civilian counterparts. They discovered that veterans earn an average of $11,000 more per year than civilians; however, this varies by age and geography.[xx]

Option 3: Associate or Bachelor's Degree

Let's assume that a potential postsecondary student is neither interested in an apprenticeship nor in joining the military. Plus, the potential student has strong marks in high school, strong standardized test scores, and good time-management skills. In that case, considering a two- or four-year program is appropriate. Great—so what prerequisites are necessary to maximize the likelihood of a positive educational outcome? Here are a few big ones:

1. *Have goals and objectives.* Enrolling in a two-year (associate degree) or four-year (bachelor's degree) program is a major commitment in time and resources. So, prior to entering, it is critical to establish goals and objectives for how to maximize the return on time and financial investment. Some goals may be to learn more about one or more

industries, to acquire a valuable skillset, to earn good grades, or to develop a network.

2. *Be academically prepared.* If a student needs remediation prior to completing a two- or four-year program, the student is significantly less likely to earn a degree. According to a 2012 study by the non-profit group Complete College America, nearly 52 percent of students enrolling in a two-year program and 20 percent of students enrolling in a four-year program were required to take remediation courses. Of students who enter remediation courses, only 9.5 percent of them successfully earn an associate degree (within three years), while 35.1 percent of students successfully earn a bachelor's degree (within six years). The remaining students fail to earn a degree.[xxi]

> ## *"The most commonly cited reason when people leave college is financial problems."*

3. *Be financially prepared.* The most commonly cited reason when people leave college is financial problems.[xxii,xxiii,8] So, before enrolling—and before applying to a college for that matter—it is important to take stock of the ability to afford college, estimate the expense of college, and develop a plan to fill the gap between estimated cost and affordability. Step one is to find out how much college will cost. Fortunately, there are now net-price online calculators that help students determine what a college will cost (link provided in the upcoming *Helpful Resources* section). If the net expense exceeds a student's or family's ability to afford college, what then? Some good options include:

   ▫ Enroll at a community college that has an *articulation agreement* with the college or university where you want to finish up your education. An articulation agreement means that some, or all, of the credits earned at a community college can be transferred to a larger, more prestigious college or university. These agreements vary by college and by field of study, so it's important to contact both the community college and the university to ensure that the credits earned at a community college can be transferred.

---

[8] 35.3 percent of respondents in a LendEDU poll and 38 percent in an EducationData poll indicated that the primary reason for leaving college was related to cost. This included an aversion to assuming debt (or additional debt).

- Apply for work-study in addition to applying for financial aid. Federal work-study provides part-time jobs for undergraduate, graduate, and professional students with financial need. There may be both on- and off-campus jobs available for students. These programs are administered by the university or college financial aid office.
- Apply for scholarships. Scholarships are either *merit-based* or *need-based*. Merit-based scholarships require that an applicant meets certain academic or skills conditions (grades, musical talent, athletic accomplishment, etc.), while a need-based scholarship is awarded based on the applicant's background and ability to afford his or her education. To learn which scholarships may be available, applicants should check with their high school counselors, the administrators at their preferred college's financial aid office, and their local businesses or foundations. They should also review online scholarship search engines (there are two listed in the upcoming *Helpful Resources* section).
- Once these options have been exhausted, then consider applying for a student loan. In general, students should first look to assume direct subsidized loans, and if need exceeds the maximum amount that can be borrowed, then a student should assume a direct unsubsidized loan. In general, students should also attempt to assume loans as late in their college careers as possible. So, if a student anticipates assuming $20,000 in debt to pay for a four-year degree, it is better to assume the $20,000 in the final two years and not the first two years of their studies.

Helpful Resources

- Find a community college:
  https://www.usnews.com/education/community-colleges/search
- Apprenticeship programs:
  https://www.apprenticeship.gov/career-seekers
- Military jobs:
  https://www.operationmilitarysdfkids.org/military-jobs/
- Military college support:
  https://www.todaysmilitary.com/education-training
- College net cost calculator:
  https://collegecost.ed.gov/net-price

- Federal student loans:
  https://studentaid.gov/understand-aid/types/loans
- DOL scholarship locator:
  https://www.careeronestop.org/toolkit/training/find-scholarships.aspx
- Private scholarship locator:
  https://scholarships360.org/

QUESTION 2: WHEN SHOULD SOMEONE CONTINUE WITH THEIR POSTSECONDARY EDUCATION?

So, assuming someone believes that they are a good candidate for an associate or bachelor's degree, when should they enroll? The conventional wisdom is that college-bound students should enroll in college immediately after high school; but, a lot of people take alternative paths. According to the U.S. Department of Education (DOE) National Center for Education Statistics, of the 19.6 million students who were enrolled in postsecondary institutions in 2019, 6.5 million are age 25 and older, while 2.6 million students are age 35 and older.[xxiv] Let's briefly take a look at the benefits and disadvantages of attending college immediately or waiting until later in life.

Option 1: Attend Directly after High School

Attending college immediately after high school is the most common path for people who enroll in college; but is that the best option for you (or your child)? Here are some considerations. Attending college immediately after high school enables students to earn their degree at a younger age. This may be particularly relevant if the student has the potential to continue with their studies after earning their bachelor's degree. For example, a law degree requires an additional three years of schooling, while becoming a doctor requires a four-year medical school plus another three to seven years of postgraduate training (residency and internship). Separately, younger learners are generally unfettered from additional familial responsibilities and thus, can dedicate more time and effort to their studies, which increases the chance that they will complete a program on time. Also of consideration, earning a degree generally increases a person's earnings potential; therefore, the earlier a person can earn their degree, the longer a person can reap the financial benefits, which reduces the implicit cost of a college degree. Finally, waiting an extended period of time to attend college has the potential to delay milestones later in life, such as marriage, buying a house, or starting a family.

Yet, with all that said, not every college-bound student should attend college immediately after high school graduation. In fact, we can get a sense of why that's the case if we parse the data from a 2021 white paper coauthored by Straighterline (an online educational company) and UPCEA (a continuing education association with around 400 members). Their paper, titled *Today's Disengaged Learner Is Tomorrow's Adult Learner*, includes a survey of 3,236 people that explains why people left college, by age group. What they found is that the youngest students (ages 18 to 19) are more likely to leave college due to *family reasons/commitments* (39% vs 32% of all students), *lack of time* (36% vs 24% of all students), and *health reasons* (26% vs 15% of all students).[xxv] How can we interpret these results as it relates to when to attend college? I believe that the *lack of time* response suggests that many of the younger students entered college before they had developed strong time-management skills. The *health reasons* response suggests that younger students may have been more prone to mental health issues while attending college—a significant and growing concern.[xxvi] The takeaway? Some students simply need more time before they are ready to attend college, which leads us to Option 2: the gap year.

Option 2: Gap Year

A *gap year* is a period of time when a student is not receiving a formal education. The duration of a gap year is actually between six months and two years—and this period typically occurs between high school and college. Gap years may involve working part-time, completing an internship, volunteering, learning another language, completing remedial course work, or traveling. These activities may or may not be a part of a structured gap-year program. According to the National Student Clearinghouse (an educational non-profit that provides educational reporting to North American colleges and universities), annually between 11,000 and 13,000 students who enrolled in college took a gap year between 2018 and 2020.[xxvii] According to the Gap Year Association (GYA) 2020 Alumni survey, the most common reasons cited for taking a gap year included desire for personal growth, desire for travel, feeling academically "burned out," wanting to volunteer, and needing time to figure out what they want to study.[xxviii]

What are the advantages of taking a gap year? According to the 2020 GYA survey of nearly 1,600 gap year alumni, nearly all respondents reported that during their gap year they experienced increased maturity and self-confidence. In addition, over 80 percent of survey respondents reported that the gap year influenced their future career ambitions, provided them with a competitive advantage when applying to college or for a job, and increased their academic motivation. Finally, 78 percent of respondents indicated that their gap year influenced what they would study once they entered college.[xxix] As a parent, would I recommend that my children take a gap year? Perhaps. I think a gap year is appropriate if a student is clearly college-bound but does not meet the three criteria mentioned earlier in this chapter—specifically, a student needs to have an objective (or goal) prior to enrolling, and the student needs to be both academically and financially prepared for the two- to four-year commitment.

So, what are the outcomes for students who take gap years? Unfortunately, as of the writing of this book, there are no longitudinal (i.e., over time) American studies that track students who do or do not take gap years. So, we cannot compare the graduation rates, job choices, incomes, or other metrics of the students with or without a gap year. Instead, we have to rely on anecdotes, studies outside the United States, and small samples, which suggest that gap year students have slightly higher GPAs and higher graduation rates[xxx] but possibly slightly lower earnings later in life.[xxxi] With all that said, there are a few risks associated with taking a gap year. First, not everybody goes to college following their gap year; according to the GYA survey, 83 percent of gap year students enroll in a college one year after the start of their gap year. Meanwhile, 13 percent entered the workforce, while the balance continued to travel, enjoyed a second gap year, or joined the military.[xxxii] Separately, students who have already been admitted to college will need to reapply for financial aid, while others may find their financial aid package has changed. Some students may also feel rusty when it comes to academic rigor.

Even so, what do you do if you or your child decides to take a gap year? First, it's still probably a good idea for students to apply to college during their senior year of high school. This means completing all standardized tests, receiving recommendation letters, receiving academic transcripts, and completing applications. If a student is accepted into a college, that student should then contact the school and request that their admittance be deferred for a year; the timing of this request should be as early as possible, but no later than when fall tuition payments are due. Depending on the college, the school may ask for an explanation as to what the student intends to do with the time; however, most colleges have become supportive of students taking gap years. If a student is not accepted into a college of choice, the student should reapply to college the following year—only this time, the student will have much more time to write a compelling essay and will have additional life experiences to reference in their application.

Option 3: Mid-Career Return to School

Nobody really goes back to college after working for a couple of years, right? Wrong! In 2015, the U.S. DOE released a study showing the demographic and enrollment characteristics of students who were enrolled in associate and bachelor's degree programs; the study included groups that enrolled in 1995, 1999, 2003, 2007, and 2011. So, what did this study find? Around one-third of students had waited more than a year to enroll in a program—and almost all of these students weren't enrolling late due to a gap year. In addition, of the roughly one-third of students who didn't enroll straight out of high school, 71 percent of students worked either full- or part-time, and the average delay prior to entering college for full-time workers was 50 months.[xxxiii] So, how do adult learners compare to the younger students in terms of their respective college experiences? A 2018 study by researchers at Grand Valley State University and Indiana University suggests that adult learners have different, albeit still positive, experiences. Specifically, adult learners are more likely to enroll part-time, take online classes, and earn their degrees at more than one institution. Adult learners generally had positive perceptions of their learning experience, although they had fewer interactions with faculty and peers.[xxxiv]

So, should you or an adult friend go back to college later in life? Perhaps. Like someone considering entering college immediately after high school, a potential adult learner should pass the three-part criteria for attending college: having goals and objectives, being academically prepared, and being financially prepared. Furthermore, because an adult learner is more likely to have dependents and potentially other obligations, the implicit cost of noncompletion of the program is higher than for a younger learner. Given the potential impediments that are unique to returning to college later in life, beginning this academic journey may be most appropriate at a community college. As will be detailed later in this chapter, community colleges are low-cost, low-commitment options that can serve as an important bridge to earning an associate or bachelor's degree. By contrast, for-profit colleges regularly target adult learners. However, the outcomes for these programs are poor since noncompletion rates and cost of attendance are both high.

Helpful Resource

- GAP year providers:
  https://www.gapyearassociation.org/providers/

QUESTION 3: HOW DO YOU CHOOSE A COLLEGE?

You've decided to apply to and, eventually, attend college. Congrats! Now, where should you go to school? Next are things to consider.

Should You (or Your Kids) Attend the Most Prestigious *School?*

One piece of conventional wisdom is that you should attend the most prestigious school possible because that prestige will confer higher earnings potential for the rest of your life. So, is that true? Maybe. On one side of the debate is five-time *New York Times* bestselling author Malcolm Gladwell. In his 2013 book *David and Goliath*, Gladwell takes aim at prestigious universities (e.g., "Big Ponds"). He argues: "Rarely do we stop and consider whether the most prestigious of institutions is always in our best interest." Instead, "The Big Pond takes really bright students and demoralizes them."[xxxv] Mr. Gladwell points out that *half* of the students who were at the very top of their class find out that when they attend the most elite schools, they are then in the bottom half of their class! In other words, imagine a class of 100 students in which each student was in the top one percent of their high school. Now that their peer group consists of only outstanding students, half of these students find that they rank in the bottom half of their peers.[9] Not able to cope with being below average, many of these (otherwise elite) students will fail to earn a degree in their area of interest.

Early studies on the topic noted that students who went to more elite schools tended to earn more later in life; however, later studies demonstrated that this can be attributed to the student (better students go to more elite schools and earn more money), and not the school (elite schools admit future high earners, as opposed to producing high earners).[xxxvi] More recently, this wisdom has been challenged. According to a 2018 paper titled *Elite Schools and Opting-In: Effects of College Selectivity on Career and Family Outcomes*, written by researchers at Virginia Tech, Tulane University, and the University of Virginia, school selectivity does matter (for some students). Specifically, school selectivity as measured by average entering class SAT scores impacts a woman's—but not a man's—future earnings potential; each 100-point increase in average SAT scores increases a woman's probability of earning an advanced degree by five percent, increases possible earnings by 14 percent, and

---

[9] I can relate. While I was an MBA student at Chicago Booth, I took a course taught by Nobel Prize winning economist Eugene Fama. The class was required for Chicago Booth Ph.D. candidates and I was clearly the least intelligent person in the room.

reduces the likelihood of marriage by four percent. The authors speculate that this occurs for two reasons: attending a selective school makes a woman less likely to start a family or conditional on starting a family, and having attended an elite school could reduce the career penalty (future earnings) caused by family formation.[xxxvii]

So, what should you do? During a 2015 lecture at New Roads School (a Santa Monica-based college preparatory school), Malcolm Gladwell suggested, "You shouldn't go to the most exclusive, best, most prestigious school, you should go to the school where you think you can succeed."[xxxviii] So what would I recommend for my kids—or for your kids? I'd take a middle ground and suggest: *of the schools where you (or your kids) think you will be successful, go to the most prestigious one.*

> *". . . of the schools where you (or your kids) think you will be successful, go to the most prestigious one."*

What Metrics Should You (or Your Kids) Care About?

If school prestige (whether measured by college rankings or some other metric) is not the most critical metric when prospective students evaluate colleges, then what is? Some considerations include: school facilities (lecture halls, gyms, libraries, etc.), accommodations (dorms or apartments), socializing opportunities (clubs and general student body composition), academic offerings (majors), campus location, campus size, and total cost. So, when my children are ready to begin evaluating colleges—after having spent the better part of a year researching and writing this book—what metrics will I prioritize when we look at colleges? Here are the four criteria that I believe are most important:

- *Graduation rate*—this rate is generally defined as the percentage of students who complete their studies within 1.5 times the expected time to graduation; that is, six years for a four-year degree and three years for a two-year degree. Why is this metric of primary concern? Well, while my children may have college objectives that include learning a certain field and/or having a great time, as a parent, my primary objective is that my children complete their programs. As shown in Chapter 3, the economic benefits (in terms of future earnings) of attending college but failing to earn a degree are minimal. Meanwhile, the economic cost in terms of forgone earnings and potential student debt is significant. So, a high graduation rate suggests that my children have the best possible chance of . . . well . . . graduating. In addition, the graduation rate is the most relevant metric that demonstrates students' collective evaluation of a university. People vote with their feet, and if students don't believe their time and financial resources are well spent at a college or university, they leave. We should listen to them. I recommend eliminating any school from consideration that has a graduation rate below 60 percent, and I recommend prioritizing schools with a graduation rate above 80 percent.[10]

- *Total cost*—as briefly described in Chapter 2, people have a tendency to fall for the *Chivas Regal Effect*, which is to say that we assign value to cost or price. In fact, the *U.S. News and World Report*'s ranking system reinforces this misconception, as per-student spending is a large (10%) input to their rankings. Basically, if two schools are identical in all respects except cost, the school with the higher cost will have a higher rank and will likely be perceived to be superior; but, it's probably not. Instead, prospective students should focus on *not overspending*. As mentioned earlier in this book, the most common factor cited by college dropouts is that the cost of attending college was too high. For this reason, I recommend only attending colleges that are within $5,000 of a person's annual budget; and by extension, limiting student debt to no more than $20,000 at graduation. Schools that are entirely within a person's budget should be given priority.

- *Course and degree offerings*—prior to enrolling in college, a student should have well-established goals and objectives. Since college is an academic institution, college goals must include an academic component. But what if my kids tell me they want to study philosophy (and love reading Kant)? My response will be, "Great! Let's find a school with a good philosophy program and a separate program that will give you a more marketable skill. You can study both while there." What type of *other* program is that? It could be any STEM (science, technology, engineering, and mathematics) field, accounting, business, or architecture (to name a few). I recommend reviewing Appendix 2 of Chapter 3 to see how college majors translate into earnings potential.

- *Fit*—what is fit? Well, does the student like the school, feel comfortable there, and identify with its student body. Some elements to consider

---

[10] The *graduation rate* metric is likely inaccurate for most, if not all, community colleges. Some students who enter community colleges may intend to take a limited number of courses to acquire a skill. Alternatively, other students may leave the community college, taking their credits with them, and earn a degree elsewhere. As a result, community college graduation rates are not an appropriate metric for evaluation.

for fit are: size (small versus large student body); location (most students stay close to home);[11] campus culture (how much emphasis is on academics versus other student activities); course offerings (can the student study what's interesting to them); and student body diversity (how racially mixed or homogenous is the population). How important is fit to a student's academic success? Very important. According to survey results that were reported by the previously mentioned Straighterline and UPCEA study, 30 percent of college dropouts cite "fit" as a reason for leaving an institution. Only financial reasons or family commitments were cited more frequently as a reason for leaving college.[xxxix] I plan on visiting the campuses and having my kids talk to some current students. I want them to learn for themselves things like: (1) where do most students live? (2) are most students active in organizations, and if so, which ones? (3) are most students happy to be here? and (4) do you know why some students leave? Then, I'll ask my kids what they think.

Building a Target List of Schools and Applying

There are a lot of considerations and figuring out which of the nearly 5,300 colleges and universities in the United States that you or your child should attend is a daunting task. Therefore, it is necessary to learn what resources are available for you to do this. I recommend starting with the Collegescorecard and CollegeRaptor websites. Both websites provide the user with the ability to search and compare college test scores and admission rates, net of assistance costs, average debt at graduation, fields of study, student body diversity, and income of graduating students. CollegeRaptor also has the unique feature of allowing students to compare financial aid packages. If a student has received a letter from a college offering grants, scholarships, or loans, then that student can create an account, upload their letter, and view other similar letters from the same college.

How should you organize your target list of schools? Most advisors recommend that students subdivide schools into three criteria: *reach* schools (where probability of admission is low as estimated by entering school grades and

---

[11] According to a 2019 study by the Higher Education Research Institute, University of California, Los Angeles, 42 percent of students attend a college within 50 miles of their home, while 84 percent attend college within 500 miles of their home. *Source*: Stolzenberg, E. B., Aragon, M. C., Romo, E., Couch, V., McLennan, D., Eagan, M. K., & Kang, N. (2020). The American Freshman: National Norms Fall 2019. Los Angeles: Higher Education Research Institute, UCLA.

scores), *target* schools (where the applicant is comfortably between the 25th and 75th percentile of the entering class's test scores and grades), and *safety* schools (where the probability of admission is high). How many schools should be on your list (and to which ones should you apply)? Simple: you should apply to 115 colleges. That's how many Jasmine E. Harrison applied to in 2018—and she got accepted by 113 of them.[xl] In all seriousness, the answer is likely somewhere between five and 20, and the answer to the *right* number of applications will vary by both student and guide. With that said, I plan to recommend to my kids that they apply to two *safety* schools, two *target* schools, and as many *reach* schools as they can justify, given the cost to apply and the time it will take them to complete a good application. So, if they apply to two *reach* schools (six schools in total), or 10 *reach* schools (14 schools in total), I'll support either of those choices.[12]

What else should a prospective candidate know or do when they start the application process? Here are a few helpful tips:

- *Start early*—the summer prior to the start of their senior year of high school is a good time to put together a list of schools, visit most (if not all) of the *target* and *reach* schools, and begin to write college application essays.
- *Nail the essays*—with the migration to *test-optional* schools, college essays are increasingly important. The essay is a window into the way a student thinks and what motivates them. The typical 16- or 17-year-old student hasn't had the benefit of a lifetime of experiences; but, a clever story about a mundane task (e.g., driving to school or having dinner as a family) can be the window that catches the attention of the admission officers. The essay should be personal, thoughtful, genuine, and (ideally) unique to the applicant.

---

[12] While researching this section, I read several blogs discussing the *right* number of schools to which a candidate should apply. Many advisors recommend a 1:1:1 or a 1:2:1 ratio of *reach* to *target* to *safety* schools. The use of a ratio makes no sense to me. In one blog, an advisor recommended that students apply to 16 colleges, including seven *reach*, five *target*, and four *safety* schools. That advisor continued that if the student wanted to apply to one additional *reach* school, then the student should also apply to one more *target* school and two more *safety* schools, bringing the ratio to 8:6:6. Why should a candidate apply to another *target* and additional *safety* schools just because he or she wants to apply to another *reach* school? Applying to more *safety* schools doesn't increase the chances of acceptance to *reach* schools. And because time is limited, applying to more *safety* schools may actually reduce the likelihood of acceptance into a *reach* school.

- *Get help*—parents, counselors, and college alumni are all good resources. There is also a large and growing market for college application consultants (or independent educational consultants—IECs). However, they are expensive, with most charging between $140 and $200 per hour. A website that will help to find an IEC near you can be found at the link provided in the upcoming *Helpful Resources* section.

Should You Go Straight to a Major University or Start at a Community College?

What if, after completing your research, you discover that you simply can't afford attending your desired school? Or, what if you don't think you will be accepted into one of your desired programs due to high school grades or test scores? Or, what if you simply can't figure out exactly what kind of bachelor's degree you want to earn? In any of these cases, entering a community college may be a good option. Community colleges are often significantly less expensive than four-year colleges and universities. Most also have *open admission* processes, meaning that the only criterion for acceptance is successfully completing an application and paying tuition. Finally, many community colleges offer a broad range of courses, which students can take to learn about potential areas of interest. So, is this a common path for college-bound students. Yes! According to the American Association of Community Colleges, 36 percent of first-time freshman and 39 percent of all U.S. undergraduates enroll in one of 1,043 community colleges throughout the country. The average annual tuition among students is $3,800, a fraction of the $10,740 at four-year public, state colleges (it's even higher for private colleges). It is possible to reduce that financial burden of college even further since 56 percent of community college students receive some form of financial aid.[xli] So, what's the catch? Well, students can't earn a four-year bachelor's degree at a community college—they can (generally) only earn a two-year associate degree. In addition, community colleges generally have significantly less *campus culture*, many students commute, and these schools are viewed as less prestigious given their open admission policies.

The solution to these issues is that students can eventually transfer to a four-year school and take most, if not all, of their academic credits with them. But how well does that work? Unfortunately, not so well. According to data from the Community College Research Center, about 80 percent of students who originally enroll in a community college intend to transfer to a four-year program in order to earn a bachelor's degree.[xlii] Of those students, less than half successfully transfer to a four-year program. Of those students who

". . . only 14 percent of students who start at a community college eventually earn a bachelor's degree."

do transfer, less than half will earn a bachelor's degree. In total, only 14 percent of students who start at a community college eventually earn a bachelor's degree.[xliii] That's a pretty bad outcome, so how can you maximize the chance that you (or your kid) are part of the 14 percent? The answer is to figure out a plan before taking the first course at a community college. Specifically, learn which colleges and community colleges have articulation agreements, and make sure that you understand what is in the agreement. An articulation agreement sets the terms by which a student can transfer from a two-year community college to a four-year college—these terms include acceptance (what grades does a community college student need to guarantee admission into a four-year program), transfer credits (which credits carry over and which don't), scholarship eligibility (do students get to take financial aid with them), and other academic course requirements. To learn about articulation agreements, a prospective student can inquire with a local community college as to whether, and with whom, the school has articulation agreements. Similarly, if the student has a specific university in mind, the student can inquire about which community colleges that specific school has articulation agreements. This is vital because the Community College Research Center estimates that students lose an average of 43 percent of their credits when they transfer, which essentially adds another year (or more) to their schooling and significantly reduces their likelihood of successfully earning a bachelor's degree.[xliv]

Helpful Resources

- DOE College Scorecard:
  https://collegescorecard.ed.gov/
- Additional College Finder and Comparison:
  https://www.collegeraptor.com/
- Other college search tools:
  https://academicinfluence.com/inflection/college-life/best-college-search-tools
- Find a college admissions consultant:
  https://www.iecaonline.com/quick-links/member-directory/

QUESTION 4: WHAT SHOULD SOMEONE WHO HAS ASSUMED DEBT DO (AND NOT DO)?

You have decided to attend a college that costs more than you are able to afford, and you've decided to plug the gap with student loans. Okay—no problem. That's an appropriate decision for millions of students. Now the question remains: what should you do and not do? Let's review so we can make sure that you have the best possible outcome.

Dos (and Don'ts)—During Schooling:

- *Earn your degree*: In a 2017 white paper, the Center for American Progress produced a powerful insight into the importance of completing a program once enrolled. Specifically, the default rate 12 years after entering a postsecondary educational program among people who earned a bachelor's or associate degree is nine and 22 percent, respectively. However, people who dropped out of a program had a 46 percent default rate.[xlv] In other words, if you drop out of a program, you are between two and five times more likely to default on your loans later in life. This high default rate can partially be attributed to the minimal economic benefit from attending but not graduating from college. According to the U.S. Bureau of Labor Statistics, the median annual income of someone with "some college, no degree" is about $5,000 higher than someone with a "high school diploma, no college" but is about $22,000 lower than someone with a bachelor's degree.[xlvi]
- *Minimize your debt*:
    - Don't take out the full amount of debt available to you: If $5,500 is available to you in the form of a direct government subsidized loan, only take out the full $5,500 if you really need it. By taking out less debt, you'll graduate with less debt, and you'll find that the extra cash isn't burning a hole in your pocket during the school year.
    - Apply for financial aid and work-study: These programs are administered by the colleges and universities and begin with the student filling out a Free Application for Federal Student Aid (FAFSA) form. Answer honestly and take full advantage of whatever programs are offered, including work-study.
    - Apply for scholarships: Around 400 colleges utilize the College Scholarship Service (CSS), which allows students to set up a profile, identify relevant scholarships, and apply for

them. Note: you should only set up a profile if your institution is a participant. If your school is not one of the 400 institutions that utilize this system, simply email or call your institution and speak with someone at the office of financial aid regarding how to apply for both academic and need-based scholarships.

   ◻ Get a summer and part-time job: Some work-study programs offer limited hours (perhaps only four hours per week), while others may only offer the student minimum wage. A part-time or summer job can be a good compliment to, or substitute for, work-study.

- *Assume debt later in your studies and begin repaying while in college if possible*: Federal direct subsidized loans do not accrue interest while in college—that's great! However, all other debt does begin accruing interest immediately. So, why does that matter? Imagine that a student borrows $10,000 their freshman year at an interest rate of five percent. This person graduates five years later and begins paying his or her loan six months after that. During that time, the $10,000 loan has grown to over $13,000. Had that student borrowed $10,000 his or her final year of college and began paying off the loan six months after graduation, the loan would have only grown to $10,760.

- *Borrow at the best terms*: In general, you want to borrow at the lowest interest rate, and preferably, that interest will not accrue while the student is enrolled. Therefore, begin with borrowing direct subsidized loans. If this amount is insufficient to meet your needs, then utilize direct unsubsidized loans. If you still need cash, then ask the school for help with finding one or more private lenders. Select the private lender with the lowest interest rate.

Dos—After Schooling:

- *Prioritize eliminating your debt*: In most cases, repaying student debt should be the top financial priority of recently graduated college students. As highlighted in Chapter 6, student debt has impaired a generation. This debt has been cited by former students as the reason for regret about attending college, delayed household formation, delayed home purchases, delayed marriages, lower entrepreneurship, lower job satisfaction, and even damaged mental health. Student debt is also significantly more difficult to discharge during bankruptcy. Get rid of it as soon as possible.

- *Enroll in an income repayment plan*: If you are struggling to keep up with your student loans and you have federal loans, consider enrolling in one of four income repayment plans. These plans generally cap monthly payments at 10 percent of your discretionary income; plus, any remaining balance after 20 or 25 years will be forgiven.
- *Refinance your loans*: Consider refinancing one or more loans if—and only if—the rate offered by a private lender is significantly (at least 0.5%) lower than the current rate that you have. For example, if your federal student loan is 4.5 percent, should you refinance if a private lender is offering you 4.25 percent? Probably not. Why? Because once you refinance with a private lender, you no longer have the option of an income repayment plan. Refinancing with a private lender also means that the borrower will no longer have access to federal loan forgiveness programs such as the Public Service Loan Forgiveness or Teacher Loan Forgiveness programs. Borrowers also lose access to federal deferment or forbearance. In addition, if the government ever chooses to forgive student loans, those forgiven loans will only be federal loans. Websites like nerdwallet.com and bankrate.com allow you to compare multiple lenders simultaneously.

Don'ts—After Schooling:

- *Consolidate debt*: The federal government allows students to consolidate multiple direct loans into a single loan with the average interest rate being the weighted average of all the underlying loans. While making a single payment may be simpler than making multiple payments, it's not a great financial move. Should you choose to partially repay one or more loans early, then you should repay the loan with the highest interest rate, first. However, if you consolidate your loans, you won't have this option.
- *Utilize deferment, or forbearance, if not necessary*: If you have an unexpected medical expense, loss of employment, or other major setback, deferment or forbearance are good options. Deferment is preferential to forbearance since interest does not accrue during this period, whereas interest continues to accrue during forbearance. Requesting deferment or forbearance ensures that you will not be considered delinquent for failing to make payments. However, since repayment of loans quickly is a high priority, this option should only be utilized if necessary.

Dos and Don'ts If You Can't Repay Your Loans (and Intend to File for Bankruptcy)

- *Do*—prioritize student loan repayment prior to bankruptcy. Student debt is significantly more difficult to discharge during bankruptcy since unlike credit card or medical debt, student debtors have to meet an *undue hardship* test during bankruptcy (see Chapter 5). So, prior to filing for bankruptcy you should maximize credit card debt and minimize student loan debt.[13] Also, while it is more difficult to discharge student loans, it is not impossible. According to a 2011 study published in the American Bankruptcy Law Journal, only about one in 1,000 people who declare bankruptcy try to jettison their student debt. That's a mistake because about 25 percent of people who try are able to fully discharge their debt.[xlvii] So, if necessary, be sure to (at least) try to discharge student loans.
- *Don't*—ignore the loans. Late fees will quickly accumulate and creditors can (and will) garnish wages if you default. This means that student debt may impact your financial outlook for the rest of your life. Speak with your lenders and possibly a bankruptcy attorney sooner rather than later.

Helpful Resources:

- Federal student aid:
  https://studentaid.gov/h/apply-for-aid
- College scholarship service profile:
  https://cssprofile.collegeboard.org/
- Student loan income repayment plans:
  https://studentaid.gov/manage-loans/repayment/plans/income
  -driven

CONCLUSION AND SUMMARY OF THOUGHTS

Postsecondary education has enormous benefits; people improve skills and income while society benefits from a healthier and more productive population. But that doesn't mean that everybody should go to college. And, it

---

[13] If it was me, I'd charge utilities, food, and rent on credit cards, and use every spare dollar to repay student loans. Then, once the student loans have been repaid, if I now have crushing credit card debt, I could file for bankruptcy.

doesn't mean that people should assume that a college degree will pay for itself in the form of higher income, nor does it mean that any amount of student debt is reasonable. It's not. As highlighted in Chapter 6, student debt has tremendously adverse impacts and should be avoided. Student debt is a trap, and like a siren singing to a sailor, it's best to chart a course away from it.

So, what are the main takeaways from this chapter—and this book? Here are a few things to consider: colleges and universities have a tacit responsibility to elevate individuals by conferring marketable skills, as well as elevate society by creating a thoughtful, well-rounded populace. Sadly, most schools are failing as this mission. But, that's not to say that university administrators are bad people. Rather, schools, like people in general, are simply responding to a host of misaligned incentives. Schools optimize on rankings because that's how they are judged by their board of trustees. Meanwhile, the government optimizes on the number of loans that are made available because that's how they are judged by their constituents. Banks optimize on maximizing the return to their shareholders because that's how they are judged by their board of directors. Students optimize on going to the most prestigious school, or any school for that matter, because that's what they are advised to do by parents, counselors, and most of society. Therefore, nobody is optimizing on maximizing the economic, social, and psychological outcomes of students as measured by their future successes (and failures) for having committed time and financial resources to their postsecondary education.

What does this mean for you or your child as a potential student? Plenty. The postsecondary system in the United States is designed to take people in, even when those students are not ready for the academic rigor or able to afford the program. As I have stated before, my advice is that before any individual even applies to college, they need to pass these three criteria: have an objective for what they want to accomplish, be academically prepared, and be financially prepared. With respect to the final criteria—financial preparation—this does not mean that a person is willing and able to maximize their student loan debt. On the contrary, it means forming a plan to graduate with $20,000 or less in student debt. With any luck, our policymakers will take the courageous steps outlined in the prior chapter to increase college affordability and improve student outcomes. Until then, students and parents need to work valiantly to ensure that the next generation of college graduates isn't *crushed* with debt.

Citations

Introduction

    i.   Trends in College Pricing and Student Aid 2021, New York: College Board. Figure SA-14.

    ii.   The Institute for College Access & Success. (2019). Quick Facts about Student Debt. http://bit.ly/1lxjskr.

    iii.   National Center for Education Statistics, Beginning Postsecondary Students 2012/17.

    iv.   Public Loan outstanding and recipient data: U.S. Department of Education. Federal Student Aid Office. Website: https://studentaid.gov/data-center/student/portfolio.

    v.   United States Census Bureau. https://www.census.gov/data/tables/time-series/demo/popest/2020s-state-total.html.

    vi.   https://ballot-access.org/2021/12/29/december-2021-ballot-access-news-print-edition/.

    vii.   https://worldpopulationreview.com/us-cities.

    viii.   Bureau of Economic Analysis. https://www.bea.gov/sites/default/files/2021-12/qgdpstate1221_1.pdf.

    ix.   Center for Microeconomic Data. New York Federal Reserve. Household Debt and Credit Report (Q2 2022).

    x.   https://www.youtube.com/watch?v=hJYLJRr3hEY.

    xi.   Lester Breslow and Michael Johnson. "California's Proposition 99 on Tobacco, and its Impact." Annual Review of Public Health 14 (1993): 585–604.

    xii.   Solar Energy Industries Association (SEIA). History of the 30% Solar Investment Tax Credit. 2012. Retrieved 8/6/2022. https://www.seia.org/sites/default/files/resources/History%20of%20ITC%20Slides.pdf.

Chapter 1

i.   Website: Harvard Research Guide. Harvard in the 17th and 18th Centuries. Harvard College Curriculum, 1640–1800: Overview and research sources. https://guides.library.harvard.edu/c.php?g=405381&p=6465805. Accessed 09/22/2020.

ii.   Samuel Eliot Morison. (1935). *The Founding of Harvard College.* Cambridge, MA: Harvard University Press. p. 249.

iii.   Website: William & Mary. History & Traditions. https://www.wm.edu/about/history/. Accessed 9/25/2020.

iv.   Historical Statistics of the United States (1949). Prepared by the Bureau of the Census with the Cooperation of the Social Science Research Council. United States Department of Commerce, Charles Sawyer, Secretary. Series B 1–12.

v.   Walter Crosby Eells. Baccalaureate Degrees Conferred by American Colleges in the 17th and 18th Centuries (Washington, 1958). Table 4: Ratio of Living Baccalaureate Graduates to Total Population 1650–1950.

vi.   Frederick Rudolph. (1962). *The American College & University.* University of Georgia Press. Athens, GA. pp. 33–35.

vii.   Frederick Rudolph. (1962). *The American College & University.* University of Georgia Press. Athens, GA. p. 40.

viii.   Roy J. Honeywell. (1931). *The Educational Works of Thomas Jefferson.* Cambridge, MA. pp. 54–56.

ix.   Louis Clinton Hatch. (1927). Portland, ME. Loring, Short, & Harmon. p. 19.

x.   Robert Lincoln Kelly. (1940). *The American Colleges and the Social Order.* New York, NY. p. 31.

xi.   D. G. Tewksbury. (1965). *The Founding of American Colleges and Universities Before the Civil War: With Particular Reference to the Religious Influences Bearing Upon the College Movement.* United States: Archon Books. p. 28.

xii.   Carroll D. Wright, Commissioner of Labor (1900). The History and Growth of the United States Census. Washington: Government Printing Office. p. 52.

xiii.   H. P. Tappan. (1851). *University Education.* United States: George P. Putnam. p. 54.

xiv.   Encyclopedia Virginia. Washington College during the Civil War. Contributed by Kanisorn Wongsrichanalai. Website: www.encyclopediavirginia.org. Accessed 10/1/2020.

xv.   T. H. English. (1966). Emory University, *1915–1965: A Semicentennial History.* United States: Emory University. pp. 4–5.

xvi.   Frederick Rudolph. (1962). *The American College & University.* University of Georgia Press. Athens, GA. pp. 244–245.

xvii.   Charles Riborg Mann. (1918). "A Study of Engineering Education," Joint Committee on Engineering Education of the National Engineering Societies. p. 7.

xviii.   July 2, 1862, ch. 130, §4. 305. §305. Conditions of Grant.

xix.   7 U.S.C. United States Code, 2015 Edition Title 7—Agriculture Chapter 13—
        Agricultural and Mechanical Colleges Subchapter I—College-Aid Land
        Appropriation Sec. 304—Investment of proceeds of sale of land or scrip.

xx.   Michael L. Whalen. (May 2001). "A Land-Grant University." Cornell University.
        p. 7.

xxi.   Charles Riborg Mann. (1918). "A Study of Engineering Education," Joint Com-
        mittee on Engineering Education of the National Engineering Societies. p. 7.

xxii.   Frederick Rudolph. (1962). The American College & University. University of
        Georgia Press. Athens, GA. pp. 257–260.

xxiii. Frederick Rudolph. (1962). The American College & University. University of
        Georgia Press. Athens, GA. pp. 389–390.

xxiv.   R. Freeman Butts (Robert Freeman). (1939). The College Charts Its Course:
        Historical Conceptions and Current Proposals. New York, NY: McGraw-Hill.
        p. 240.

xxv.   Claudia Goldin and Lawrence F. Katz. "The Shaping of Higher Education:
        The Formative Years in the United States, 1890 to 1940." Journal of Economic
        Perspectives. Volume 13, Number 1. Winter 1999. pp. 37–62.

xxvi.   National Center for Education Statistics. (1993). 120 Years of American Educa-
        tion: A Statistical Portrait. U.S. Department of Education Office of Educational
        Research and Improvement. Editor: Thomas D. Snyder. Table 23.

xxvii. Walter Crosby Eells: Baccalaureate Degrees Conferred by American Colleges
        in the 17th and 18th Centuries (Washington, 1958). Table 4: Ratio of Living
        Baccalaureate Graduates to Total Population 1650–1950.

xxviii. Frederick Rudolph. (1962). The American College & University. University of
        Georgia Press. Athens, GA. pp. 59–60.

xxix.   Claudia Goldin and Lawrence F. Katz. "The Shaping of Higher Education:
        The Formative Years in the United States, 1890 to 1940." Journal of Economic
        Perspectives—Volume 13, Number 1—Winter 1999—pp. 37–62.

xxx.   National Center for Education Statistics. (1993). 120 Years of American Educa-
        tion: A Statistical Portrait. U.S. Department of Education Office of Educational
        Research and Improvement. Editor: Thomas D. Snyder. Table 23.

xxxi.   Claudia Goldin and Lawrence F. Katz. "The Shaping of Higher Education:
        The Formative Years in the United States, 1890 to 1940." Journal of Economic
        Perspectives—Volume 13, Number 1—Winter 1999—pp. 37–62.

xxxii. College Blue Book. (1933). Huber William Hurt and Harriett-Jeanne Hurt, eds.
        Hollywood by-the-Sea, FL: The College Blue Book.

xxxiii. Daniel Staroh. (1930). The Income of the American Family. Consultant in
        Commercial Research. New York, NY. p. 6.

xxxiv. Department of Commerce, Bureau of the Census. 1975. Historical Statistics of
        the United States from Colonial Times to 1970. Washington, D.C.: GPO. Series
        Y 682–709.

xxxv.   C. Wellmon and P. Reitter. (2017). The Rise of the Research University: A Source-
        book. United States: University of Chicago Press. p. 2.

xxxvi. N. Diamond and H. D. Graham. (2004). *The Rise of American Research Universities: Elites and Challengers in the Postwar Era*. United Kingdom: Johns Hopkins University Press. p. 10.

xxxvii. Johnathan Cole. *The Triumph of America's Research University*. The Atlantic. September 20, 2016.

xxxviii. Arthur G. Beach. (1935). *A Pioneer College: The Story of Marietta*. p. 293.

xxxix. Frederick Rudolph. (1962). *The American College & University*. University of Georgia Press. Athens, GA. pp. 466–467.

xl. National Center for Education Statistics. (1993). 120 Years of American Education: A Statistical Portrait. U.S. Department of Education Office of Educational Research and Improvement. Editor: Thomas D. Snyder. Table 23.

xli. Walter Crosby Eells: Baccalaureate Degrees Conferred by American Colleges in the 17th and 18th Centuries (Washington, 1958). Table 4: Ratio of Living Baccalaureate Graduates to Total Population 1650–1950.

xlii. Crimson News Staff. "College Life During World War II Based on Country's Military Needs." December 7, 1956.

xliii. V. R. Cardozier. (1993). *Colleges and Universities in World War II*. ABC-CLIO, 1993. pp. 211–229.

xliv. Glenn Altschuler and Stuart Blumin. (2009). *The GI Bill: The New Deal for Veterans* (Pivotal Moments in American History). Oxford University Press; Illustrated Edition.

xlv. V. R. Cardozier. (1993). *Colleges and Universities in World War II*. ABC-CLIO, 1993. pp. 222–224.

xlvi. Walter Crosby Eells. Baccalaureate Degrees Conferred by American Colleges in the 17th and 18th Centuries (Washington, 1958). Table 4: Ratio of Living Baccalaureate Graduates to Total Population 1650–1950.

xlvii. National Center for Education Statistics. (1993). 120 Years of American Education: A Statistical Portrait. U.S. Department of Education Office of Educational Research and Improvement. Editor: Thomas D. Snyder. Table 23.

xlviii. V. R. Cardozier. (1993). *Colleges and Universities in World War II*. ABC-CLIO, 1993. p. 225.

xlix. H. Truman. (1947). Statement by the President Making Public a Report of the Commission on Higher Education. Retrieved from https://www.presidency.ucsb.edu/documents/statement-the-president-making-public-report-the-commission-higher-education.

l. The State Higher Education Executive Officer and the Public Good: Developing New Leadership for Improved Policy, Practice, and Research. (2018). United States: Teachers College Press. p. 29.

li. National Center for Education Statistics. (1993). 120 Years of American Education: A Statistical Portrait. U.S. Department of Education Office of Educational Research and Improvement. Editor: Thomas D. Snyder. Table 23.

lii. U.S. Public law. 85-864. 72 Stat. 1580.

liii.   National Center for Education Statistics. (1993). 120 Years of American Education: A Statistical Portrait. U.S. Department of Education Office of Educational Research and Improvement. Editor: Thomas D. Snyder. Table 29.

liv.   Julian E. Zelizer. The Fierce Urgency of Now: Lyndon Johnson, Congress, and the Battle for the Great Society. New York, NY: Penguin Press, 2015.

lv.   House bill: H.R. 9567 (89th Congress).

lvi.   Kery Murakami. (April 15, 2020). The Higher Education Act and the Pandemic. https://www.insidehighered.com/.

lvii.   Public Law 89-329. 89th United States Congress. Effective: November 8, 1965.

lviii.   National Center for Education Statistics. (1993). 120 Years of American Education: A Statistical Portrait. U.S. Department of Education Office of Educational Research and Improvement. Editor: Thomas D. Snyder. Table 26.

lix.   Public Law 92-318. 92nd United States Congress. Effective: June 23, 1972.

lx.   Public Law 89-329. 89th United States Congress. Effective: November 8, 1965.

lxi.   National Center for Education Statistics. (1993). 120 Years of American Education: A Statistical lxii Portrait. U.S. Department of Education Office of Educational Research and Improvement. Editor: Thomas D. Snyder. Table 26.

lxii.   Arthur M. Cohen and Florence B. Brawer. (1996). *The American Community College* (3rd ed.). San Francisco, CA: Jossey-Bass Publishers. p. 214.

lxiii.   W. Crosby Eells. (1963). Degrees in Higher Education. Washington: Center for Applied Research in Education. p. 96.

lxiv.   Arthur M. Cohen and Florence B. Brawer. (1996). *The American Community College* (3rd ed.). San Francisco, CA: Jossey-Bass Publishers. p. 215.

lxv.   Arthur M. Cohen and Florence B. Brawer. (1996). *The American Community College* (3rd ed.). San Francisco, CA: Jossey-Bass Publishers. Table 1.1.

lxvi.   Arthur M. Cohen. (1999). Governmental Policies Affecting Community Colleges. Chapter 1 of Community Colleges: Policy in the Future Context. Barbara Townsend, Ed.

lxvii.   Arthur M. Cohen and Florence B. Brawer. (1996). *The American Community College* (3rd ed.). San Francisco, CA: Jossey-Bass Publishers. Table 1.1.

lxviii. American Association of Community Colleges. Website. Fast Facts. https://www.aacc.nche.edu/2022/02/28/42888/.

lxix.   National Center for Education Statistics. (1993). 120 Years of American Education: A Statistical Portrait. U.S. Department of Education Office of Educational Research and Improvement. Editor: Thomas D. Snyder. Table 23.

lxx.   J. Thelin, J. Edwards, and E. Moyan. (n.d.). Higher Education in the United States: Historical Development, System. Retrieved from StateUniversity.com.

lxxi.   G. A. Gurin. (1971). A Study of Students in a Multiversity. Final report, contract no. OE-6-10-034. Ann Arbor, MI: Office of Education, University of Michigan.

lxxii.   Urban Research Corporation, On Strike . . . Shut It Down! A Report on the First National Student Strike in U.S. History, May 1970. (Chicago: 1970).

lxxiii.   J. Thelin, J. Edwards, and E. Moyan. (n.d.). Higher Education in the United States: Historical Development, System. Retrieved from StateUniversity.com.

lxxiv.   United States. National Commission on Excellence in Education. (1983). A Nation at Risk: the Imperative for Educational Reform. Washington, D.C. The National Commission on Excellence in Education.

lxxv.   National Center for Education Statistics. (1993). 120 Years of American Education: A Statistical Portrait. U.S. Department of Education Office of Educational Research and Improvement. Editor: Thomas D. Snyder. Table 23.

lxxvi.   United States. National Commission on Excellence in Education. (1983). A Nation at Risk: the Imperative for Educational Reform. Washington, D.C. The National Commission on Excellence in Education. Recommendation B.

lxxvii.   National Center for Education Statistics. Digest of Education Statistics. Table 303.10. Total fall enrollment in degree-granting postsecondary institutions, by attendance status, sex of student, and control of institution.

lxxviii.   Education Amendments of 1972, Pub. L. No. 92-318, tit. I, pt. D, §417B(a), 86 Stat. 235, 258, replaced by Education Amendments of 1980, Pub. L. No. 96-374, 94 Stat. 1367 (codified as amended at 25 U.S.C. §640c-2, scattered sections of 28 U.S.C., and 42 U.S.C. §2753 (2006 & Supp. IV 2011)).

lxxix.   Sarah E. Turner. "For-Profit Colleges in the Context of the Market for Higher Education" in *Earnings from Learning: The Rise of For-Profit Universities*, supra note 2, at 51, 55.

lxxx.   W. Beaver. (April 17, 2016). "The Rise and Fall of the For-Profit Higher Education." American Association of University Professors. Retrieved from https://www.aaup.org/article/rise-and-fall-profit-higher-education#.YxeXWqHMJPY.

lxxxi.   National Center for Education Statistics. Digest of Education Statistics. Table 303.10. Total fall enrollment in degree-granting postsecondary institutions, by attendance status, sex of student, and control of institution.

lxxxii.   U.S. Department of Education. (October 30, 2014). Obama Administration Announces Final Rules to Protect Students from Poor-Performing Career College Programs.

lxxxiii.   The Institute for College Access & Success. (2019). Quick Facts about Student Debt. http://bit.ly/1lxjskr.

lxxxiv.   U.S. Department of Education. FY 2018 Official National Cohort Default Rates with Prior Year Comparisons. https://www2.ed.gov/offices/OSFAP/defaultmanagement/schooltyperates.pdf. Accessed 7/15/22.

lxxxv.   U.S. Department of Education. (October 30, 2014). Obama Administration Announces Final Rules to Protect Students from Poor-Performing Career College Programs.

lxxxvi.   National Center for Education Statistics. Digest of Education Statistics. Table 303.10. Total fall enrollment in degree-granting postsecondary institutions, by attendance status, sex of student, and control of institution.

lxxxvii.   Education Department on 07/01/2019. Program Integrity: Gainful Employment. Federal Register. The Daily Journal of the United States Government. https://www.federalregister.gov/documents/2019/07/01/2019-13703/program-integrity-gainful-employment.

lxxxviii.   Case 5:20-cv-00455 Document 1 Filed 01/22/20.

lxxxix.   Source: Declaration of James Richard Kvaal—#48, Att. #1 in American Federation of Teachers v. DeVos (N.D. Cal., 5:20-cv-00455)—CourtListener.com.

xc.   Frederick Rudolph. (1962). *The American College & University*. University of Georgia Press. Athens, GA. pp. 59–60.

Chapter 2

i.   U.S. Department of Education, National Center for Education Statistics, Projections of Education Statistics to 1986–87; Higher Education General Information Survey (HEGIS), "Institutional Characteristics of Colleges and Universities" surveys, 1969–70 through 1985–86; "Fall Enrollment in Institutions of Higher Education" surveys, 1963 through 1985; Integrated Postsecondary Education Data System (IPEDS), "Fall Enrollment Survey" (IPEDS-EF:86-99) and "Institutional Characteristics Survey" (IPEDS-IC:86-99); IPEDS Spring 2001 through Spring 2019, Fall Enrollment component; and IPEDS Fall 2000 through Fall 2020, Institutional Characteristics component. (This table was prepared June 2022.)

ii.   U.S. Census Bureau, Current Population Survey, Annual Social and Economic Supplements (CPS ASEC). Table H-3. Mean Household Income Received by Each Fifth and Top 5 Percent, All Races: 1967 to 2020.

iii.   Jack Stripling. (October 15, 2017). "The Lure of the Lazy River." The Chronicle of Higher Education.

iv.   NCES. Table 317.10. Degree-granting postsecondary institutions, by control and level of institution: Selected years, 1949–50 through 2018–19; Table 105.30. Enrollment in degree-granting postsecondary institutions; Table 303.10. Total fall enrollment in degree-granting postsecondary institutions, by attendance status, sex of student, and control of institution.

v.   The United States Census Bureau.

vi.   Median family income: U.S. Census Bureau (1950). All other data points: U.S. Federal Reserve. Inflation Adjustment: U.S. Federal Reserve.

vii.   James B. Hunt Jr. (May 2006). Educational Leadership for the 21st Century. National Center for Public Policy and Higher Education.

viii.   R. Collins. (1979). *The Credential Society: An Historical Sociology of Education and Stratification*. New York, NY: Academic Press. p. 63.

ix.   R. Collins. (1979). *The Credential Society: An Historical Sociology of Education and Stratification*. New York, NY: Academic Press. pp. 120–121.

x.   "Moving the Goalposts: How Demand for a Bachelor's Degree Is Reshaping the Workforce." Boston: Burning Glass Technologies, 2014. Online. Internet. (December 25, 2020). Available: http://burning-glass.com/research/credentials-gap/.

xi.   Joseph Fuller. (December 20, 2017). "Why Employers Must Stop Requiring College Degrees for Middle-Skill Jobs." *Forbes*.

xii.   U.S. Federal Reserve. https://www.newyorkfed.org/research/college-labor -market/college-labor-market_underemployment_rates.html.

xiii. https://www.youtube.com/watch?v=_1yAOK0nSb0&index=493&list
=LL2kj7HykNVs5L0o01nYKtHQ.

xiv. Before COVID-19, Private College Tuition Discount Rates Reached Record
Highs. (May 20, 2020). Press Release. National Association of College and
University Business Officers.

xv. William J. Bennett. (February 18, 1987). "Our Greedy Colleges." *The New York
Times*.

xvi. NCES. Table 317.10. Degree-granting postsecondary institutions, by control
and level of institution: Selected years, 1949–50 through 2019–20; Table 105.30.
Enrollment in degree-granting postsecondary institutions; Table 303.10.

xvii. https://collegescorecard.ed.gov/.

xviii. Michael Stratford. (September 14, 2015). The New College Scorecard. Inside
Higher Education. www.insidehighered.com.

xix. U.S. Bureau of Labor Statistics. Tickers include: CPIFABSL, CPIHOSSL,
CPIAPPSL, CUSR0000SETA01, CPIMEDSL, CUSR0000SEHF01,
CUSR0000SAS, CUSR0000SETB, CPIAUCSL, CUUR0000SEEB01.

xx. U.S. Department of Education, National Center for Education Statistics (2019).
Digest of Education Statistics, 2018 (NCES 2020-009), Table 330.10.

xxi. United States Census Bureau. Table H-3. Mean Household Income Received by
Each Fifth and Top 5 Percent, All Races: 1967 to 2018.

xxii. The Cost of Federal Regulatory Compliance in Higher Education: A Multi-
Institutional Study. October 2015. Vanderbilt University. White Paper. https://
news.vanderbilt.edu/files/Cost-of-Federal-Regulatory-Compliance-2015.pdf.

xxiii. R. G. Ehrenberg. (2009). *Tuition Rising*. United States: Harvard University
Press. p. 11.

xxiv. Michael C. Jensen and William H. Meckling. "Theory of the Firm: Managerial
Behavior, Agency Costs and Ownership Structure." *Journal of Financial Economics*, Volume 3, Issue 4, 1976, pp. 305–360, ISSN 0304-405X.

xxv. William J. Bennett. (February 18, 1987). "Our Greedy Colleges." *The New York
Times*.

xxvi. Howard R. Bowen. (1980). "The Costs of Higher Education: How Much Do
Colleges and Universities Spend per Student and How Much Should They
Spend?" San Francisco, CA: Josey-Bass Publishers. pp. 18–19.

xxvii. Robert B. Archibald and David H. Feldman. The Journal of Higher Education,
Volume 79, Number 3, May/June 2008, pp. 268–295.

xxviii. William J. Baumol and William G. Bowen. (1966). *Performing Arts, The Economic Dilemma: a Study of Problems Common to Theater, Opera, Music, and
Dance*. Cambridge, MA: M.I.T. Press.

xxix. Eric Helland and Alexander Tabarrok. (2019). "Why Are the Prices So Damn
High? Health, Education, and the Baumol Effect" (pdf). Mercatus Center.

xxx. Susan Tifft. (September 25, 1989). "Education: Sticker Shock at the Ivory
Tower." *Time Magazine*. https://content.time.com/time/subscriber/article/
0,33009,958634,00.html.

xxxi.   Two Decades of Change in Federal and State Higher Education Funding. (October 2019). The Pew Charitable Trusts.

xxxii.   Douglas A. Webber. (2017). "State Divestment and Tuition at Public Institutions," *Economics of Education Review*, 60: 1–4.

xxxiii.   "University Prepares to Have State Funding Slashed in Half." (February 25, 2015). *LSU Reveille* (student newspaper).

xxxiv.   Nick Martin. (February 12, 2016). "Louisiana Governor Threatens to Cut LSU Football over Budget Concerns." *The Washington Post*.

xxxv.   E. G. Bogue and Kimberely B. Hall. (2003). *Quality and Accountability in Higher Education: Improving Policy, Enhancing Performance*. Westport, CT: Praeger. Print.

xxxvi.   M. Luca and J. Smith. (2013). "Salience in Quality Disclosure: Evidence from the *U.S. News* College Rankings." Journal of Economics & Management Strategy, 22: 58–77. https://doi.org/10.1111/jems.12003.

xxxvii.   Robert Morse and Eric Brooks. (September 13, 2020). "How *U.S. News* Calculated the 2022 Best Colleges Rankings." https://www.usnews.com/education/best-colleges/articles/how-us-news-calculated-the-rankings.

xxxviii.   James Harvey, et al. (February 1998). "Straight Talk about College Costs and Prices." Report of The National Commission on the Cost of Higher Education. American Institutes for Research, Washington, D.C.; American Council on Education, Washington, D.C.; National Commission on the Cost of Higher Education, Washington, D.C. ISBN-1-57356-225-4.

xxxix.   National Center for Education Statistics. Table 330.10. Average undergraduate tuition and fees and room and board rates charged for full-time students in degree-granting postsecondary institutions, by level and control of institution: Selected years, 1963–64 through 2018–19.

xl.   U.S. Bureau of the Census. Table H-3. Mean Household Income Received by Each Fifth and Top 5 Percent, All Races: 1967 to 2018.

xli.   Public Law 110–84. 110th Congress. September 27, 2007. [H.R. 2669].

xlii.   U.S. Department of Education. https://studentaid.gov/data-center/student/loan-forgiveness/pslf-data. Data accessed 4/5/22.

Chapter 3

i.   College Board. (2019). Education Pays 2019: the Benefits of Higher Education for Individuals and Society. Retrieved from https://research.collegeboard.org/pdf/education-pays-2019-full-report.pdf.

ii.   Retrieved from https://research.collegeboard.org/trends/education-pays. Retrieved 12/08/2021.

iii.   U.S. Bureau of Labor Statistics, Table A-4. Employment status of the civilian population 25 years and over by educational attainment: Monthly, Seasonally Adjusted; https://www.bls.gov/news.release/empsit.t04.htm.

iv.   Federal Reserve Bank of New York. Retrieved from https://www.newyorkfed.org/research/college-labor-market/college-labor-market_compare-majors.html.

v.   U.S. Bureau of Labor Statistics, Unemployment Rate—[Level of Education], 25 Yrs. & over [LNS14027662, LNS14027689, LNS14027659, LNS14027659], retrieved from FRED, Federal Reserve Bank of St. Louis; https://fred.stlouisfed .org/series/LNS14027659, November 21, 2021.

vi.   "Annual Update of the HHS Poverty Guidelines." Federal Register. Vol. 86, No. 19. Monday, February 1, 2021.

vii.   Jessica Semega, Melissa Kollar, John Creamer, and Abinash Mohanty. U.S. Census Bureau, Current Population Reports, P60-266(RV), Income and Poverty in the United States: 2018. U.S. Government Printing Office. Washington, D.C., 2020.

viii.   Michael D. King. (May 12, 2021). "Those With a High School Diploma or Less Make Up Majority of Government Assistance Recipients." United States Census Bureau. https://www.census.gov/library/stories/2021/05/more-than-one-in -seven-social-safety-net-recipients-in-2017-were-college-graduates.html.

ix.   P. M. Hauser and E. M. Kitagawa. (1973). *Differential Mortality in the United States: A Study in Socioeconomic Epidemiology*. United States: Harvard University Press.

x.   M. A. Freedman, G. A. Gay, J. E. Brockert, P. W. Potrzebowski, and C. J. Rothwell. (1988). The 1989 revisions of the U.S. Standard Certificates of Live Birth and Death and the U.S. Standard Report of Fetal Death. *American Journal of Public Health* 78, 168–172, https://doi.org/10.2105/AJPH.78.2.168.

xi.   National Vital Statistics Reports, Vol. 69, No. 13, January 12, 2021, Table I-7.

xii.   U.S. Bureau of Labor Statistics, Current Population Survey, Census of Fatal Occupational Injuries, December 2020. Fatal occupational injuries, total hours worked, and rates of fatal occupational injuries by selected.

xiii.   U.S. Department of Health and Human Services. The Health Consequences of Smoking—50 Years of Progress: A Report of the Surgeon General. Atlanta: U.S. Department of Health and Human Services, Centers for Disease Control and Prevention, National Center for Chronic Disease Prevention and Health Promotion, Office on Smoking and Health, 2014.

xiv.   P. Jha, C. Ramasundarahettige, V. Landsman, et al. (2013). "21st Century Hazards of Smoking and Benefits of Cessation in the United States. *New England Journal of Medicine*. 368:341–50.

xv.   D. de Walque. (2004). "Education, Information, and Smoking Decisions: Evidence from Smoking Histories, 1940–2000." (World Bank Policy Research Working Paper No. 3362).

xvi.   S. R. M. Coleman, D. E. Gaalema, T. C. Nighbor, A. A. Kurti, J. Y. Bunn, and S. T. Higgins. "Current Cigarette Smoking Among U.S. College Graduates." Prev Med. 2019 Nov; 128:105853. doi: 10.1016/j.ypmed.2019.105853. Epub 2019 October 22. PMID: 31654730; PMCID: PMC6879857.

xvii.   NCHS, National Health Interview Survey. (2018).

xviii.   X. Z. He and D. W. Baker. "Differences in Leisure-Time, Household, and Work-Related Physical Activity by Race, Ethnicity, and Education." *J Gen Intern Med*. 2005 Mar;20(3):259-66. doi: 10.1111/j.1525-1497.2005.40198.x. PMID: 15836530; PMCID: PMC1490074. "Ethnicity, and Education." Xiaoxing Z. He, MD, MPH1 and David W. Baker, MD, MPH1.

xix. Life Expectancy in Adulthood Is Falling for Those Without a BA Degree, but as Educational Gaps Have Widened, Racial Gaps Have Narrowed. Anne Case, Angus Deaton Proceedings of the National Academy of Sciences. March 2021, 118 (11) e2024777118; doi:10.1073/pnas.2024777118.

xx. Gary S. Becker. (1993). *Human Capital: A Theoretical and Empirical Analysis with Special Reference to Education.* 3rd Edition. Chicago, IL: The University of Chicago Press.

xxi. D. M. Cutler and A. Lleras-Muney. (2010). "Understanding Differences in Health Behaviors by Education." *J Health Econ.* Jan;29(1):1–28. doi:10.1016/j .jhealeco.2009.10.003. Epub 2009 Oct 31. PMID: 19963292; PMCID: PMC2824018.

xxii. P. Farrell and V. R. Fuchs. (1982). "Schooling and Health: the Cigarette Connection." *J Health Econ.* Dec;1(3):217–30. doi:10.1016/0167-6296(82)90001-7. PMID: 10263956.

xxiii. Michael Spence. (1973). "Job Market Signaling." *Quarterly Journal of Economics* 87: 355–374.

xxiv. Kim Hayoung, et al. (December 7, 2021). "COVID-19 and U.S. Higher Education Enrollment: Preparing Leaders for Fall." MCKINSEY & CO., https:// www.mckinsey.com/industries/public-and-social-sector/our-insights/ covid-19-and-us-highereducation-enrollment-preparing-leaders-for-fall.

xxv. *Associated Press.* 10 Tampa Bay. "Gov. DeSantis Proposes College 'Bill of Rights' to Party." (September 24, 2020).

xxvi. Anjelica Cappellino, J.D. (September 9, 2021). "More than 70 Universities Sued for Refunds Following COVID-19 Campus Closure." Expert Institute.

xxvii. https://www.linkedin.com/pulse/new-survey-reveals-85-all-jobs-filled-via -networking-lou-adler/. Accessed 12/5/2001.

xxviii. "Job Networks through College Classmates: Effects of Referrals for Men and Women," Maria Zhu. Working paper. http://www.mariazhu.com/uploads/ 1/2/5/4/125452305/zhu_jmp_fall18.pdf Paper.

xxix. Erica York. (February 2021). Summary of the Latest Federal Income Tax Data, 2021 Update. Tax Foundation. FISCAL FACT, No. 743.

xxx. College Board. (2019). "Education Pays 2019: the Benefits of Higher Education for Individuals and Society." p. 40.

xxxi. College Board. (2019). "Education Pays 2019: the Benefits of Higher Education for Individuals and Society." p. 41.

xxxii. NCES. Table 202.20. Percentage of 3- to 5-year-old children enrolled in school, by age and selected child and family characteristics: 2010 through 2019.

xxxiii. NCES. Table 207.10. Percent of children participating in literacy activity with family member.

xxxiv. NCES. Table 207.20. Percentage of kindergartners through fifth-graders whose parents reported doing education-related activities with their children in the past month, by selected child, parent, and school characteristics: 2012, 2016, and 2019.

xxxv.   John Bound, Michael F. Lovenheim, and Sarah Turner. (2010). "Why Have College Completion Rates Declined? An Analysis of Changing Student Preparation and Collegiate Resources." American Economic Journal: Applied Economics 2.3: 129–57. Table 2.

xxxvi.   National Center for Education Statistics. Beginning Postsecondary Students. 2012/2017.

xxxvii.   College Dropouts and Student Debt. (February 17, 2021). Mike Brown. DebtLendEDU. https://lendedu.com/blog/college-dropouts-student-loan-debt/. Accessed 12/12/2021.

xxxviii.   Melanie Hanson. "College Dropout Rates." EducationData.org. https://educationdata.org/college-dropout-rates. Accessed 12/12/21.

xxxix.   U.S. Bureau of Labor Statistics, Current Population Survey. (2020). Earnings and Unemployment Rates by Educational Attainment.

xl.   Retrieved from https://research.collegeboard.org/trends/education-pays. Retrieved 12/08/2021.

xli.   NCES. Table 330.10. Average undergraduate tuition and fees and room and board rates charged for full-time students in degree-granting postsecondary institutions, by level and control of institution: (This table was prepared December 2019).

xlii.   Retrieved from https://research.collegeboard.org/trends/education-pays. Retrieved 12/08/2021.

xliii.   J. E. Brand and D. Davis. (2011). "The Impact of College Education on Fertility: Evidence for Heterogeneous Effects." Demography. 48:863–887. [PubMed: 21735305].

xliv.   The Labor Market for Recent College Graduates. Federal Reserve Bank of New York. Last updated: February 12, 2021. https://www.newyorkfed.org/research/college-labor-market/index.html#/outcomes-by-major. Accessed 12/15/21.

xlv.   C. Kim, C. R. Tamborini, and A. Sakamoto. (2015). "Field of Study in College and Lifetime Earnings in the United States." Sociology of education, 88(4), 320–339. https://doi.org/10.1177/0038040715602132.

xlvi.   Anthony P. Carnevale, Ban Cheah, and Emma Wenzinger. "The College Payoff: More Education Doesn't Always Mean More Earnings." Washington, D.C.: Georgetown University Center on Education and the Workforce, 2021. cew.georgetown.edu/ collegepayoff2021.

xlvii.   Preston Cooper. "Is College Worth It? A Comprehensive Return on Investment Analysis." 10/19/21. FreOpp. https://freopp.org/is-college-worth-it-a-comprehensive-return-on-investment-analysis-1b2ad17f84c8. Accessed 12/16/21.

xlviii.   Jackson Gruver. (June 25, 2019). "Biggest College Regrets." Payscale.com. https://www.payscale.com/data/biggest-college-regrets.

Chapter 4

i.   Victor Fleischer. (August 19, 2015). "Stop Universities from Hoarding Money," *The New York Times*. https://www.nytimes.com/2015/08/19/opinion/stop-universities-from-hoarding-money.html. Accessed 3/29/22.

ii.   NPR Staff. (August 22, 2015). "In Elite Schools' Vast Endowments, Malcolm Gladwell Sees 'Obscene' Inequity." NPR. https://www.npr.org/2015/08/22/433735934/in-elite-schools-vast-war-chests-malcolm-gladwell-sees-obscene-inequity. Accessed 3/29/22.

iii. 2021 NACUBO-TIAA Study of Endowments. https://www.nacubo.org/research/2021/nacubo-tiaa-study-of-endowments.

iv.   Katy McCreary and Lauren Post. Press Release. (1/30/2020). U.S. Educational Endowments Report 5.3 Percent Average Return in FY19. National Association of College and University Business Officers.

v.   National Center for Education Statistics. Table 333.90. Endowment funds of the 120 degree-granting postsecondary institutions with the largest endowments, by rank order: Fiscal year 2020.

vi.   Alfred C. Potter. (March 1903). "The College Library." *Harvard Illustrated Magazine*, vol. IV no. 6, p. 105.

vii. https://www.yale.edu/about-yale/traditions-history.

viii. July 2, 1862, Ch. 130, §4. 305. §305. Conditions of Grant.

ix.   Abigail Ayres Van Slyck. *Free to All*, University of Chicago Press. (1995). ISBN 978-0-226-85031-3.

x.   George S. Bobinski. (December 1968). "Carnegie Libraries: Their History and Impact on American Public Library Development." Vol. 62, No. 11. pp. 1361–1367. Published By: American Library Association.

xi.   https://www.carnegie.org/about/our-history/.

xii. Annual Report. FY 2020–2021. Carnegie Corporation of New York. https://www.carnegie.org/about/financials/.

xiii. D. F. Swensen and C. D. Ellis. (2000). *Pioneering Portfolio Management: An Unconventional Approach to Institutional Investment*. United Kingdom: Free Press. p. 10.

xiv. D. F. Swensen and C. D. Ellis. (2000). *Pioneering Portfolio Management: An Unconventional Approach to Institutional Investment*. United Kingdom: Free Press. pp. 13–14.

xv.   George Judson. (August 13, 1992). "Bar Group Approves Transfer of U. of Bridgeport Law School." *The New York Times*. The New York Times Company. p. B7.

xvi. Evan Ramstad and Stephen Miller. (September 3, 2012). "Unification Church Founder Rev. Moon Dies." The *Wall Street Journal*.

xvii. "University of Bridgeport Cuts Ties with Unification Church." (May 24, 2019). www.ctinsider.com.

xviii. Scott Jaschik. (February 22, 2018). "Evergreen Calls Off 'Day of Absence.'" Inside Higher Ed.

xix. Bradford Richardson. (June 5, 2017). "Student Takeover of 'Hippie School' Could Happen Anywhere, Academics Warn." *The Washington Times*.

xx.   Scott Jaschik. (May 30, 2017). "Who Defines What Is Racist?" Inside Higher Ed.

xxi. Lilah Burke. (January 10, 2020). "A New Path for Evergreen." Inside Higher Ed.

xxii. AR 2017-18 Financial Statement. The Evergreen State College. Retrieved November 22, 2019.

xxiii. D. F. Swensen and C. D. Ellis. (2000). *Pioneering Portfolio Management: An Unconventional Approach to Institutional Investment.* United Kingdom: Free Press. pp. 17–23.

xxiv. Susan N. Gary. (January 2007). UMIFA Becomes UPMIFA, ABA Property & Probate Journal.

xxv. Source for asset class returns: Aswath Damodaran, Professor of Finance at the Stern School of Business at New York University, and author's calculations.

xxvi. 2019 NACUBO-Commonfund Study of Endowments. Average Annual Effective Spending Rates for U.S. College and University Endowments and Affiliated Foundations, Fiscal Years 2009 to 2019.

xxvii. U.S. Educational Endowments Report 5.3 Percent Average Return in FY19. Press Release. (January 30, 2020). NACUBO.org.

xxviii. 2021 NACUBO-TIAA Study of Endowments. https://www.nacubo.org/research/2021/nacubo-tiaa-study-of-endowments.

xxix. D. F. Swensen and C. D. Ellis. (2000). *Pioneering Portfolio Management: An Unconventional Approach to Institutional Investment.* United Kingdom: Free Press. p. 29.

xxx. Rick Seltzer. (January 31, 2019). Endowment Returns Slow; Survey Offers Peek at Spending. Inside Higher Ed.

xxxi. 2019 NACUBO-TIAA Study of Endowments: Summary Results and Key Insights. NACUBO and TIAA.

xxxii. Dylan Matthews. (June 3, 2015). Malcolm Gladwell Mercilessly Mocks John Paulson's Obscene $400 Million Gift to Harvard. www.vox.com.

xxxiii. Lisa Hagen. (July 10, 2020). Trump Threatens Tax-Exempt Status of Schools and Universities. *U.S. News and World Report.*

xxxiv. National Center for Education Statistics. Endowment sizes. Table 333.90. Endowment funds of the 120 degree-granting postsecondary institutions with the largest endowments, by rank order: Fiscal year 2020. Number of degree-granting institutions. Table 317.10. Degree-granting postsecondary institutions, by control and level of institution: Selected years, 1949–50 through 2018–20.

xxxv. Sandy Baum. (September 10, 2019). Endowments Won't Solve College Affordability Problems. Urban Institute.

xxxvi. Paul Arnsberger, Melissa Ludlum, Margaret Riley, and Mark Stanton. A History of the Tax-Exempt Sector: An SOI Perspective. Internal Revenue Service. www.irs.gov.

xxxvii. The American Economic Review. (December 1917). Vol. 7, No. 4. pp. 791–815.

xxxviii. National Center for Education Statistics. Endowment sizes. Table 333.90. Endowment funds of the 120 degree-granting postsecondary institutions with the largest endowments, by rank order: Fiscal year 2020.

xxxix. 2021 NACUBO-TIAA Study of Endowments. https://www.nacubo.org/research/2021/nacubo-tiaa-study-of-endowments.

xl. Charlie Eaton. (2018). "The Ivory Tower Tax Haven: the State, Financialization, and the Growth of Wealth College Endowments." Berkeley, CA: Haas Institute for a Fair and Inclusive Society, University of California, Berkeley. haasinstitute.berkeley.edu/justpublicfinance. p. 4.

xli. Charlie Eaton. (2018). "The Ivory Tower Tax Haven: the State, Financialization, and the Growth of Wealth College Endowments." Berkeley, CA: Haas Institute for a Fair and Inclusive Society, University of California, Berkeley. haasinstitute.berkeley.edu/justpublicfinance. p. 9.

xlii. Joint Committee on Taxation. (2017). "Estimated Budget Effects of the Conference Agreement for H.R. 1, the 'Tax Cuts and Jobs Act'." JCX-67-17. Washington, D.C.: Joint Committee on Taxation.

xliii. W. Espeland and M. Sauder. (2007). "Rankings and Reactivity: How Public Measures Recreate Social Worlds." *American Journal of Sociology* 113: 1–40.

xliv. Charlie Eaton. (2018). "The Ivory Tower Tax Haven: the State, Financialization, and the Growth of Wealth College Endowments." Berkeley, CA: Haas Institute for a Fair and Inclusive Society, University of California, Berkeley. haasinstitute.berkeley.edu/justpublicfinance. pp. 15–19.

xlv. U.S. Department of Education. (October 30, 2014). Obama Administration Announces Final Rules to Protect Students from Poor-Performing Career College Programs.

xlvi. Andrew Kreighbaum. (July 2, 2019). DeVos Issues Final Repeal of Gainful Employment. Inside Higher Education.

xlvii. Kery Murakami. (January 16, 2020). "Many Nonprofit College Programs Would Fail Gainful Test." Inside Higher Education.

xlviii. https://www.texaspolicy.com/college-earnings-and-debt/.

Chapter 5

i. Emma Kerr and Sarah Wood. (September 14, 2021). "See 10 Years of Average Total Student Loan Debt." *U.S. News.*

ii. Melanie Hanson. (November 17, 2021). "Student Loan Debt Statistics." EducationData.org. https://educationdata.org/student-loan-debt-statistics. Accessed 1/26/2022.

iii. Emma Kerr and Sarah Wood. (September 14, 2021). "See 10 Years of Average Total Student Loan Debt." *U.S. News.*

iv. Melanie Hanson. (November 17, 2021). "Student Loan Debt Statistics" EducationData.org. https://educationdata.org/student-loan-debt-statistics. Accessed 1/26/2022.

v. Melanie Hanson. (July 10, 2021). "Average Student Loan Debt." EducationData .org. https://educationdata.org/average-student-loan-debt.

vi. Public Loan outstanding data: U.S. Department of Education. Federal Student Aid Office. Website: https://studentaid.gov/data-center/student/portfolio. Accessed 1/26/22.

vii.   Private loan outstanding data: MeasureOne. The MeasureOne Private Student Loan Report. (December 15, 2021).

viii.   William R Emmons. (December 2, 2016). "The End Is in Sight for the U.S. Foreclosure Crisis." Federal Reserve Bank of St. Louis.

ix.   Thomas O'Toole. (October 4, 1982). "When Sputnik Shocked Us." *The Washington Post.*

x.   Terry O'Neill. (2001). *The Nuclear Age*: Volume 9. San Diego, CA: Greenhaven Press, Inc. p. 146.

xi.   Public law: 85-864. U.S. Congress.

xii.   Pamela Ebert Flattau, et al. (March 2006). The National Defense Education Act of 1958: Selected Outcomes. Science & Technology Policy Institute. II-2.

xiii.   President Lyndon B. Johnson. (January 12, 1965). Special Message to the Congress: "Toward Full Educational Opportunity."

xiv.   20 U.S.C. §1075 (b) (1) (A).

xv.   PUBLIC LAW 90-460-August 3, 1968.

xvi.   The Guaranteed Student Loan Program (GSLP) was established by the Higher Education Act of 1965, Pub. L. No. 89-329, tit. IV, pt. B, 79 Stat. 1219 (codified as amended at 20 U.S.C. §§1071-1097 (1976 & Supp. V 1981)).

xvii.   Sandra Baum. "Financial Aid to Low-Income College Students: Its History and Prospects," IRP Discussion Paper no. 846-87; and W. Lee Hansen and Jacob O. Stampen, "Economics and Financing of Higher Education: The Tension between Quality and Equity," revised version, April 1987, of a paper presented at the annual meeting of the Association for the Study of Higher Education, San Diego, CA.

xviii.   U.S. Bureau of Labor Statistics, Consumer Price Index for All Urban Consumers: All Items in U.S. City Average [CPIAUCSL], retrieved from FRED, Federal Reserve Bank of St. Louis; https://fred.stlouisfed.org/series/CPIAUCSL, February 3, 2022.

xix.   Amendments to the Higher Education Act of 1965, Pub. L. 92-318, Sec. 133(a) 20 USC §1087-1, signed by President Nixon, June 22, 1972.

xx.   SLMA Annual Report 1973, pp. 1–2; SLMA Annual Report 1974, p. 3.

xxi.   PL 93-224, 87 Stat 937.

xxii.   PUBLIC LAW 94-482—October 12, 1976. 20 USC 1078-1.

xxiii.   Sandy Baum. *The Evolution of Student Debt in the United States.* Chapter 2. pp. 11–36 in: *Student Loans and the Dynamics of Debt.* Brad Hershbein and Kevin M. Hollenbeck, eds.

xxiv.   20 U.S.C. §1087-1 (1976 & Supp. V 1981); 34 C.F.R. §§682.301-.302 (1982).

xxv.   PUBLIC LAW 96-374—October 3, 1980. (c) Section 428(f)(3)(A).

xxvi.   34 CFR §682.302—Payment of special allowance on FFEL loans.

xxvii.   Government Sponsored Enterprises and Their Implicit Federal Subsidy: The Case of Sallie Mae. Congress of the United States Congressional Budget Office. December 1985. Table 3.

xxviii.   Government Sponsored Enterprises and Their Implicit Federal Subsidy: The Case of Sallie Mae. Congress of the United States Congressional Budget Office. December 1985. Table 2.

xxix.   Timothy D. Naegele. (1983). The Guaranteed Student Loan Program: Do Lenders' Risks Exceed Their Rewards. Hastings Law Journal. Volume 34, Issue 3.

xxx.   Sandy Baum. Data 1963 to 1990: *The Evolution of Student Debt in the United States*. Urban Institute. Chapter 2. pp. 11–36 in: *Student Loans and the Dynamics of Debt*. Brad Hershbein and Kevin M. Hollenbeck, eds. Kalamazoo, MI: W.E. Upjohn Institute for Employment Research, 2015.

xxxi.   College Board. (2013). Data 1993 to 2000: Trends in Student Aid, 2013. New York: College Board. https://trends.collegeboard.org/sites/default/files/student-aid-2013-full (accessed December 28, 2021).

xxxii.   Data 2003 to Present: Board of Governors of the Federal Reserve System (U.S.), Student Loans Owned and Securitized [SLOAS], retrieved from FRED, Federal Reserve Bank of St. Louis; https://fred.stlouisfed.org/series/SLOAS,

xxxiii.   Nancy L. Ross. (February 21, 1983). "Sallie Mae Works a Risk-Free Arena," *The Washington Post*.

xxxiv.   Subcommittee on Education, Arts and Humanities, Committee on Labor and Human Resources, United States Senate, Oversight of Student Loan Marketing Association. Sallie Mae. (August 12, 1982). p. 135.

xxxv.   Education Amendments of 1980. (P.L. 96-374). United States statutes at large, 94 Stat. 1424. Sec. 419. Retrieved from http://www.gpo.gov/fdsys/pkg/STATUTE-94/pdf/STATUTE-94-Pg1367.pdf.

xxxvi.   Omnibus Budget Reconciliation Act of 1981. (P.L. 97-35). United States statutes at large, 95 Stat. 455. Sec. 535. Retrieved from http://history.nih. gov/research/downloads/PL97-35.pdf.

xxxvii.   Willie Schatz. (May 15, 1990). SALLIE MAE'S FIRST, ONLY PRESIDENT RESIGNS. *The Washington Post*.

xxxviii.   Josh Mitchell. *The Debt Trap*. Simon & Schuster. p. 62.

xxxix.   Josh Mitchell. (July 23, 2021). "Al Lord Profited When College Tuition Rose. He Is Paying for It." The *Wall Street Journal*.

xl.   Higher Education Amendments of 1986. (P.L. 99-498). United States statutes at large, 100 Stat. 1375. Sec. 428(b)(3). Retrieved from http://www.gpo.gov/fdsys/pkg/STATUTE-100/pdf/STATUTE-100-Pg1268.pdf.

xli.   Omnibus Budget Reconciliation Act of 1990. (P.L. 101-508). United States statutes at large, 104 Stat. 1388-26. Sec. 3004. Retrieved from http://www.gpo.gov/fdsys/pkg/STATUTE-104/pdf/STATUTE-104-Pg1388.pdf.

xlii.   National Student Loan Two-Year Default Rates. Federal Student Aid. The U.S. Department of Education. https://www2.ed.gov/offices/OSFAP/default management/defaultrates.html. Accessed 2/15/22.

xliii.   Omnibus Budget Reconciliation Act of 1993. (P.L. 103-66). United States statutes at large, 107 Stat. 342. Sec. 453(a)(1). Retrieved from http://www.gpo.gov/fdsys/pkg/STATUTE-107/pdf/STATUTE- 107-Pg312.pdf.

xliv.   M. Pitsch. (March 4, 1992). "Pell Provision Dropped, Senate Passes Student-Aid Bill." Education Week. Retrieved from https://www.edweek.org/education/pell-provision-dropped-senate-passes-student-aid-bill/1992/03. Accessed 2/15/22.

xlv.   John R. Thelin. (2007). Higher Education's Student Financial Aid Enterprise in Historical Perspective, in Footing the Tuition Bill 19, 32–35. Frederick M. Hess, ed.

xlvi.   Student Loan Marketing Association Reorganization Act of 1996. Pub. L. 104-208, div. A, title I, Sec 101(e) [title VI], September 30, 1996, 110 Stat. 3009-233, 3009-275.

xlvii.   Press Release. Sallie Mae. (April 16, 2007). "Investor Group to Buy Sallie Mae for $25 Billion."

xlviii.   Travis L. Packer. (2008). College Cost Reduction and Access Act: A Good Step, but Only a Step. North Carolina Banking Institute. Volume 12, Issue 1.

xlix.   H. R. 3221. 111th CONGRESS. 1st Session. Text - H.R.3221—111th Congress (2009–2010): Student Aid and Fiscal Responsibility Act of 2009 | Congress.gov | Library of Congress.

l.   Joelle Scally and Donghoon Lee. (2018). Student Loan Update. Federal Reserve Bank of New York Consumer Credit Panel. https://www.newyorkfed.org/microeconomics/topics/student-debt. Accessed 2/18/22.

li.   Federal Student Aid. U.S. Department of Education. Federal Student Loan Portfolio. https://studentaid.gov/data-center/student/portfolio. Accessed 2/18/22.

lii.   Judith Scott-Clayton and Jing Li. (October 20, 2016). "Black-White Disparity in Student Loan Debt More than Triples After Graduation.". Evidence Speaks Reports, Vol. 2, #3. Brookings Institution.

liii.   Ibid.

liv.   Ben Miller. (October 16, 2017). "New Federal Data Show a Student Loan Crisis for African American Borrowers." Center for American Progress. Table 4.

lv.   National Center for Education Statistics. (October 2017). U.S. Department of Education. Repayment of Student Loans as of 2015 Among 1995–96 and 2003–04. First-Time Beginning Students. NCES 2018-410. Table 3.

lvi.   Adam Looney and Constantine Yannelis. "Fall 2015. A Crisis in Student Loans? How Changes in the Characteristics of Borrowers and in the Institutions They Attended Contributed to Rising Loan Defaults." Brookings Institute. Table 9.

lvii.   Ben Miller. (October 16, 2017). New Federal Data Show a Student Loan Crisis for African American Borrowers. Center for American Progress. Table 4.

lviii.   Meta Brown, Andrew F. Haughwout, Donghoon Lee, Joelle Scally, and Wilbert van der Klaauw. (February 15, 2015). "Looking at Student Loan Defaults Through a Larger Window." Liberty Street Economics. U.S. Federal Reserve Bank of New York.

lix.   Iuliano, Jason. (July 24, 2011). "An Empirical Assessment of Student Loan Discharges and the Undue Hardship Standard." 86 American Bankruptcy Law Journal 495 (2012). Available at SSRN: https://ssrn.com/abstract=1894445 or http://dx.doi.org/10.2139/ssrn.1894445.

lx.   https://studentaid.gov/understand-aid/types/loans/interest-rates. Accessed 1/10/2022.

lxi.   Federal Student Loans Made Through the William D. Ford Federal Direct Loan Program: Terms and Conditions for Borrowers. (September 24, 2019). Congressional Research Service. https://crsreports.congress.gov/. R45931.

lxii.   PUBLIC LAW 116–136—March 27, 2020.

lxiii. Federal Code of Regulations. Title 34, Subtitle B, Chapter VI, Part 601, Subpart B, §601.10.

lxiv.   15 U.S.C., 2011 Edition, Title 15—COMMERCE AND TRADE, CHAPTER 41—CONSUMER CREDIT PROTECTION, SUBCHAPTER IV—EQUAL CREDIT OPPORTUNITY.

lxv.   PUBLIC LAW 90-321-May 29, 1968.

lxvi.   PUBLIC LAW 95-109—September 20, 1977.

lxvii. Sandra Baum. "Financial Aid to Low-Income College Students: Its History and Prospects," IRP Discussion Paper no. 846-87; and W. Lee Hansen and Jacob O. Stampen, "Economics and Financing of Higher Education: The Tension between Quality and Equity," revised version, April 1987, of a paper presented at the annual meeting of the Association for the Study of Higher Education, San Diego, CA. [Includes author's calculations].

lxviii. H.R. REP. No. 95-595, at 536–537 (1977).

lxix.   Pub. L. 89-329, title IV, §439A, as added Pub L. 94-482, title I §439(a), Oct 12, 1976 Stat 2141.

lxx.   95–598, 92 Stat. 2549, November 6, 1978.

lxxi.   In re Brunner, 46 B.R. 752, 753 (S.D. N.Y. 1985).

lxxii. 46 B.R. 752 (S.D. N.Y. 1985), aff'd sub nom. Brunner v. N.Y. State Higher Educ. Servs. Corp., 831 F. 2d 395 (2d Cir. 1987).

lxxiii. In re Brunner, 46 B.R. 752, 753 (S.D. N.Y. 1985).

lxxiv. https://thecollegeinvestor.com/34921/statute-of-limitations-on-student -loan-debt/. Accessed 1/17/22.

lxxv.   (July 14, 2021). Warren, Booker, Pressley, Colleagues to Education Department: What Steps Are You Taking to Protect Student Borrowers' Wages and Benefits When Payments Resume? https://www.warren.senate.gov/newsroom/ press-releases/.

lxxvi. Courtney Nagle. (April 10, 2019). "Student Loan Debt Could Affect Your Job in 13 States." https://www.usnews.com/.

Chapter 6

i.   CEA (2016). "Investing in Higher Education: Benefits, Challenges, and the State of Student Debt," Council of Economic Advisers Report.

ii. Thomas Dee. (2004). "Are There Civic Returns to Education?" *Journal of Public Economics* 88: 1697–1720.

iii.   Lance Lochner and Enrico Moretti. (2004). "The Effect of Education on Crime: Evidence from Prison Inmates, Arrests, and Self-Reports." *The American Economic Review* 94(1): 155–189.

iv.   M. Gurgand, A. Lorenceau, and T. Mélonio. (2011). "Student Loans: Liquidity Constraint and Higher Education in South Africa." Agence Française de Développement Working Paper No. 117.

v.   Alex Solis. (2013). Credit access and college enrollment, Working Paper, No. 2013:12, Uppsala University, Department of Economics, Uppsala, http://nbn-resolving.de/urn:nbn:se:uu:diva-204400.

vi.   Stephen Sun and Constantine Yannelis. (2015). "Credit Constraints and Demand for Higher Education: Evidence from Financial Deregulation." The Review of Economics and Statistics.

vii.   National Tracking Poll #200926. (September 2020). Table MCFI20.

viii.   National Tracking Poll #190331. (March 2019). Table IMM10.

ix.   Jackson Gruver. (June 25, 2019). "Biggest College Regrets." Payscale.com. https://www.payscale.com/data/biggest-college-regrets.

x.   Richard Fry. (2016). "For First Time in Modern Era, Living with Parents Edges Out Other Living Arrangements for 18- to 34-Year-Olds." Washington, D.C.: Pew Research Center, May.

xi.   Lisa Dettling and Joanne Hsu. (2014). "Returning to the Nest: Debt and Parental Co-Residence Among Young Adults." SSRN Electronic Journal. 10.2139/ssrn.2511411.

xii.   K. Parker. (2012). "The Boomerang Generation." Pew Social and Demographic Trends Report, Pew Research Center, Washington, D.C.

xiii.   "Boomerang Generation, Returning to the Nest." (May 2019). TD Ameritrade.

xiv.   U.S. Census Bureau. Housing Vacancies and Homeownership (CPS/HVS); Historical Tables; Table 19. Homeownership Rates by Age of Householder: 1994 to Present.

xv.   Alvaro A. Mezza, Daniel R. Ringo, Shane M. Sherlund, and Kamila Sommer. (2016). "Student Loans and Homeownership," Finance and Economics Discussion Series 2016-010. Washington: Board of Governors of the Federal Reserve System, https://doi.org/10.17016/FEDS.2016.010r1.

xvi.   D. Gicheva. (2016). "Student Loans or Marriage? A Look at the Highly Educated," 53:207–216.

xvii.   R. Bozick and A. Estacion. "Do Student Loans Delay Marriage? Debt Repayment and Family Formation in Young Adulthood." Demographic Research. 2014; 30:1865–1891.

xviii.   Fenaba Addo, Jason Houle, and Sharon Sassler. (2019). "The Changing Nature of the Association Between Student Loan Debt and Marital Behavior in Young Adulthood." *Journal of Family and Economic Issues* 40:86–101.

xix.   Kimberly Lawson. (December 18, 2018). "A New Study Found More Couples Are Delaying Marriage Due to Crushing Student Debt." www.brides.com.

xx. Fenaba Addo, Jason Houle, and Sharon Sassler. (2019). "The Changing Nature of the Association Between Student Loan Debt and Marital Behavior in Young Adulthood." *Journal of Family and Economic Issues* 40:86–101.

xxi. Jonathan Vespa. (2017). "The Changing Economics and Demographics of Young Adulthood: 1975–2016." Current Population Reports, pp. 20–579. U.S. Census Bureau, Washington, D.C.

xxii. "Boomerang Generation, Returning to the Nest." (May 2019). TD Ameritrade.

xxiii. M. Nau, R. E. Dwyer, and R. Hodson. (2015). "Can't Afford a Baby? Debt and Young Americans." *Res Soc Stratif Mobil* 42:114–122. doi:10.1016/j.rssm.2015.05.003.

xxiv. J. E. Brand, D. Davis. (2011). "The Impact of College Education on Fertility: Evidence for Heterogeneous Effects." *Demography* 48:863–887. [PubMed: 21735305].

xxv. *Age and Fertility. A Guide for Patients.* Revised 2012. American Society for Reproductive Medicine under the direction of the Patient Education Committee and the Publications Committee. https://www.reproductivefacts.org/.

xxvi. "Dynamism in Retreat: Consequences for Regions, Markets and Workers." (February 2017). Economic Innovation Group.

xxvii. Ewing Marion Kauffman Foundation. (2020). "Student Loans and Entrepreneurship: An Overview." Entrepreneurship Issue Brief, No. 5, Kansas City, Missouri.

xxviii. Gallup and Purdue University. (2015). "Great Jobs, Great Lives. The Relationship Between Student Debt, Experiences and Perceptions of College Worth." Gallup-Purdue Index 2015 Report.

xxix. Small Business Majority and Young Invincibles. (2016). Opinion Poll: Millennials Identify Student Debt, Retirement Savings as Barriers to Entrepreneurship.

xxx. Krishnan and Wang. (2019). "The Cost of Financing Education: Can Student Debt Hinder Entrepreneurship?" Management Science.

xxxi. U.S. Small Business Administration. Office of Advocacy. (August 2018). Frequently Asked Questions About Small Business. https://www.sba.gov.

xxxii. Krishnan and Wang. (2019). "The Cost of Financing Education: Can Student Debt Hinder Entrepreneurship?" Management Science.

xxxiii. American Student Assistance. 2015 Edition. "Life Delayed: The Impact of Student Debt on the Daily Lives of Young Americans."

xxxiv. Sandy Baum and Marie O'Malley. (2003). "College on Credit: How Borrowers Perceive Their Education Debt." NASFAA Journal of Student Financial Aid. Vol. 33, No. 3. http://publications.nasfaa.org/jsfa/vol33/iss3/1.

xxxv. Jesse Rothstein and Cecilia Elena Rouse. (2011). "Constrained After College: Student Loans and Early-Career Occupational Choices." *Journal of Public Economics*, Volume 95, Issues 1–2. pp. 149–163, ISSN 0047-2727, https://doi.org/10.1016/j.jpubeco.2010.09.015.

xxxvi. Katrina M. Walsemann, Gilbert C. Gee, and Danielle Gentile. (2015). "Sick of Our Loans: Student Borrowing and the Mental Health of Young Adults in the United States." *Social Science & Medicine*, Volume 124. pp. 85–93, ISSN 0277-9536, https://doi.org/10.1016/j.socscimed.2014.11.027.

xxxvii. Donna C. Jessop, Matthew Reid, and Lucy Solomon. (2020). "Financial Concern Predicts Deteriorations in Mental and Physical Health Among University Students." *Psychology & Health* 35:2, 196-209, doi:10.1080/08870446 .2019.1626393.

xxxviii. K. M. Walsemann, J. A. Ailshire, C. S. Hartnett. (August 2020). "The Other Student Debt Crisis: How Borrowing to Pay for a Child's College Education Relates to Parents' Mental Health at Midlife." *The Journals of Gerontology*. Series B, Psychological Sciences and Social Sciences. 75(7):1494–1503. doi:10.1093/ geronb/gbz146.

xxxix. Josh Mitchell. "Student Loan Losses Seen Costing U.S. More than $400 Billion." (November 21, 2020). The *Wall Street Journal*.

xl. Student Loan Programs—CBO's May 2019 Baseline. https://www.cbo.gov/ system/files?file=2019-05/51310-2019-05-studentloan.pdf. Accessed 4/10/2022.

xli. Monthly Budget Review: Summary for Fiscal Year 2019. November 7, 2019. Congressional Budget Office. https://www.cbo.gov/system/files/2019-11/ 55824-CBO-MBR-FY19.pdf. Accessed 4/10/2022.

xlii. U.S. Department of Education, Fiscal Year 2021. Agency Financial Report, Washington, D.C. Figure 9.

xliii. Datalab. https://datalab.usaspending.gov/americas-finance-guide/spending/ categories/. Accessed 4/10/22.

Chapter 7

i. Peggy McIntosh. (1988). White Privilege and Male Privilege. https://national seedproject.org/images/documents/White_Privilege_and_Male_Privilege _Personal_Account-Peggy_McIntosh.pdf. Accessed 5/11/22.

ii. N. Quadlin and J. A. Conwell. (2021). Race, Gender, and Parental College Savings: Assessing Economic and Academic Factors. Sociology of Education, 94(1), pp. 20–42. https://doi.org/10.1177/0038040720942927.

iii. Linda Darling-Hammond. "Unequal Opportunity: Race and Education." Brookings Review, vol. 16, no. 2, Spring 1998, p. 28+. Gale Academic OneFile, link.gale.com/apps/doc/A20505589/AONE?u=anon~7d843774&sid=google Scholar&xid=533719ed. Accessed May 13, 2022.

iv. State and Local Financing of Public Schools. Updated August 26, 2019. Congressional Research Service. https://fas.org/sgp/crs/misc/R45827.pdf. Accessed 5/13/22.

v. Serrano v. Priest - 5 Cal.3d 584 - Mon, 08/30/1971 | California Supreme Court Resources.

vi. Joshua Seth Lichtenstein. (1991). "Abbott v. Burke: Reaffirming New Jersey's Constitutional Commitment to Equal Educational Opportunity," Hofstra Law Review: Vol. 20: Issue 2, Article 6. Available at: http://scholarlycommons.law .hofstra.edu/hlr/vol20/iss2/6.

vii. Campaign for Fiscal Equity Inc. v. State, 86 N.Y.2d 306 (1995), found Cornell Law School Legal Information Institute. Accessed 5/13/22.

viii. $23 Billion. Edbuild. (February 2019). https://edbuild.org/content/23-billion/ full-report.pdf. Accessed 5/13/22.

ix. C. Han, O. Jaquette, and K. Salazar. (2019). Recruiting the Out-of-State University: Off-Campus Recruiting by Public Research Universities.

x. Christopher Avery, Andrew Fairbanks, and Richard Zeckhauser. (2001). "What Worms for the Early Bird: Early Admissions at Elite Colleges." Working Paper Series. Harvard University. John F. Kennedy School of Government.

xi. Jennifer A. Giancola and Richard D. Kahlenberg. (2016). "True Merit: Ensuring Our Brightest Students Have Access to Our Best Colleges and Universities." Lansdowne, VA: Jack Kent Cooke Foundation.

xii. Harold O. Levy. (January 12, 2017). "Colleges Should Abandon Early Admissions." Insight HigherEd. https://www.insidehighered.com/views/2017/01/12/ discrimination-inherent-early-admissions-programs-essay.

xiii. C. Coffman, T. O'Neil, and B. Starr. (2010). "An Empirical Analysis of the Impact of Legacy Preferences on Alumni Giving at Top Universities." In R. D. Kahlenberg (Ed.), *Affirmative Action for the Rich: Legacy Preferences in College Admissions*. pp. 101–212. Century Foundation Press. https://s3-us-west-2 .amazonaws.com/production.tcf.org/app/uploads/2016/03/08201915/2010-09 -15-chapter_5.pdf.

xiv. National Center for Education Statistics (NCES). Table 302.20. Percentage of recent high school completers enrolled in college, by race/ethnicity: 1960 through 2020. https://nces.ed.gov/programs/digest/d21/tables/dt21_302.20.asp.

xv. National Center for Education Statistics (NCES). Table 302.60. Percentage of 18- to 24-year-olds enrolled in college, by level of institution and sex and race/ ethnicity of student: 1970 through 2020. https://nces.ed.gov/programs/digest/ d21/tables/dt21_302.60.asp.

xvi. Lorelle L. Espinosa, Jonathan M. Turk, Morgan Taylor, and Hollie M. Chessman. (2019). "Race and Ethnicity in Higher Education: A Status Report." Washington, D.C.: American Council on Education. Table 3.2.

xvii. Lorelle L. Espinosa, et al. (2019). "Race and Ethnicity in Higher Education: A Status Report."

xviii. Tomas Monarrez and Kelia Washington. Racial and Ethnic Representation in Postsecondary Education. (June 2020). Center on Education Data and Policy. The Urban Institute. White Paper. https://www.urban.org/sites/default/files/ publication/102375/racial-and-ethnic-representation-in-postsecondary -education_1.pdf. Accessed 5/21/22.

xix. A. Carnevale, M. L. Fasules, A. Porter, and J. Landis-Santos. (2016). "African Americans: College Majors and Earnings." Report by The Georgetown University Center on Education and the Workforce.

xx.   U.S. Department of Education, National Center for Education Statistics, Integrated Postsecondary Education Data System (IPEDS). Fall 2019 and Fall 2020. Table 322.30. Bachelor's degrees conferred by postsecondary institutions, by race/ethnicity and field of study: 2018–19 and 2019–20.

xxi.   U.S. Department of Education, National Center for Education Statistics, Integrated Postsecondary Education Data System (IPEDS), Winter 2016–17, Graduation Rates component. Table 326.10.

xxii.   D. Shapiro, A. Dundar, F. Huie, P. Wakhungu, X. Yuan, A. Nathan, and Y. Hwang. (April 2017). "A National View of Student Attainment Rates by Race and Ethnicity." Fall 2010 Cohort. (Signature Report No. 12b). Herndon, VA: National Student Clearinghouse Research Center.

xxiii.   U.S. Department of Education, National Center for Education Statistics, Integrated Postsecondary Education Data System (IPEDS), Fall 2019 and Fall 2020. Table 331.37. Percentage of part-time or part-year undergraduates receiving financial aid, and average annual amount received, by type and source of aid and selected student characteristics: Selected years, 1999–2000 through 2015–16.

xxiv.   Judith Scott-Clayton and Jing Li. (October 20, 2016). "Black-White Disparity in Student Loan Debt More than Triples After Graduation." Evidence Speaks Reports, Vol. 2, #3. Brookings Institution.

xxv.   Rachel Louise Ensign and Shane Shifflett. (August 7, 2021). "College Was Supposed to Close the Wealth Gap for Black Americans. The Opposite Happened." The *Wall Street Journal*.

xxvi.   Judith Scott-Clayton and Jing Li. (October 20, 2016). "Black-White Disparity in Student Loan Debt More than Triples After Graduation." Evidence Speaks Reports, Vol. 2, #3. Brookings Institution.

xxvii.   J. E. Scott-Clayton. (2018). "The Looming Student Loan Crisis Is Worse than We Thought." Brookings Institution Evidence Speaks Report, Vol. 2, #34.

xxviii.   Janelle Jones and John Schmitt. (2014). "A College Degree Is No Guarantee," CEPR Reports and Issue Briefs 2014-08, Center for Economic and Policy Research (CEPR).

xxix.   M. Cominole, E. Thomsen, M. Henderson, E. D. Velez, and J. Cooney. (2021). "Baccalaureate and Beyond (B&B:08/18): First Look at the 2018 Employment and Educational Experiences of 2007–08 College Graduates." (NCES 2021-241). U.S. Department of Education. Washington, D.C.: National Center for Education Statistics. Retrieved from https://nces.ed.gov/pubsearch/pubsinfo.asp?pubid=2021241.

xxx.   Janelle Jones and John Schmitt. (2014). "A College Degree Is No Guarantee," CEPR Reports and Issue Briefs 2014-08, Center for Economic and Policy Research (CEPR).

xxxi.   Devah Pager. (2003). "The Mark of a Criminal Record." *American Journal of Sociology*, Vol. 108, No. 5, pp. 937–976.

xxxii.   Devah Pager, Bart Bonikowski, and Bruce Western. (2009). "Discrimination in a Low-Wage Labor Market: A Field Experiment." *American Sociological Review*, Vol. 74, No. 5, pp. 777–779.

xxxiii. Nextions. (2014). "Written in Black & White: Exploring Confirmation Bias in Racialized Perceptions of Writing Skills." Yellow Paper Series. Chicago, IL.

xxxiv. Christopher Parsons, Johan Sulaeman, Michael Yates, and Daniel Hamermesh. (2009). "Strike Three: Umpires' Demand for Discrimination." American Economic Review. 10.2139/ssrn.1318858.

xxxv. S. N. Bleich, M. G. Findling, L. S. Casey, R. J. Blendon, J. M. Benson, G. K. SteelFisher, J. M. Sayde, and C. Miller. (2019). "Discrimination in the United States: Experiences of Black Americans." Health services research, 54(S2), 1399–1408. https://doi.org/10.1111/1475-6773.13220.

xxxvi. B. Hussar, J. Zhang, S. Hein, K. Wang, A. Roberts, J. Cui, M. Smith, F. Bullock Mann, A. Barmer, and R. Dilig. (2020). "The Condition of Education 2020." (NCES 2020-144). U.S. Department of Education. Washington, D.C.: National Center for Education Statistics. Retrieved from https://nces.ed.gov/pubsearch/pubsinfo.asp?pubid=2020144.

xxxvii. 2013–2014 Civil Rights Data Collection: A First Look. Washington, D.C.: U.S. Department of Education. Office for Civil Rights. (2016b).

xxxviii. M. Taylor, J. Turk, H. Chessman, and L. Espinosa. (2020). "Race and Ethnicity in Higher Education: 2020 Supplement." American Council on Education, Washington, viewed May 31, 2022. https://www.equityinhighered.org/resources/report-downloads/.

xxxix. U.S. Department of Education. National Center for Education Statistics, Integrated Postsecondary Education Data System (IPEDS). Winter 2016–17. Graduation Rates component. Table 326.10.

xl. N. Quadlin and J. A. Conwell. (2021). "Race, Gender, and Parental College Savings: Assessing Economic and Academic Factors." Sociology of Education, 94(1), 20–42. https://doi.org/10.1177/0038040720942927.

xli. Emily A. Shrider, Melissa Kollar, Frances Chen, and Jessica Semega. (September 2021). U.S. Census Bureau, Current Population Reports, pp. 60–273. Income and Poverty in the United States: 2020, U.S. Government Publishing Office, Washington, D.C.

xlii. U.S. Department of Education, National Center for Education Statistics, Integrated Postsecondary Education Data System (IPEDS), Fall 2019 and Fall 2020. Table 331.37. Percentage of part-time or part-year undergraduates receiving financial aid, and average annual amount received, by type and source of aid and selected student characteristics: Selected years, 1999–2000 through 2015–16.

Chapter 8

i. Dean Randy, L. Diehl, and the Executive Leadership Team. College of Liberal Arts. (July 2011). "Maintaining Excellence and Efficiency at The University of Texas at Austin."

ii. Kevin James. "Bernie's Bad College Idea." (May 27, 2015). *U.S. News and World Report*. https://www.usnews.com/opinion/knowledge-bank/2015/05/27/why-bernie-sanders-free-public-college-plan-is-a-bad-idea. Accessed 2/23/22.

iii.   Andrew Kreighbaum. (April 4, 2017). "Sanders, Democratic Colleagues Introduce New Free-College Bill." Inside Higher Ed. https://www.insidehighered.com/news/2017/04/04/sanders-democratic-colleagues-introduce-new-free-college-bill. Accessed 2/23/22.

iv.   Carmen Reinicke. (April 21, 2021). "Sen. Bernie Sanders Introduces Bill to Make College Free and Have Wall Street Pay for It." CNBC. https://www.cnbc.com/2021/04/21/sen-bernie-sanders-introduces-bill-to-make-college-free-and-have-wall-st-pay-for-it.html. Accessed 2/23/22.

v.   Robert Pollin, James Heintz, and Thomas Herndon. (2018). The Revenue Potential of a Financial Transaction Tax for U.S. Financial Markets. International Review of Applied Economics, 32:6, 772–806, doi:10.1080/02692171.2018.1485634.

vi.   Jo Blanden and Stephen Machin. (2004). "Educational Inequality and the Expansion of U.K. Higher Education." *Scottish Journal of Political Economy* 51(2), pp. 230–249. ISSN 0036-9292.

vii.   Jon Marcus. (October 18, 2016). "How Free College Tuition in One Country Exposes Unexpected Pros and Cons." https://hechingerreport.org/free-college-tuition-one-country-exposes-unexpected-pros-cons/.

viii. "How Swiss Is Trump's New 'Apprentice'?" https://www.swissinfo.ch/eng/how-swiss-is-trump-s-new-apprentice/43337348. Accessed 2/27/22.

ix.   National Center for Education Statistics. Beginning Postsecondary Students 2012/2017.

x.   SUMMARY OF FUEL ECONOMY PERFORMANCE. (December 15, 2014). U.S. DEPARTMENT OF TRANSPORTATION. NHTSA, NVS-220.

xi.   https://www.ecfr.gov/current/title-49/subtitle-B/chapter-V/part-531. Accessed 7/12/22.

xii.   James Harvey, Roger M. Williams, Rita J. Kirshstein, Amy Smith O'Malley, and Jane V. Wellman. *Straight Talk about College Costs and Prices*. Report of The National Commission on the Cost of Higher Education. ISBN-1-57356-225-4. 2/1/1998. p. 115.

xiii. 2019 NACUBO-Commonfund Study of Endowments. Average Annual Effective Spending Rates for U.S. College and University Endowments and Affiliated Foundations, Fiscal Years 2019 to 2009.

xiv.   D. F. Swensen and C. D. Ellis. (2000). *Pioneering Portfolio Management: An Unconventional Approach to Institutional Investment*. United Kingdom: Free Press.

xv.   James McWilliams. (January 3, 2019). Chuck Grassley's Crusade to Tax University Endowments. Pacific Standard.

xvi.   Senator Charles Grassley. "Grassley Urges Continued Look at College Endowment Growth, Student Affordability." Press release, September 8, 2008, http://www.grassley.senate.gov/news/news-releases/grassley-urges-continued-look-college-endowment-growth-student-affordability.

xvii. 2019 NACUBO-Commonfund Study of Endowments. Average Annual Effective Spending Rates for U.S. College and University Endowments and Affiliated Foundations, Fiscal Years 2019 to 2009.

xviii. Matt Willie. (2012). "Taxing and Tuition: A Legislative Solution to Growing Endowments and the Rising Costs of a College Degree." BYU L. Rev. 1665.

xix. J. Klor de Alva and Mark Schneider. (2015). "Rich Schools, Poor Students: Tapping Large University Endowments to Improve Student Outcomes." San Francisco, CA: Nexus Research and Policy Center.

xx. Sandy Baum and Victoria Lee. (July 2019). "The Role of College and University Endowments." Research Report. The Urban Institute.

xxi. Peter Baker and David Herszenhorn. (March 30, 2010). "Obama Signs Overhaul of Student Loan Program." *The New York Times.* https://www.nytimes .com/2010/03/31/us/politics/31obama.html.

xxii. Bureau of Labor Statistics, U.S. Department of Labor, The Economics Daily, 62.7 percent of 2020 high school graduates enrolled in college, down from 66.2 percent in 2019 at https://www.bls.gov/opub/ted/2021/62-7-percent-of-2020 -high-school-graduates-enrolled-in-college-down-from-66-2-percent-in-2019 .htm (visited March 16, 2022).

xxiii. National Center for Education Statistics. https://nces.ed.gov/programs/digest/ d20/tables/dt20_326.15.asp (visited March 16, 2022).

xxiv. Preston Cooper. (October 19, 2021). Is College Worth It? A Comprehensive Return on Investment Analysis. FreOpp. https://freopp.org/is-college -worth-it-a-comprehensive-return-on-investment-analysis-1b2ad17f84c8. Accessed 12/16/21.

xxv. Federal Student Aid. U.S. Department of Education. Federal Student Loan Portfolio. https://studentaid.gov/data-center/student/portfolio. Accessed 2/18/22.

xxvi. Joe Biden Speech on Economic Recovery Plan Transcript. (November 16, 2020). http://edition.cnn.com/TRANSCRIPTS/2011/16/cnr.14.html. Accessed 3/18/22.

xxvii. Elizabeth Warren. (September 17, 2020). https://www.warren.senate.gov/ newsroom/press-releases/schumer-warren-the-next-president-can-and -should-cancel-up-to-50000-in-student-loan-debt-immediately-democrats -outline-plan-for-immediate-action-in-2021. Accessed 3/18/22.

xxviii. Bernie Sanders. https://berniesanders.com/issues/free-college-cancel-debt/. Accessed 3/18/22.

xxix. Adam Looney. (February 12, 2021). "Putting Student Loan Forgiveness in Perspective: How Costly Is It and Who Benefits?" Brookings Institute. https://www .brookings.edu/blog/up-front/2021/02/12/putting-student-loan-forgiveness -in-perspective-how-costly-is-it-and-who-benefits/. Accessed 3/18/22.

xxx. Ibid.

xxxi. "Partial Student Debt Cancellation Is Poor Economic Stimulus." (June 3, 2001). Committee for a Responsible Federal Budget. https://www.crfb.org/blogs/ partial-student-debt-cancellation-poor-economic-stimulus. Accessed 3/18/22.

xxxii. Pub. L. 89-329, title IV, §439A, as added Pub L. 94-482, title I §439(a), Oct 12, 1976 Stat 2141.

Chapter 9

i.   M. Lövdén, L. Fratiglioni, M. M. Glymour, U. Lindenberger, and E. M. Tucker-Drob. (2020). "Education and Cognitive Functioning Across the Life Span." Psychological Science in the Public Interest. 2020; 21(1):6–41. doi:10.1177/1529100620920576.

ii. S. R. M. Coleman, D. E. Gaalema, T. D. Nighbor, A. A. Kurti, J. Y. Bunn, and S. T. Higgins. (October 22, 2019). "Current Cigarette Smoking Among U.S. College Graduates." Prev. Med. 2019 Nov; 128:105853. doi:10.1016/j.ypmed.2019.105853. Epub. PMID: 31654730; PMCID: PMC6879857.

iii. X. Z. He and D. W. Baker. (2005). "Differences in Leisure-Time, Household, and Work-Related Physical Activity by Race, Ethnicity, and Education." *J Gen Intern Med.* Mar; 20 (3):259-66. doi:10.1111/j.1525-1497.2005.40198.x. PMID: 15836530; PMCID: PMC1490074.

iv. College Board. (2019). "Education Pays 2019: the Benefits of Higher Education for Individuals and Society."

v.   Retrieved 12/08/2021 from https://research.collegeboard.org/trends/education-pays.

vi. U.S. Bureau of Labor Statistics. Table A-4. Employment status of the civilian population 25 years and over by educational attainment: Monthly, Seasonally Adjusted. https://www.bls.gov/news.release/empsit.t04.htm.

vii. 2019 Society for Human Resource Management. "The Global Skills Shortage. Bridging the Talent Gap with Education, Training and Sourcing." https://www.shrm.org/hr-today/trends-and-forecasting/research-and-surveys/pages/skills-gap-2019.aspx.

viii. https://www.apprenticeship.gov/employers/program-comparison. Accessed 6/5/2022.

ix. D. Farnbauer. (2021). "Bridging German and U.S. Apprenticeship Models: The Role of Intermediaries, Lumina Foundation for Education." Retrieved from https://policycommons.net/artifacts/2441428/bridging-german-and-us-apprenticeship-models/3463152/ on 05 Jun 2022. CID: 20.500.12592/207w1j.

x.   The U.S. Department of Labor. Career Seeker Fact Sheet. https://www.apprenticeship.gov/sites/default/files/Career_Seeker_Fact_Sheet.pdf. Accessed 6/5/2022.

xi. U.S. Bureau of Labor Statistics. Employed full time: Wage and Salary Workers: High School Graduates, No College: 25 Years and Over [LEU0252917000A], retrieved from FRED, Federal Reserve Bank of St. Louis; https://fred.stlouisfed.org/series/LEU0252917000A. June 5, 2022.

xii. U.S. Department of Education, National Center for Education Statistics, Integrated Postsecondary Education Data System (IPEDS), Fall 2010 through Fall 2020, Completions component. See Digest of Education Statistics 2021, Table 318.40.

xiii.   Veronica Minaya and Judith Scott-Clayton. Labor Market Trajectories for Community College Graduates: How Returns to Certificates and Associate's Degrees Evolve Over Time. Education Finance and Policy 2022; 17(1): 53–80. doi: https://doi.org/10.1162/edfp_a_00325.

xiv.   Jim Garamone. (May 16, 2019). DOD Official Cites Widening Military-Civilian Gap. U.S. Department of Defense. https://www.defense.gov/News/News-Stories/Article/Article/1850344/dod-official-cites-widening-military-civilian-gap/.

xv.   2018 Demographics. Profile of the Military Community. Department of Defense (DoD), Office of the Deputy Assistant Secretary of Defense for Military Community and Family Policy (ODASD (MC&FP)).

xvi.   https://corporate.walmart.com/askwalmart/how-many-people-work-at-walmart. Accessed 6/5/22.

xvii.   AMAZON.COM, INC. Form 10-K for the Fiscal Year Ended December 31, 2021. Securities and Exchange Commission.

xviii.   https://www.usa.gov/join-military. Accessed 6/5/2022.

xix.   https://www.military.com/join-armed-forces/making-commitment.html. Accessed 6/5/2022.

xx.   https://www.hillandponton.com/veteran-civilian-pay-statistics/#average-incomes.

xxi.   Complete College America. (April 2012). "Remediation: Higher Education's Bridge to Nowhere." Washington, D.C.: Author. Retrieved from http://completecollege.org/docs/CCA-Remediation-final.pdf.

xxii.   "College Dropouts and Student Debt." (February 17, 2021). Mike Brown. DebtLendEDU. https://lendedu.com/blog/college-dropouts-student-loan-debt/. Accessed 6/12/2021.

xxiii.   Melanie Hanson. "College Dropout Rates." EducationData.org. https://educationdata.org/college-dropout-rates. Accessed 12/12/21.

xxiv.   United States Department of Education, National Center for Education Statistics. Table 303.40. Total fall enrollment in degree-granting postsecondary institutions, by attendance status, sex, and age of student: Selected years, 2001 through 2030. https://nces.ed.gov/programs/digest/d21/tables/dt21_303.40.asp.

xxv.   Dr. Wally Boston. (November 2021). "Today's Disengaged Learner Is Tomorrow's Adult Learner." White paper. Straighterline and UPCEA. https://partners.straighterline.com/disengagedlearnersstudy. Accessed 6/16/22.

xxvi.   Sarah Ketchen Lipson, Sasha Zhou, Sara Abelson, Justin Heinze, Matthew Jirsa, Jasmine Morigney, Akilah Patterson, Meghna Singh, and Daniel Eisenberg. "Trends in College Student Mental Health and Help-Seeking by Race/Ethnicity: Findings from the National Healthy Minds Study, 2013–2021." *Journal of Affective Disorders*, Vol. 306, 2022, pp. 138–147, ISSN 0165-0327, https://doi.org/10.1016/j.jad.2022.03.038.

xxvii.   National Student Clearinghouse Research Center. (2021). High School Benchmarks 2021. National College Progression Rates.

xxviii.   Nina Hoe Gallagher and Kempie Blythe. (October 2020). Gap Year Alumni Survey 2020. Gap Year Association.

xxix.   Ibid.

xxx.   Blog. Bob Clagett on Taking a Gap Year. http://collegeadmissionbook.com/blog/bob-clagett-taking-gap-year.

xxxi.   Jonathan Cribb. "Gap Year Takers: Uptake, Trends and Long-Term Outcomes." DFE research report, no. DFE-RR252. [London]: Department for Education, 2012. Online. Internet. June 13, 2022. Available: https://www.education.gov.uk/publications/eOrderingDownload/DFE-RR252.pdf.

xxxii.   Nina Hoe Gallagher and Kempie Blythe. (October 2020). Gap Year Alumni Survey 2020. Gap Year Association.

xxxiii.   U.S. Department of Education, National Center for Education Statistics. (2015). Demographic and Enrollment Characteristics of Nontraditional Undergraduates: 2011–12. https://nces.ed.gov/pubs2015/2015025.pdf Google Scholar.

xxxiv.   Karyn E. Rabourn, Allison BrckaLorenz, and Rick Shoup. (2018). "Reimagining Student Engagement: How Nontraditional Adult Learners Engage in Traditional Postsecondary Environments." The Journal of Continuing Higher Education, 66:1, 22-33, doi:10.1080/07377363.2018.1415635.

xxxv.   Malcolm Gladwell. (October 1, 2013). David and Goliath: Underdogs, Misfits, and the Art of Battling Giants. Little, Brown and Company. ISBN-10:0316204366.

xxxvi.   Stacy Berg Dale and Alan B. Krueger. (2002). "Estimating the Payoff to Attending a More Selective College: An Application of Selection on Observables and Unobservables." The Quarterly Journal of Economics 117(4): 1491–1527.

xxxvii.   Suqin Ge, Elliott Isaac, and Amalia R. Miller. (August 5, 2019). "Elite Schools and Opting In: Effects of College Selectivity on Career and Family Outcomes." Available at SSRN: https://ssrn.com/abstract=3284635 or http://dx.doi.org/10.2139/ssrn.3284635.

xxxviii.   Jeff Goodman. (April 24, 2015). "Malcolm Gladwell: College Applicants 'Seduced by Prestige.'" https://www.smdp.com/malcolm-gladwell-college-applicants-seduced-prestige/.

xxxix.   Dr. Wally Boston. (November 2021). Today's Disengaged Learner Is Tomorrow's Adult Learner. White paper. Straightline and UPCEA. https://partners.straighterline.com/disengagedlearnersstudy. Accessed 6/16/22.

xl.   Christine Hauser. (May 3, 2018). "She Was Accepted to 113 Colleges: 'I Could Go Anywhere, and Discover Who I Am.'" The New York Times.

xli.   The American Association of Community Colleges (AACC). Fast Facts. (2022). https://www.aacc.nche.edu/wp-content/uploads/2022/05/AACC_2022_Fact_Sheet-Rev-5-11-22.pdf.

xlii.   Community College Research Center. "What We Know About Transfer." Research Overview. (January 2015). https://ccrc.tc.columbia.edu/media/k2/attachments/what-we-know-about-transfer.pdf.

xliii. Community College Research Center. Community College Transfer. Policy Fact Sheet. (July 2021). https://ccrc.tc.columbia.edu/media/k2/attachments/community-college-transfer.pdf.

xliv. Ibid.

xlv. Ben Miller. (October 16, 2017). New Federal Data Show a Student Loan Crisis for African American Borrowers. Center for American Progress. Table 4.

xlvi. U.S. Bureau of Labor Statistics, Current Population Survey. Earnings and unemployment rates by educational attainment. (2020).

xlvii. Jason Iuliano. (July 25, 2011). "An Empirical Assessment of Student Loan Discharges and the Undue Hardship Standard." 86 American Bankruptcy Law Journal 495 (2012), Available at SSRN: https://ssrn.com/abstract=1894445 or http://dx.doi.org/10.2139/ssrn.1894445.

Index